Celtic Indian Boy of Appalachia:
A Scots Irish Cherokee Childhood

by

Rickey Butch Walker

© Copyright 2013

**Bluewater Publications
Protected**

All rights reserved. No part of this publication may be reproduced or transmitted in any form or by any means, electronic or mechanical, including photocopying, recording, or by any information storage and retrieval system, without prior written permission from the Publisher.

Published by:
Bluewater Publications
1812 CR 111
Killen, Alabama 35645
www.BluewaterPublications.com

Bluewater Publications Books by Rickey Butch Walker

Warrior Mountains Indian Heritage - Teacher's Edition,
ISBN 978-1-934610-27-5, $39.95

Warrior Mountains Indian Heritage - Student Edition,
ISBN 978-1-934610-66-4, $24.95

Warrior Mountains Folklore,
ISBN 978-1-934610-65-7, $24.95

Doublehead: Last Chickamauga Cherokee Chief,
ISBN 978-1-934610-67-1, $19.95

Chickasaw Chief George Colbert: His Family and His Country,
ISBN 978-1-934610-71-8, $19.95

Appalachian Indians of the Warrior Mountains,
ISBN 978-1-934610-72-5, $14.95

Celtic Indian Boy of Appalachia: A Scots Irish Cherokee Childhood,
ISBN 978-1-934610-75-6, $14.95

Pending in Publication

Appalachian Indian Trails of the Chickamauga: Lower Cherokee Settlements

Hiking Sipsey: A Family's Fight for Eastern Wilderness

Works in Progress

When Cotton Was King: White Gold of the Muscle Shoals

Black Folk Tales of Appalachia: Slavery to Survival

Soldiers Wife: Cotton Fields to Berlin and Tripoli

Contents

INTRODUCTION 1
    WHO AM I? 1
    FAMILY WREATH 4
    APPALACHIA: MY HEART, MY SOUL 7

MOM, DAD, AND SISTERS 13
    MIGRANT WORK 13
    GONE WEST 15
    SCHOOL DAYS 20

LIFE IN THE HOLLOW 26
    SISTERS, STORMS, AND WASH PANS 26
    DYNAMITE OUR WELL 30
    RED NECKS AND SISTER'S WEDDING 34
    FIRECRACKER FIGHT 39
    EATING ROCKS, CURES, AND CUTS 42
    UNKNOWN BROTHER 46
    HARD LOVE 48
    MOTHER'S CHURCH 51

MATERNAL GRANDPARENTS 53
    RAT POISON GAP 53
    DRUNK DUCKS AND MATTRESSES 56
    QUILT OF LOVE 58
    STORYTELLER 61
    HORSEFLIES, CANDY BARS, AND COTTON POISON 67
    HAPPY BIRTHDAY GRANDPA 70

MOONSHINE AND GAMBLING 75
    WHISKEY THIEF SHOT 75
    WILDCAT, WHITE LIGHTNING 78
    THE CRAP GAME 81
    SHORT AND SLIM 83

PATERNAL GRANDPARENTS 88
    GRANDMA'S HUGE BISCUITS 88
    SHOTGUN WEDDING 94
    OUTHOUSE 96
    TOBACCO PLUGS AND SNUFF 99

    Death Calls and Body Bag 101

WAYS OF THE WILD 108
    Walks in my Home Land 108
    Fiddle Worms and Rattlesnakes 110
    Quail Trap 115
    Turtle and Wild Meat 117
    Fresh Possum 119

HUNTING DOGS 122
    Squirrel Dogs 122
    Blue John 125

BACKWOODS FUN 128
    Grapevines and Saplings 128
    Truck Wagon 130
    Corn Cobs and Cotton Bolls 131

HILL COUNTRY RECREATION 134
    Skinny Dipping Plowboys 134
    Cow Pasture Baseball 136
    County Fair 141
    Coon on the Log 144
    Fighting Game Cocks 147

MOUNTAIN WORK AND SURVIVAL 152
    Hog Killing 152
    Murder and Wood Cutting 155
    Cotton Picking 158
    Sawmill and Softball 160

FISHING ADVENTURES 168
    Night I Never Forgot 168
    Mountain Rifle Fishing 171
    Fishing Hole 174
    Buried Waterfall 177

TRAPPING IN HILL COUNTRY 181
    Trap Line 181
    Bobcat Hole 186
    Mink for Christmas 190

HUNTING IN APPALACHIA **194**
   Bow for an Indian Boy 194
   Grandpa's Love 197

CONCLUSION **200**
   Finishing a Dream at Oakville 200
   Good or Bad; did I choose? 203

INDEX **208**

Introduction

Who Am I?

When I was real small, I asked questions all the time; one of the most frequently asked was, *"Who am I?"* My grandma Ila Wilburn would always say, *"Son you are Arsh and Indian."* At that time, we ate a lot of Arsh taters; therefore I surmised that our ancient folks grew taters. My Walker folks always told me that I was Cherokee, Creek, and Scots.

My Walker aunt had our traditional family Scots kilt with its bright colors of red, blue, and green. I knew that Indians were about wild in all the old cowboy shows; my dad was a perfect role model for the Indians on television. I figured we were people who wore those short dresses, blew bagpipes, carried a tomahawk, used a scalping knife, and shot a bow.

When I asked, *"What kind of Indian am I?"* I was always told that I was part Creek and part Cherokee, but I was never told that I was part Arsh and part Scots. The dilemma was that I never did figure out which part was Cherokee, which part was Creek, which part was Scots, or which part was Arsh. However, when my friends and I played cowboys and Indians, I was always the Indian. I really had this desire to scalp one of those cowboys, but I was always the one that was supposed to die.

At a very young age, I was taught to love who I was and where I came from; the hills and hollows of the lower foothills of southern Appalachia was my folks' home for generations. My Indian and Celtic heritage was an important part of my life; my dad Brady Walker told me stories about his Indian grandmother smoking her corn cob pipe. When I was only seven years old, my great grandpa George Curtis made me my first Cherokee long bow from a white oak tree; he allowed me to help in the completion of my handmade white oak bow. My Grandpa Arthur Wilburn taught me to live off the land and what Mother Nature provided. I was aware of the spirits of my ancestors who walked these lands years before I came along; I learned the old ways, to walk in the way of the wild, to honor traditions, and to respect all the ancestral bloodlines that flowed through my being.

Butch Walker-Celtic Warrior

Picture-*Butch Walker is in his Scots Irish family colors of red, blue, and green kilt, and five foot Celtic broad sword!*

Fast forward fifteen years; one day a friend and I were going to the student lounge at the University of North Alabama in Florence. I told him I was going to get a hamburger and Arsh taters for dinner; everybody at college called it lunch but that was a word I never heard my parents or my grandparents say-it was always breakfast, dinner, and supper.

My friend looked at me very strange and asked, *"Where did you grow up?"* I told him, *"I was raised up in the foothills of the mountains of southern Lawrence County, Alabama."* He said, *"That is what I thought, and the correct name of the food you are going to eat is Irish potatoes."* I said to my friend, *"Are you sure there is not an ethnic group of people that are Arsh?"*

I was just out of high school and was not aware of the correct pronunciation; my friend assured me that no such Arsh ethnic group existed and that was just southern slang for Irish people. At that moment, I was somewhat embarrassed; later, I tried to find out for sure if Arsh people did exist. But, I finally had a realization that I was actually of Irish ancestry and not descended from an Arsh potato grower.

None of my parents, grandparents, or great grandparents had a high school education; they all talked in southern hill country slang and some of those old words still come to mind. It took me a long time to lose that hillbilly style of talking; today, I still use terms that I grew up speaking. My language is not out of ignorance but out of years of hearing and speaking my grandparents' style of hillbilly communication. I really hate that we have lost most of our unique southern Appalachian words that was considered by the educated to be slang; those words were such an important part of my early childhood and our Warrior Mountains colloquial heritage.

Since I believed everything my grandma told me, I had no reason to doubt her answer to the question, *"Who am I?"* When I was in grade school, we were never taught anything about our true ancestry; therefore, my grandparents taught me all I learned about who I was, and they used the word Arsh. The elementary and high schools I attended did not teach us about our Scots, Irish, Creek, and Cherokee mixed-blood people. They just wanted us to learn about the English (Anglo Saxon), French, and Spanish. Our Indian ancestors were talked about like they were Chinese or some distant far away people.

Not too many years ago, the editor and publisher of the elementary history book for the State of Alabama came to my office at the Oakville Indian Mounds Education Center where I worked with Lawrence County Schools' Indian Education Program. They wanted me to recommend and endorse their Alabama history book for fourth grade students in public schools across Alabama. I knew what I had missed when I was taught Alabama history in elementary and high school; I wanted to see if things had changed.

In front of these educated people, I opened the book to the back where the index was located and did not say a word. After looking for several minutes in the book, they asked what I was looking for; I told them that the words Scots, Irish, or Celtic was not in the book and there was no mention of mixed-blood Indian people. I also told them that a very large percentage of people and students in the southeast and North Alabama have Celtic ancestry and some 20 percent of the early arriving Celtic people have mixed Indian blood.

The PhD editor looked at me and said, *"Mr. Walker, Alabama history is like generic medication; it is the same from the Tennessee State Line to Dauphin Island."* I kindly told both the editor and publisher, *"I will never endorse a book that does not teach our children who they really are!"* Today, as far as I know, our history books still do not talk about our Celtic, Indian, or mixed blood heritage so common along the Appalachian Mountains.

Family Wreath

Well folks, I could call my ancestral lineage a family tree, but on my mother's side of the family, my older generations of blood kinfolks formed a family circle or straight line like a pine tree rather than an oak tree. Another way it could be described would be, a tree trunk forked into branches and the branches grew back together to form another trunk. Therefore, I feel compelled to call my maternal historical roots a family wreath instead of a family tree.

Lockey B. Welborn, 1/4 Cherokee
7/13/1834-1/13/1918

Since I had four great, great, great grandparents who were brothers and sisters, quarter blood Cherokee Indian and Scots Irish people, I am very much kin to myself. Those third great grandparents who were a brother and sister combination were Lockey B. Welborn and his sister Mary Elizabeth Welborn, and Pascal Sandy Segars and his sister Martha Segars. Many mixed blood Indian people with dark complexions would many times call themselves Black Dutch or Black Irish, and it was no different with some of my folks.

Personally, it does not bother me in the least to be kin to myself, but so far, I have not kept the family tradition alive and married one of my cousins. I would be willing to marry a cousin for the survival of family traditions and to keep the hillbilly flavor of my ancestors; however, a good looking one has not asked me for my hand in marriage.

Of course, I have been told many times that you could tell if you were from Lawrence County, Alabama, if your family tree was a straight line or circle. It was common and acceptable for first cousins in the Warrior Mountains to marry, but in my case, my great, great grandparents were double first cousins and had the same grandparents.

I will tell it like it was for my great, great, great grandparents; a brother and sister married a brother and sister and two of their kids married who were double first cousins. They had the same blood as a brother and sister and the same grandparents. This is an easy way to avoid having to meet new in-laws because you are already kin to everyone in your spouse's family.

But there is another saying in the Warrior Mountains of the lower Appalachian foothills of North Alabama; it is better to marry your cousin than it is to ride a mule twenty miles through the mountains to find someone who is not kin to you. By the time you found that beauty which was not a cousin, you would be worn out or bruised too bad to do anything about it; therefore, it was better to marry your cousin next door that you could walk to in a few miles than it was to get a woman which required a ride through mountainous and rough terrain on the back of a mule.

Of course, there are big problems with marriage among family members; one is the increase in some abnormalities in the children from these unions, and I am as abnormal as many of my kinfolks. But, there is also special benefits for people like me that are strong introverts; you do not have to worry about searching and asking people about your family tree because you already know your double kinfolks.

You see most of your double cousins at funerals and weddings on both sides of the family; therefore, all marriages and funerals are like family reunions. My family ancestry is just about one big circle or nearly a straight line. Another thing that some genealogists say is a direct result of family inbreeding is the red hair and freckles which is common features of Celtic people; my family has its share of red headed freckled faced relatives and kinfolks which I proudly claim.

Now my family wreath or circle does not stop with my great, great grandparents; the kinfolk's marriage tradition continued for several generations. A brother and a sister of the children of my double first cousin great, great grandparents married another brother and sister who I do not believe were double first cousins but all of their kids were double first cousins. One set of the brother and sister duo was the parents of my maternal grandpa, and my grandpa was one of those double first cousins. I am not aware that these double first cousins ever married each other, but two of my maternal grandpa's sisters married brothers so all their children were also double first cousins.

Then a sister in the family of my mother's mother, my maternal grandma, married her husband's, my maternal grandpa, uncle; therefore my grandpa could also call his uncle his brother-in-law. Then to top that all off, my daddy's sister married my mother's uncle; so my mother could call him uncle or brother-in-law. The situation of whether to call some of our kinfolks a brother-in-law, uncle or aunt, or just cousin was tough when I was a young Celtic Indian boy growing up in the Warrior Mountains.

Augustive T. Welborn, 1/4 Cherokee
12/7/1861-10/20/1920

Since the four parents of my two of great, great grandparents that started my family wreath were one fourth Cherokee Indian and three fourths Scots Irish, I have a good explanation for the inter-family relationships or kinfolk marriages. It was acceptable for Celtic cousins to intermarry in order to keep the family ties strong and to increase the strength of the family clan. The kinfolk's marriage provided loyal family recruits that were needed to increase the numbers of relatives involved in feuds with belligerent neighbors. In addition, in the southeastern Indian culture, children could not marry into the mother's family or their maternal clan; however, it was acceptable for Indian people to marry their paternal cousins or their father's nieces or nephews. Now this may not be a good excuse for marrying family members, but it is the one that I am using to justify closely related marriage in my family.

Now believe it or not, I am going to try to identify all my

relatives involved in my family wreath. The four brothers and sisters were Lockey B. Welborn and Mary Elizabeth Welborn who married Pascal Sandy Segars and Martha Segars. Lockey B. Welborn and Martha Segars had several children but one of those kids was my great, great grandpa Gus Welborn. Pascal Sandy Segars, a Confederate casualty of Cedar Run, and Mary Elizabeth Welborn also had several children and one of those kids was my great, great grandmother Sarah Mandy Segars.

Gus Welborn and Sarah Mandy Segars had Pascal Sandy Welborn and Celia Welborn who married a brother and sister, Robert Johnson and Dora Johnson. Pascal Sandy Welborn and Dora Johnson had two of my Grandpa Arthur's sisters, Nathie and Williemyrl, that married brothers Ara and W. D. Proctor. Also, Pascal Sandy Welborn's brother Howard married Minnie Curtis who was a sister to my Grandpa Arthur's wife, Ila Curtis. Finally, my grandpa's brother Willard Welborn married my daddy's sister Violine Walker; therefore, my mother could call my Uncle Willard uncle or brother-in-law.

Now that was a mouth full, but family cousins did marry to make our kinship circle a little tighter, and this tradition of family marriage arrangements continued for many years. The intermarriage custom was common and acceptable years ago; people did not frown on being married to a cousin. Today, I have first cousins that have been together for several years and are keeping an old family tradition alive for future generations to write about. Look at it this way; they already know their kinfolks because they are from the same family and do not have to worry about new people in their partner's family.

Appalachia: My Heart, My Soul

I grew up in the southern foothills of lower Appalachia; the southwestern end of this Appalachian mountainous area was known for hundreds of years as the Warrior Mountains that covered a vast portion from northern Alabama into northeastern Mississippi. The Warrior Mountains is made up of the hills and hollows that drain the Warrior River Basin and eventually into Mobile Bay.

Many of the first white settler families of Appalachia mixed with the aboriginal Indian people of the area; the majority of these mixed families were of Celtic and Indian blood. During the turmoil of encroachment onto native lands, the Warrior Mountains afforded isolation and protection from removal for my family and other families of mixed American Indian and Celtic ancestry because the area was rugged, remote, and sparsely settled.

The Celtic group of my folks included Scots and Irish while my Indian folks included Cherokee and Creek. The relationship between the two cultures began with the first Celtic traders of the English merchants in the colonies around the middle of the 1700's; many Scots Irish men married women of Cherokee, Creek, or Chickasaw lineage, and on both sides of my family, it was no different. My mixed Walker ancestors were traders to the Indians occupying the area of the Warrior Mountains. Initially many of these traders had a white wife in their colonial home and an Indian wife in the area of lower Appalachia; I reckon that my third great grandpa William B. Walker, Sr. had three wives, and at the age of eighty, he had five children with the youngest James W. Walker being only five years old.

Brady Walker 3/8 Cherokee
5/2/1925-12/29/2001

My mixed blood Celtic Indian folks migrated through the Appalachian Mountains from Virginia, the Carolinas, east Tennessee, and northwestern Georgia leaving a trail of Walker surnames to areas and counties through which they passed. The gradual migration of my Scots Irish Cherokee people occurred over some 250 years; a few of my family ancestors finally settled out in the southern foothills of lower Appalachia in an area known as the Warrior Mountains of northern Alabama. Eventually some of my direct mixed blood ancestors migrated all the way through Alabama, Mississippi, Louisiana, and Arkansas, into the western states of Oklahoma and Texas where some of my relatives remain to this day along the Red River and other places in the west.

The southern foothills of Appalachia in northern Alabama formed the upper drainage of the Warrior River Basin in the counties of Blount, Jefferson, Cullman, Morgan, Lawrence, Franklin, Colbert, Winston, and Marion Counties. At times my mixed blood Celtic Indian people scattered and roamed throughout these vast Appalachian foothills of the Warrior Mountains all the way into the hill country of northeastern Mississippi. It was in these foothills of Appalachia that my people hunted, trapped, raised small patches of corn, planted their gardens, cared for the small numbers of livestock they depended on for food, raised their families, and struggled to survive on the poor mountainous soils.

I have great grandparents on both sides of my family buried throughout Appalachia from Virginia, North Georgia, into North Alabama, through northeastern Mississippi; some of my great grandparents are buried all the way into eastern Texas. I have not visited all their gravesites but have pictures of some of my great grandparents' tombstones from Georgia, Alabama, Mississippi, and Texas. My hardy Celtic Indian ancestors that moved across our great southern states had the urge to find a better life; I have no idea if they ever found what they were looking for, but their desire to move scattered their children from Georgia westward through Texas.

Part of my late 1700's family on both sides got stuck in the lower portion of the southern Appalachian hill country of the Warrior Mountains and raised seven generations of folks down to me; this was a very rugged and isolated area where my relatives intermarried with each other. It was in these Appalachian Mountain foothills where the kinship ties were strong enough to fight one another and then band together like brothers and sisters when the family was threatened. The members of my interrelated mixed blood people moved as a unit or group through the vast area of mountain ranges for protection and to maintain strong family ties.

On both sides of my family, kinfolks moved westward with a lot of aunts, uncles, cousins, and other relatives seeking opportunities which they thought were better; the grass is always greener on the other side of the fence. Today, I am thankful that a few of my people remained in Appalachia; the land of the Warrior Mountains where my family roots have grown very deeply within the sandy mountain soil and surrounding red clay valleys.

Since the first white Europeans landed in our country, my Indian and Celtic grandpas fought and died in nearly every conflict through the Civil War. As Indian people, they fought white encroachment; my Cherokee Indian ancestors White Raven and Kingfisher fought to protect their children and way of life on Appalachian lands that had been theirs for hundreds of years, but their Indian children began marrying Celtic traders and rapidly the native blood quantum of those offspring begin to decrease. These mixed Celtic Indian children started assimilating and marrying more frequently into the massive Celtic migration moving south and west into the lands of the Cherokee, Creek, and Chickasaw of the southeastern United States.

My mixed blood fourth great grandpa William Walker was born about 1760; he was one quarter Scots Irish and three quarters Cherokee and fought with the "Scots Irish over the Mountain Men" against the British at the Battle of King's Mountain; mixed Indian people fought on both sides of the conflict. He later fought with the American forces during the Indian wars. Another fourth great grandpa Joel Legg was born May 28, 1758; he fought the British during the Revolutionary War. Joel served in eight different Massachusetts units at various times from 1775 through 1781; his mother was an Indian lady by the name of Experience Fish.

My folks fought on both sides of the Civil War; my second great grandpa William B. Walker, Jr., born March 15, 1820, was three eighths Cherokee and was from Old Houston, Winston County, Alabama. The area became known as the "Free State of Winston" because the people voted at Looney's Tavern on the Old Jasper Road to remain neutral during the war.

William initially fought for the Confederacy and then joined the Union Army at Camp Davies, Mississippi, on December 14, 1863, and was discharged July 19, 1865. William lived through the Civil War and signed the "Loyalty Oaths" along with his father William, Sr. and his brother Jonathan on August 12, 1867, in Winston County, Alabama. Earlier his brother Jonathan was listed as a prisoner of war as of March 10, 1865, at Monroe Crossroads near Fayetteville, North Carolina; Jonathan Walker was mustered out in Nashville, Tennessee, on July 9, 1865.

When my great, great, grandpa William, Jr.'s seventh child Hulda Christine Walker was born on March 19, 1871, his wife Mary Ann Vaughn died shortly thereafter; then in May 1871, he quickly married Elizabeth Nelson of Morgan County, Alabama, and moved to Mississippi where they had several more children. William died in December 1886, at the age of sixty six of pneumonia; he is buried in the Walker-Big Spring Cemetery in Yalobusha County, Mississippi.

My third great grandpa Confederate Second Sergeant Pascal Sandy Segars was born in Georgia about 1831; he was a rebel soldier that died on August 9, 1862, along with 72 other soldiers in the 48th Alabama at the Battle of Cedar Run in Virginia while fighting with General Stonewall Jackson. Pascal Sandy Segars was enlisted for the war in the Forty Eighth Regiment of the Alabama Volunteers on April 7, 1862, and served only four months and three days before being killed; he left behind six small children with the youngest being Sarah Mandy Segars, my great, great grandmother. He was buried in Virginia in a mass grave with some seventy other rebel soldiers.

Mary E. Welborn, age 75
1/4 Cherokee
5/2/1838-12/24/1913

Pascal Sandy Segars' wife Mary Elizabeth Welborn was born May 2, 1838, and died December 24, 1913; she is buried at Old Bulah on top of the mountain ridge overlooking Indian Tomb Hollow. Both Pascal Sandy Segars and Mary Elizabeth Welborn were quarter blood Cherokee and three quarters Scots Irish. My parents and maternal grandparents are buried less than a mile north of Indian Tomb Hollow in the Welborn Cemetery close to Pascal and Mary's daughter Sarah Mandy Segars Welborn who married her double first cousin Augustive (Gus) T. Welborn.

In the northern portion of what was once known as the Black Warrior Forest of the Warrior Mountains, I have a seventh generation great, great, great, great, grandmother Martha Elzey Welborn, who was the wife of Gideon Welborn. She was born on June 20, 1797, and died in 1887; she was the mother of Lockey B. Welborn and Mary Elizabeth Welborn. Grandma Martha lies buried beneath the sandy mountain soil within a few miles of where I have spent the vast majority of my life. Martha's grave is in Bankhead Forest at the Cave Springs Cemetery which is located at the junction of the Leola Road and the Old Jasper Road (Highway 41) near the southeastern corner of Lawrence County, Alabama.

My roots are deep in the backwoods, hollows, and hills of a land that I roamed over with my grandpa at a very early age; a landscape where I was taught the old ways and the ways of the wild even before starting to school. A place where I carried a bow and arrow handmade by my great grandpa before the time I had enough strength to pull it back; the place I trapped and hunted from my earliest remembrance. This was a place that time left behind for many years; a place where the Appalachian foothills merge with the flat plain of the Moulton Valley. This place is the Warrior Mountains where I grew to manhood; still in my mind, a place of the old ways where I walked in the ways of the wild of years ago.

It is my desire that my grandchildren be raised in my land of deep family roots. I want my grandkids to appreciate the green crowned hills and deep misty hollows of my youth; the same land of the youth of their ancestors. I want my grandchildren to raise their families in an area that still slows time to an era steeped in family traditions and cultural awareness of the area where many of their preceding generations of people lay buried.

This land is my heart and my soul, the land of the Warrior Mountains where my ancestral spirits from long ago still calls me home. Because of these feelings and for these reasons, I dedicate this book *"Celtic Indian Boy of Appalachia"* to all my grandchildren; may they forever love this land as did their grandparents before them.

Mom, Dad, and Sisters

Migrant Work

In the early 1950's, my dad, Brady Walker, and my mom, Novel Wilburn, could not find work and survived by living in an old clap board house on my grandpa Dan Walker's place. My daddy would help with farm work; milk some 40 dairy cows and do other odd jobs he could find. Times were extremely tough for my parents to make ends meet and the old wooden house was not much, but it was free from rent and all Grandpa Dan expected was a little help on the farm with his milking and row crops in return for living in the house.

Grandpa Dan Walker had a pair of mules, a bunch of milk cows, hogs, chickens, and several acres of crop land that was planted every spring. He and his kids had cleared the 130 acre farm; they survived the depression through hard work and self-sufficiency. My dad and his other siblings would help grandpa milk his old cows in his small dairy operation and put the milk into big metal cans to be sold.

The milk truck would come by on a regular basis to pick up the milk and then send grandpa a check. Grandpa Walker's farm was on the old Jasper Road (present-day Highway 41) in Morgan County, Alabama, about five miles south of Danville. When I was a small boy, the old road was a dusty dirt road that would have big mud holes during wet weather.

Being desperate for work, my folks were willing to pick up the small amount of essential belongings and go where ever they could make a little money. During this period of time, a lot of people in the North Alabama area were out of work; these poor families around the Warrior Mountains area would take off north during the spring and summer to Michigan to pick cherries and other fruit in order to survive.

Many of these poor southern families would make up the migrant labor force for the northern fruit farmers. Sometimes people who migrated from the south to the north for fruit picking would wind up getting jobs in the factories and stay; therefore, many families in North Alabama have kinfolks in Michigan and other northern states. The times when large numbers of southerners went north to pick fruit were prior to the mass migration of Mexican farm laborers which began flooding the country for agricultural work during the 1970's.

Novel Wilburn and Brady Walker

Anyway, when I was a small boy and my two older sisters were not in school, my dad and his younger brother Kenneth Walker had this brilliant idea that they could make a killing picking fruit in the north. Uncle Kenneth, my dad, my mom and three small kids, which included me, packed up the old car and headed to Kalamazoo, Michigan. To say the least, riding conditions were not the best with a carload of people, much less all the junk we had to have to survive on for the entire spring and summer in the north land.

    We were kind of like the Clampets headed to Hollywood, but this trip would not be a life of luxury. After being on the road for hours, we finally made it to our destination in Michigan. Memory does not serve me or my sisters as to where we stayed when we got up north, but I do remember my dad telling how tough it was to wind up with any profit. Everything that he made picking fruit was used to just keep food for us to eat and a place to stay.

    After a few months in the north on the fruit picking expedition, Uncle Kenneth and my dad tried to save enough money from their hard work to make it back to Alabama. Dad told me many times that we were lucky to make it back home; when we finally got back to Alabama, he and Uncle Kenneth were flat broke. Our fruit picking adventure was a bust; we were glad to be back in the familiar country of the Warrior Mountains.

Upon our arrival back to Grandpa Dan Walker's, another farm and milk hand had moved into our old house; therefore, we had to find another place to live. Two of my daddy's brothers, Uncle William Roy Walker and Uncle Thurman Walker, lived in the Addison area and helped my dad get a farm job with Mr. Waymon Elam. Mr. Elam had a big farm with lots of cattle and several fine horses.

Dad got to go to work for Mr. Elam at Addison and we moved into a small house he had for his farm hands. The little house we lived in was next to Mr. Elam's big house in downtown Addison, Alabama. Mr. Elam even had a concrete walkway going up to his house and we thought it was grand to walk on his sidewalk. My oldest sister Diane went through the first grade at Addison Elementary.

While at Addison, I remember riding with Mr. Elam on his big red horse. He would set me in front of him and ride me all over the farm. He had a bunch of horses and we would ride across his pastures checking on all the stock. However, my dad and mom still had not settled our little family into one location and would soon be on the move again and again. It was not long that my Aunt Ida came home and told my dad about her restaurant in Springfield, Colorado. She promised my mom a job as a waitress; therefore, look out west here we come.

Gone West

My folks were barley scraping by with three small children, times were extremely difficult, and finding steady work in the 1950's was hard to come by; therefore, we were on the move for several years so that my parents could make enough money to survive. My Aunt Ida told my dad that my mother could do waitress work at her restaurant in Springfield, Colorado, and that she was sure that he could find a job.

Within a short time after my dad heard the good news about job opportunities, we were on the way out west. We found a small house in Springfield and my daddy got a job working at a flying horse service station and mother started her job as a waitress. This area was a strange land for a Celtic Indian boy from the Warrior Mountains of North Alabama. The area was fairly flat, arid, and dusty, but I remember the little horny toads that we loved to play with. These were actually fat short lizards with little spikes all over their bodies.

Mother would sometimes babysit two little girls that used to stay with us while their mother worked and their names were Charlotte and Denny. The thing I hated about having these two girls at our house was that my momma would put all three of us in a big tub at the same time and give us all a bath in the same water; their plumbing was a whole lot different than mine and I did not like them examining me every time we took a bath.

Brady holding Denny, Novel holding Charlotte, Butch, June, Diane

Charlotte was the older one and was always getting into trouble and at the same time she managed to get me in deep trouble. One day while we were playing hide and seek outside, Charlotte told me to get in an old refrigerator that was out back of the house where we lived. After I crawled in the refrigerator, Charlotte slammed the door shut locking me on the inside.

I pushed on the door of that old refrigerator and it would not open; I hollered to the top of my lungs for someone to come let me out of that death trap. After a long time, mother started looking for me and Charlotte eventually told her that I was in the refrigerator. When I was finally rescued, I was wet with sweat and about to pass out. I was extremely glad to be out of that trap that could have easily been my demise. I honestly believe that I would have been dead within a couple more hours.

On another occasion, I got mad at the girls who were picking on me and run in the house with my baseball. The old lady across the street saw what was going on and decided to come over to my house to comfort me. She had a bunch of bananas that she was going to give me as a treat; however, little did she know that I was behind our couch with the baseball in my hand. I was waiting to ambush one of the girls; but, instead I heard the precious old lady opening the door.

I stayed hid thinking it was one of my tormentors who were coming through the door. As the door stopped moving, I come up from behind the couch throwing my baseball and was deadly accurate. The baseball hit the old lady smack dab on the middle of her nose and knocked her completely out the front door. I knew immediately that I had made a grave mistake.

I run out to help her with a bleeding nose and knew that I had a whipping coming as soon as my folks got home from work. Sure enough, when momma got home, she grabbed her belt and gave me a good whipping and the same thing happened when my daddy got home. That was one thing that I really hated, but I will never forget the event that happened in Springfield, Colorado.

The weather was different in Springfield than what I was used to in the Warrior Mountains because it was windy and dry. One Sunday afternoon, my family decided to go on a ride and look over the country. As we were headed out of the little town, we saw a very dark cloud in the distance. You could see for miles and at first my parents had no idea what was on the horizon; therefore, we drove on toward the black cloud that was all the way to the ground. My dad finally realized that the black wall we were approaching was a huge dust storm; therefore, he turned the car around and headed back to our little house.

By the time we got back home, the dust storm was already hitting the area with a vengeance. Mother grabbed towels and stuffed them in the cracks under the door; suddenly it became darker than night on the outside and the wind and dust were howling. The dust storm lasted well into the night and the next morning everything including our bodies was covered with dust as fine as flour. My mother had to take all the dishes which were full of dust out of the cabinets; and she washed not only the dishes, but also all of our clothes. The entire floor had about an inch of dust as fine as flour covering everything in sight including all the furniture. I will never forget my first and last dust storm in Springfield, Colorado.

In addition to the dust storm, I got to see the largest snow storm that I ever got to witness. It was extremely cold in Colorado during the winter but the dry air made it seem not so cold; however, one afternoon, it decided to snow and did not stop for several hours. The next day I remember going out to see a snow well over two feet deep, but looking across the country, the snow was a beautiful sight. Even though Springfield was east of the Rockies, it still got a large snow storm that winter we were in Colorado; finally my parents decided that we needed to go back home to the land of our ancestors which made us all excited to go back and see our grandparents.

In the spring, we headed back to the Warrior Mountains of North Alabama and this time mother wanted to settle near her parents who lived on the northern eastern edge of William B. Bankhead National Forest. When we got back to Alabama, my dad found us an old clap board house on the old Alexander Plantation and he started to work as a farm hand for Mr. Joe Jacobs who was the son-in-law of Mr. Jake Alexander. Joe Jacobs, who was married to Quillar Alexander the daughter of Jake, had taken over the farming operations on the old plantation; he had a bunch of farmhands that worked the fields, took care of the livestock, and ran the old cotton gin.

I remember picking cotton for Mr. Tom Hall who rented the place after Joe Jacobs quit farming the land. One particular day, we were picking cotton in what the local folks called the mound field; in 1924, an Indian mound in that cotton patch had been excavated by the Smithsonian. A lot of Indian artifacts were still scattered across a huge area of the field; it was that hot dry day that I was busy picking cotton when I found my first perfect arrowhead. I was so excited that I ran through the cotton to my Grandma Ila Wilburn to show her my find; for the rest of that afternoon, all I did was look for more arrowheads.

Our old house on the Alexander Plantation was just 500 yards west of the gin lot and on the south side of the old Poplar Log Cove Road. Our plank dwelling was within walking distance of the big hickory tree where all the farmhands would gather in the morning waiting for their orders for the day. The big hickory tree was just to the west of the plantation house that was built by Thomas Jefferson Alexander and about 75 yards east of the old log barn that was built seven years before the Civil War. Today, the old log barn is still standing and has been covered with a metal roof; the old plantation house that I played in as a child has long since been destroyed.

Our share cropper's house on the farm was old, but it did have electricity and on the front porch my mother had an old wringer washing machine. Sometimes the clothes would get stuck trying to go through the drying rollers that would squeeze the water out of the clothes; mother would take her finger and push the clothes so they would pass through the rollers. After watching her, I decided that I would push the clothes with my index finger; however, my finger got stuck in the rollers and was nearly pulled off my hand. Today, I still have the scar where my finger was torn about an inch before the rollers finally got hung up and stalled.

Even though I had a bad experience at the old Alexander share cropper's house, I was glad to be back near my Grandpa and Grandma Wilburn's home. The old board house on the Alexander Place was close to my mother's folks. Shortly after arriving back in the area, my Wilburn Grandparents gave my mother and daddy a piece of land to build a house.

After about a year on the Alexander Plantation, my dad and Grandpa Walker had completed us a little frame house just downhill from my mother's parents. I was tickled to death to be next door to my Wilburn Grandparents because I loved my Grandpa Arthur who was the best grandpa a young boy could ever have; I would stay all night with my Grandpa and Grandma Wilburn often.

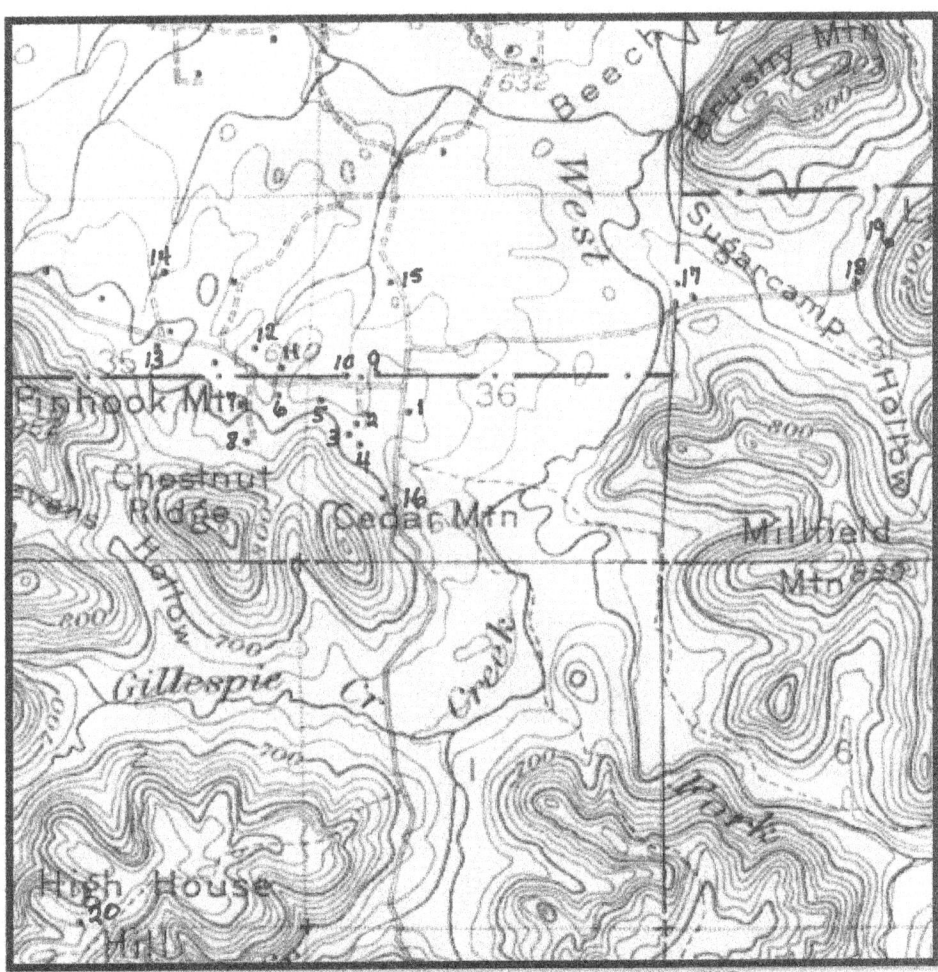

1. Alexander House 2. Nola & Monroe Welborn 3. Nola Welborn 4. McDonald, Jimmy & Odis 5. John Sterling & Brady Walker 6. Wes & Mamie Hardin 7. Frank & Celia Johnson 8. K McVay 9. Joe & Quillar Jacobs 10. Kay Melson 11. Willard & Violine Welborn 12. G. H. Melson 13. Gus Welborn 14. Rayford Welborn 15. Terrell 16. G. H. Melson 17. Sandy Welborn 18. Jim Johnson 19. Arthur Wilburn 20. William Alexander-High House

Alexander Plantation Map 1933 to 1935-Other families lived on the Alexander place including Frankie Slaten, Shirley Johnson, Luther Melson, Bobbie Nell Cheatham, Lucy Bolan, Linda Sherrill, Meherg, Mann, and Curtis Wilburn.

My mother would not let me stay over six nights per week at my Wilburn Grandparents; she made me sleep at home at least one night each week. I was very happy to be back near my Grandpa Arthur where I could hunt, fish, and trap with him in the land of my ancestors.

School Days

Our little frame house in the hollow next to Grandpa Wilburn was some seven miles from the nearest school; when I finally went to school, an old yellow school bus driven by Mr. Manco White would pick up me and my two sisters. I was nearly seven years old when I started to Speake School; it was the same school that my mother Novel Wilburn and her two brothers Curtis and Cadle Wilburn attended but neither one of them graduated. My two older sisters Diane and June were already attending Speake, but I was not very anxious to get started. I had not been around a lot of people and was not in a hurry to make new friends; my home was isolated and I spent my time with my grandpa and my dogs.

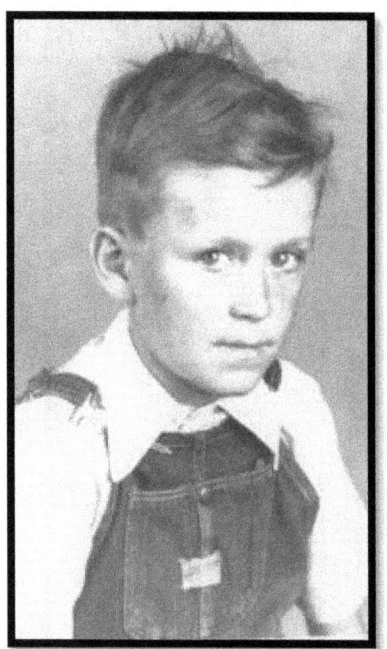

Cadle Wilburn
Speake Elementary

My life was very satisfactory to a young Celtic Indian boy who wanted to roam the woods and hunt squirrels and rabbits; my parents thought that I needed an education, but if it had been my choice, I would probably not know how to read or write to this day. I turned six on November 12 but did not get to start school until the following fall; the only good thing about starting school in fall was that I did not have to pick cotton every day. However, I found out very quickly that they let school out for six weeks for cotton picking time each fall!

I will never forget that first day that my dad, Brady Walker, took me to Speake School and cussed out the principal Mr. Smith; I had enough sense to know that it would not be in my best interest to start school with my dad and the principal in a cuss fight over a little piece of paper. My parents had lost my birth certificate or had never gotten one; the principal had to have proof of my age. My dad insisted that the principal could look at me and tell that I was old enough to start school. After Mr. Smith told my dad that he was going to call the law if he did not leave, daddy took me by the arm and we left school; wow, I was relieved that I would not have to go to school but that did not last but a few days.

Since I was born in a small upstairs clinic in Hartselle, Alabama, my parents had failed to get a copy of my birth certificate or they had misplaced the one that I had; somehow my folks finally got the certificate to prove to the principal that I was old enough to start school. Finally on the second trip to get me started to school, mother took me and that little piece of paper to the school principal since my dad did not like the little boss man that was going to put him in jail if he showed up again at his school. Mother showed the principal the piece of paper and he agreed to let me start school that day which was about a week late.

At the time I entered the first grade of school, black children were not allowed in the white school and neither were black teachers; I knew that I had

Brady Walker

been told all my life that I was Indian and Arsh but it was acceptable as long as you were not black. It was not until my senior year that the first black students came to Speake School. The male student who was the first in my high school class enrolled in 1968; he eventually quit probably because of the treatment he received from the other white male students especially during physical education classes.

I felt very bad for the black student and always thought of my own Indian heritage when I witnessed bullying by other white students just because he was different.

I was never taught by a black teacher until I went to college; some of my black professors were the best instructors of my college career. Governor George Wallace fought integration of Alabama schools; he was finally forced to change state policies when federal troops escorted the first black students into the University of Alabama, but it took a few more years before some people accepted the change.

Back to starting my first year of school; the second time my folks tried to enroll me at Speake School was evidently successful. The principal and my mother walked me down the hall and put me in the first grade classroom with a bunch of ugly white boys and pretty girls that I had never laid eyes on except my first cousin Sylvia Prater. My first grade teacher was an older mean white woman by the name of Kathleen Glover; I thought Ms. Glover was mean because she would not let me go to the bathroom. She said you have to use the bathroom only at the designated time, but my bowels were not waiting for the designated bathroom break; I sat there squirming for what seemed an eternity before I finally said that was enough and just shit in my britches.

The good thing about me taking that dump in my pants was that I felt immediate relief and it was one of those very hard turds; I kind of eased up off the lump like one of my bantam chicken hens setting on eggs so that it would not squish the hard ball of crap in my pants. As luck would have it, Ms. Glover said it was time to go to lunch; I will never forget walking in a straight line down the hall quiet as a church mouse to the lunch room that was in the basement. As I walked in that line, I managed to shake that hard lump of dodo down my britches leg and on to the floor; I was relieved that the mess was out of my britches. I am sure that one of the other kids stepped on the crap because I smelled it for the rest of the day or the smell might have just stayed in my blue jeans. From that day on when Ms. Glover give us a bathroom break, I tried to make sure I finished my business in the rest room!

Ms. Glover's husband Richard Hansel Glover also taught at Speake High School; when I was in the eleventh grade Mr. Glover taught me chemistry. On four occasions, I thought that I was going to get expelled from school; the first account came when a friend of mine James Steele was making some sort of dye in a gallon round bottomed flask. James asked for an ingredient; I gave him a big spoon of dry powder sodium peroxide which is extremely explosive when mixed with water. James dumped the chemical into the flask and it blew into a million pieces covering Mr. Glover and James; it turned James' bright yellow shirt and Mr. Glover's white shirt dark brown spotted. James was still holding the top of the big flask; he and Mr. Glover tried to clean up as best they could.

On another fateful chemistry lab day in Mr. Glover's class, I took a stick of sodium metal from a quart jar of kerosene; I threw the block of metal toward a nearby mud hole but missed. Larry Vernon, whom I played basketball with, slipped outside and kicked the sodium in the mud hole; the pure sodium metal reacted rapidly with the water creating a lot of hydrogen gas which exploded with the sound of a stick of dynamite. That little act cost me another whipping and warning of being expelled.

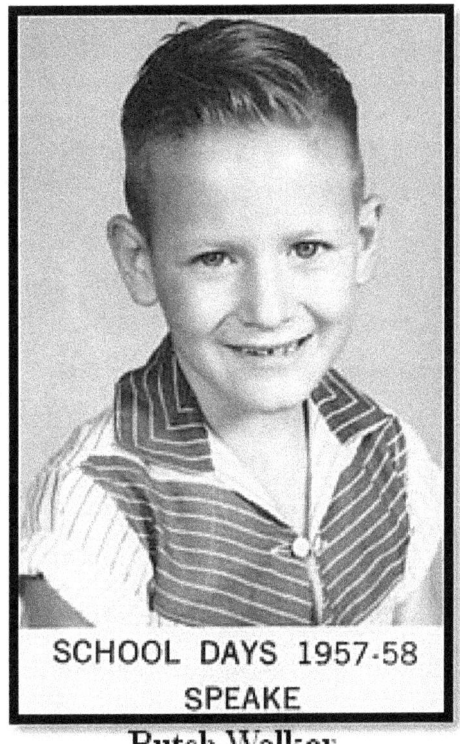

SCHOOL DAYS 1957-58
SPEAKE
Butch Walker

The third act that got Mr. Glover's attention was the making of nitroglycerin; we had the concentrated nitric acid, glycerin, and concentrated sulfuric acid which I mixed together according to the directions to form a highly explosive chemical. When my mixture started smoking, I confessed to Mr. Glover and he immediately evacuated the classroom; he made me stay and help dilute the concoction and we avoided an explosion. Today, most high school chemistry labs do not have highly dangerous materials accessible to all students.

The final act that got me another paddling was the making of hydrogen sulfide; as quickly as the foul rotten egg gas started coming out of my beaker, students begin running to the door. This time Mr. Glover put his foot down and carried me to the office with the threat of expulsion if I pull another trick in his chemistry lab. After another paddling, I settled on peaceful terms with Mr. Glover.

Now, back to elementary school; first grade was tough because Ms. Glover would make us set in a circle and read about Dick, Jane, and Spot; I did not like saying Dick especially in front of the girls because I had heard too many drunken men use that word in a way that was not very nice or appropriate in front of females. Since it did not bother Ms. Glover, I just went ahead and call Dick just as loud as the other words and many times I would hear the other boys that were not in the reading group giggle; I knew exactly what they were laughing about. Ms. Glover seemed oblivious to the word and must have been hard of hearing because she always made us read real loud. I can hear the sentences in the book to this very day; *"See Dick run. See Jane run. See Spot run."* Of course, Spot was the dog and I liked dogs!

Well I survived the first grade and got moved on to second grade which was about as boring as first, but at least I had a new teacher whose name was Ms. Lora Dale Armor; I do not believe that Ms. Armor was ever married and would not weigh 100 pounds soaking wet and carrying 20 pounds of books. Later Ms. Armor was moved to the high school where she taught English; I was in her English class one day when Boyce Reeves was kidding me about my girlfriend, Barbara Johnson. At the time, I was wearing a cast for a broken left arm from a wrestling fight in the gym with Roger Keenum; I was in the twelfth grade and had moved back to Speake High School from Mt. Hope High School.

While Ms. Armor was in front of class teaching, I got out of my chair and went to the door where coke bottles were placed in a wooden crate; with my good right hand, I picked up the crate and dumped out all the bottles. I brought the crate back to the desk of Boyce Reeves and dared him to stand up; about that time, Mr. Jackie Shelton, who had been walking down the hall, come running in the class and grabbed me. He proceeded to escort me into the hall and pushed me up against the lockers; I grabbed his tie and twisted it in my right hand and shoved him into the lockers before the principal Harold Beason came to the rescue. I was threatened with expulsion but mother came to the school and got Mr. Beason to give me a severe paddling instead. Mr. Shelton later became the preacher at Pleasant Grove Baptist Church at Wren, Alabama.

Me and my broken arm!

The third grade was as uneventful as the first and second, but again I had a new white woman teacher who was Ms. Doshia Jacobs; I thought Ms. Jacobs was as old as the hills and she was pretty strict, but at least she let us go to the bathroom in case of emergency. Third grade was not very interesting; however, I caught on quickly and made very good on my report card.

Eventually I made a few friends, but I still liked to be by myself when I got home. Usually the first thing I would do after school was grab my gun and go to the woods where my dog was treed; after a few hours hunting, I would rush back home and complete my chores. I never worried about homework because I hated it with a passion; I could not believe that teachers would have you to sit in that classroom all day long, bore you to death, and then expect you to have your homework completed the next day.

The fourth grade got very interesting with my new teacher Ms. Ava Johnson; I remember one time her hose needed to be tightened up. I watched her when she pulled up her skirt, then pulled down the garter strap, and refastened her hose. She did not seem to think much of the innocent act, but it about made my eyes bug out to see my teacher's thigh that high up on her leg; best I remember she had nice looking legs and the image has stayed with me to this day!

Now, I liked my fourth grade teacher Ms. Johnson, but I was always getting into trouble in her class; one afternoon I had to go to the restroom and decided that I would just go ahead and get on the bus. Mr. Burly Smith was my bus driver and always got to school about an hour before it was dismissed; that day Mr. Smith asked what I was doing getting on the bus early and I told him the teacher let me go. Ms. Johnson did let me go to the bathroom, but I was supposed to return to class and not to get on the bus.

Ms. Johnson reported me missing when I failed to return to class; the next day, I got a paddling for leaving school early. Another time I got a good paddling from Ms. Johnson was when we were practicing for a Christmas program in the auditorium; Larry Hogan handed me a cap gun while we were in a group practicing Christmas carols. During the middle of rehearsal of a Christmas song, I pulled the trigger of the gun and it made a very loud sound; Ms. Johnson was scared and screamed. I got another paddling for firing the cap gun; all Larry Hogan got was a big belly laugh.

Marie Freeman was my fifth grade teacher; I do not remember much about the fifth grade and stayed out of trouble. But when I went to Ms. Hattie Harrison's sixth grade class, I found another mean teacher; she would twist your ears and pull your hair for not paying attention. Ms. Hattie would make you learn all these poems and recite them in her class. Kentucky Bell was her favorite poem and it was long; I will never forget, *"The summer of 63 sir, Conrad had gone away, gone to the country town sir to sell our first load of hay. We lived in a log house yonder, poor as ever you seen..."* Anyway, we had to recite that poem word for word; I also related to the poem by being a poor Celtic Indian boy growing up in the foothills of Appalachia!

Life in the Hollow

Sisters, Storms, and Wash Pans

When I think of growing up as a young Celtic Indian boy in the mountains of Lawrence County, my two older sisters come to mind; my oldest sister was Diane Walker and she was usually in charge when my parents were not at home and she had her hands full with me. My youngest sister June Walker took orders real good from Diane and never tried to make me mind; she left that job to Diane. I really hate to admit it, but I was a handful for my sister when I was a small boy growing up on a dirt road in an isolated hollow between Brushy, Cedar, and Mull Johnson Mountains; Mull Johnson Mountain was also known as Larrymore Mountain. Only my kinfolks lived in that flat valley between those mountains and I had no one to play with until my cousins came for a visit.

Diane, June, and Butch in our house

Most days before school my younger cousins Joan and Mike Wilburn would come to the house to catch the school bus; this provided me great opportunity to pick on them until Diane stepped in to make me mind. If I got mad enough at Diane for making me behave, I usually took off to the woods; of course, I did not have far to go but for some reason my sisters would not follow me to the mountainside. Diane would get out in the yard and holler for me to come back home and promise that she would not tell daddy; after my temper tantrum settled down, I came back to the house to avoid having my sisters tell on me for being mean because that meant a whipping when my daddy got home.

My dad acted real tough on the boys that dated my sisters Diane and June but I believe it was just rough talk; I never saw anything other than hearing his words which sometimes were pretty bad. Dad did not mind embarrassing my sisters or their dates, and the best I remember, he was pretty strict on the hours that they were expected to be home.

Our home was not that big but the boys were expected to come in the house to be looked over by my dad before they could take his daughters off the premises.

Dad usually told the boys that dated my sisters in no uncertain words what he expected and did it with a lot of conviction; it is a wonder that a guy stuck around long enough to marry one of his daughters. My dad certainly did not put up with any rough neck boys like he was; he knew from personal experience how bad boys act because he was one. I never remember dad allowing a bad boy like that around our house except me; the only reason he allowed me to hang around was that I was his son.

My oldest sister was dad's favorite child when he was drunk and moaning; she would take care of him. June and I just tried to stay out of his reach but Diane would take cold wash cloths and put on his face and on the back of his neck. She would hold his hand when some rot gut whiskey was making him sick as a rattlesnake bit dog and even clean up after him when he was puking drunk; she would say, *"Daddy, I wish you would not get drunk."* My dad would act like he was so sick that he was going to die and my big sister would be so upset and worried because she really thought that he was going to die; he would holler, gag, spit up, groan, vomit, and beg for help. My mother would get fed up with his actions and just leave him alone, but Diane would pet him until he finally went to sleep.

Some might say that it was my dad's Cherokee blood that made him get staggering drunk, but his brothers, my paternal uncles, were not that way. My daddy's brothers were hard working family men who had survived the great depression; they were decent hill country folks that had property, nice houses, and made a good living for their families. My dad loved his five brothers and four sisters that survived to adulthood; all are now dead except one surviving aunt.

Dad worked just as hard as his brothers and sisters; all his family had a very strong work ethic and for the most part they were just hard working people. However, daddy's siblings seemed to possess a different philosophy of life than that of my dad; I heard him say many times, *"I am going to live hard and die young."* Dad did make life hard and rough on himself by the way he lived when he was young, but he still managed to live until he was 76 years old.

When my oldest sister started dating, we lived in a small wood frame house that probably was no more than 800 square feet; the house was on a dirt road just downhill from my maternal grandparents. The sides of the little house were covered with wide lap siding material and the roof was tin. Initially our house had only four rooms, one small living room, a small kitchen and dining room combination, my sisters' room, my parents room, and later as an add on I had a small room in the back corner of the house. Prior to the back room added on our little house, I spent five to six nights per week at my maternal grandparents; I know they thought of me as more than just a grandson.

Our little frame house next to my Wilburn grandparents

Man, I loved to sleep at either my grandparents or my house under a pile of quilts in the winter time when it was pouring down rain on top of the tin roof. Since neither house had ceiling insulation, the sound of the rain made a thunderous noise. Now that was some great sleeping weather; except when we had to get up in the middle of the night during terrible storms and run across the yard to a hole that we called a storm pit. Daddy and I had dug the hole into the red clay bank about 100 yards south of the house because of the fear of tornadoes.

I well remember waiting on the storm to really intensify before my parents would say we had to go to that dreaded hole in the red clay bank. We would all run for the storm pit in a downpour so hard you could barely see where you were going except for the brilliant flashes of lightning going across the sky. Many times the wind would be blowing so hard that you had to lean into the wind just to get started making a run for safety. By the time we made it to our storm shelter, we would all be soaking wet and usually cold; after being in the pit for a while we would all emerge with our feet covered in red clay mud. I remember squishing that mud between the toes of my bare feet; actually it felt real good.

The roof of the storm pit had tin on top of cedar poles; then a layer of clay and dirt about three feet thick was placed on top of the tin. Weeds would grow on top of our storm shelter; the storm pit was a snake haven and muddy water always run down the sides and across the floor. The door was made from heavy oak boards and opened into a narrow trench leading downhill where the muddy water would flow out of our hole. The bottom of the storm shelter was usually about two to three inches deep in mud by the time the storm was over. If the storm pit roof had collapsed, we would all be dead; sometimes there was only standing room in that death trap because neighbors that did not have a storm shelter would huddle inside our muddy pit.

Our little house did not have indoor plumbing and we all took a wash pan, bar of soap, and wash cloth to bathe; we were made to take a bath at least one time each day and my mom was the inspector. She would always check to see if I was clean and I never remember her checking my older sisters. My mother always made me wash behind my ears and that was the first thing she would do is grab me by the ears and look in them then behind my ears.

Butch and Storm Pit

If I missed a spot, mother would make me pay because she would grab that rag and nearly rub my hide off. Sometimes we would be in the car going somewhere and she would spot a little dirt that I had accidently missed; immediately she would grab a handkerchief, spit on it, and start rubbing the dirt and hide off me. I never remember her giving my sisters a spit bath; they must have been pretty good with the wash cloth.

During the winter time, the wash pan filled about half full of water was placed on top of our coal burning heater in the living room; you guessed it, it was my job to bring in all the coal we use in a tin coal bucket. When it was cold weather, we heated the wash pan of water on top of that old potbellied heater prior to our bath. Since we had an electric cook stove, we heated the bath water in that wash pan on a cooking eye during the summer time; it would be so hot in that kitchen that we set an electric fan in our window to get cool air. I remember just one tin wash pan for all of us to use which meant only one person could take a rag bath at a time.

The water we used to bathe in had to be drawn for our well which was about fifty yards behind our house; prior to us getting a well pump, it was my job to draw all the water for bathing and drinking. The well was actually about 100 yards downhill from our one hole outhouse and my hog pen was uphill from the well about 50 yards. Since the well contained sulfur water, we would never know by the smell if the well was contaminated. I must admit that it was hard getting use to bathing and drinking sulfur water because it stunk like rotten eggs, but I reckon it got us clean with a bar of soap that smelled a lot better than that water. Such was life when I was a young Celtic Indian boy growing up in Appalachia.

Dynamite Our Well

In the early days of my childhood, most all folks that built a house in the area of the Warrior Mountains either had a hand dug well or a spring near their home as a primary water supply. My grandparents were no different; my mother's folks had a spring just uphill from their house that they called the Hattie Hogan Spring; the spring was named for the lady they bought the land from. This spring that my mother grew up using had the sweetest tasting water that came right out of the mountain side and never went dry.

My dad's folks, Dan and Vady Walker, had a hand dug well; dad grew up using water from that well which was some 30 feet deep, about four feet in diameter, and lined with field stones to prevent the sides from caving into the hole. Next to the well, my Walker grandparents had three big black wash pots; with twelve kids in the family, my Grandma Walker stayed busy washing everybody's clothes. Of course, she used her old rub boards and homemade lye soap; she usually had the water heated pretty hot with the fire at the base of the cast iron wash pots. After the clothes were washed and rinsed, grandma had a clothes line near the well where she would hang the clothes to dry in the sun.

Also located next to the Walker well was a rack for hanging hogs; once the hogs were killed, the water was drawn from the well and boiled in the pots. The scalding water was then poured over the hogs to loosen the hair so that the animals could be scraped clean with big bladed butcher knives prior to processing. Many activities requiring lots of water was done near the well to prevent having to tote the water a long distance.

Whether the water supply was a spring or hand dug well, both had to be cleaned out eventually. I remember helping my Grandma Wilburn clean out her spring; over the years, the spring would collect a lot of leaves from the nearby trees. The old leaves would just about fill up the spring, and the only way to remove them was to get into the spring and dig them out. After the cleaning job was completed, it did not take long for the spring water to clear up and be ready for use. Prior to my Grandmother Wilburn's death, we installed a concrete tank at the spring and ran a pipe to her house; she had running water because the spring was up hill from the house some 300 yards.

About the same thing would happen to the big open hand dug wells which were usually not covered; trash, leaves and other debris would fall into the well over time. Therefore in the driest time of the year, a person would be let down into the well to clean out all the debris that collected in the bottom of the well. Over the years, the leaves, trash, and mud would build up in the well; someone would have to go down and dig it out and haul the trash to the surface to be discarded.

When I was about six years old, my dad and Grandpa Walker had completed our little frame house; by that time, people had drilling machines that would pound a hole into the ground for a well. We got Mr. Newt Hill to witch for water prior to having the well drilled by Mr. A. J. Oliver and his son Glenn Oliver; Mr. Oliver's well machine actually beat a hole into the ground in our back yard some 60 feet deep. The old drilling machine had a 20 solid iron pole with a chisel bit about six inches wide at the bottom; the metal pole was attached to the machine by a steel cable and beat in two foot strokes. I will never forget the constant pounding sound that the drilling made while punching a hole into the earth.

Newt Hill

Mr. Newt, who was three-eighths Creek and Cherokee Indian, cut a forked peach tree limb and held it out in front of his chest and started walking across our yard witching for water. At one point, the end of the fork started turning toward the ground with such great force that the bark on the forked stick actually twisted off the limbs that Mr. Newt was holding. He cut another forked peach tree limb and started toward the location from another direction and the fork twisted in his hands so hard that the bark peeled off again. Mr. Newt put a stake in the ground and said that we should hit water within 40 feet and sure enough we did.

Nearly everybody I knew always had someone to witch for water prior to digging their well; the person was supposed to have special powers in order to witch for a good stream of water and most old time well witchers use a fruit tree fork to find water. Some water witchers would use iron rods while other people finding water underground would use heavy copper wires in order to detect the stream of water prior to wasting money drilling a dry hole. When the rods that were held parallel crossed, the well witchers knew that a stream of water was not far below ground. Of course, those men that were productive in finding great streams of water had good reputations throughout the community and were highly sought after for finding water supplies.

Our machine dug well was just about 25 yards from our back door; and, it took a great effort of my parents especially with their small paychecks to pay the well driller to pound a hole for our well. The fee charged by Mr. Oliver was two dollars per foot and it took him about three days to dig our well. After the well was dug, dad placed two big cedar posts on each side of the hole and one cross pole attached to the two upright poles; the cross pole had a pulley attached in the middle with about fifty feet of well chain and a long metal well bucket that would hold about three gallons of water.

It was my job to keep the water bucket in the house filled with water. The water bucket had a dipper that everybody used to get a drink of water; after which, the dipper was placed back into the water bucket without being cleaned. It is a wonder that we all did not catch the same illness every time someone was sick, and who knows, we may have and was just not aware of what was causing the sickness.

Everyone that visited our house also drank water out of the same dipper, and both sets of my grandparents also had a water bucket for everyone to drink from. I never remember seeing that dipper being washed or cleaned after someone got a drink; it always put back and stayed in the water bucket. Many times when we went to the cotton patch, the water bucket and dipper went to the field; everybody working would drink from the same dipper and out of the same bucket.

The only problem with our well was that there was just not enough water to suit my dad. The water in the well would get real low during the dry part of late summer and fall. Therefore, my dad had this brilliant idea; he and my uncle who were both about drunk decided to go to the sheriff's department and ask for some dynamite. I could not believe it when they came back with six long sticks of the explosive; on top of all that, they decided to drop all six sticks into the well at one time.

Daddy got some tape and placed all the sticks together so that they would easily go to the bottom of the well; they also decided to use a long fuse to make sure the dynamite had time to get to the bottom of the hole. They did not have any experience with dynamite and had no idea what would happen; but they lit the fuse and dropped the explosive down the well.

We all backed up a little from the hole and did not think that the well which was 60 feet deep would create much of a racket, but to our surprise, the well full of dynamite acted like a huge cannon. Mud, water, rocks, and most dangerous was the well bucket and cross pole that shot upwards toward the sky. I vividly remember seeing all that stuff going nearly out of sight.

We all started running for our lives and debris finally started raining down all over the house and back yard. Of course the ground shook and vibrated for what seemed a long time, but I knew it could not have been for a second. After the well bucket, cross pole, rocks, mud, and water finally got back to earth, we went over to the hole to examine my dad's mind boggling experiment.

My dad thought that the explosion would let a lot more water come into the well and it did. The big problem was that from that day on, our well water was sulfur tasting and smelled awful. I do not know if he hit a sulfur stream or if it was all the sulfur in that six sticks of dynamite. After several years of using and drinking that sulfur water, I concluded that he opened up a sulfur stream of water, but we did not ever run low of water again.

It was one of my daily chores to draw enough water to be used in the house to drink, cook, bathe, wash clothes, and water for all my hogs, chickens, dogs, and other animals. I hated to draw water because it was an unending task. On warm summer days, I would have to draw enough to fill a number three wash tub, but it felt good to climb into that tub and take a nice warm bath. Most of our bathing was done with a wash pan that would hold about a gallon of water. Each morning, we would set our wash pan full of water on the heater or stove to warm before our bath; mother would always tell me to use her bath water.

When I was in the seventh grade, I got to stay all night with a friend that had an indoor toilet and a bath tub. He told me to go into the bathroom and take a bath; since this was my first tub bath, I had no idea how much water to run in the tub because I knew how hard it was to draw all that water. I was not going to let my friend know that it was the first time I ever took a bath in a regular bath tub; therefore, I did not ask how much water to put into the tub.

When the bottom of the tub was slightly covered with water, I cut the water off because I sure did not want to waste all that extra water by filling the tub. I remember thinking, do these people actually fill this tub all the way up. Anyway I got my bath with about one inch of water in the tub, and I will always remember that experience of taking my first bath in a regular bath tub in an indoor toilet; such was the life of a Celtic Indian boy growing up in the mountains of southern Appalachia.

Red Necks and Sister's Wedding

My oldest sister Diane was the first of my immediate family to get married; she had graduated from Speake High School in May and got married in June. Mother and her two brothers had attended Speake, but did not graduate. Mother eventually had to quit school to help with the farming activities on the small mountainside forty acre farm; mother's brothers, Curtis and Cadle, had also quit school before they graduated. Her older brother Curtis could not read or write; he was named for my grandmother's people whose surname was Curtis.

In the days when my mother attended school and until my oldest sister graduated, most all the children that attended Speake were poor country kids whose parents were small farmers. A few of the lucky families had people who had landed a job in Decatur working at one of the large industrial plants along the Tennessee River such as Montesano also known as Chemstrand.

At the time my sister got married, we lived in the small wood frame house that my dad and my Grandpa Walker had built just downhill from mother's parents. The little house was located at the northern base of the Warrior Mountains in Hickory Flats Hollow and was next to the border of United States Forest Service Property; my grandparents and great grandparents had cleared the fields from mature woodlands. My mother had grown up in poverty and was determined to make a good living for her children and labored all her life in the garment business.

Mother finally managed a shirt factory for Ms. Annie Mae Hambrick and eventually bought the business interest of the Hambrick family. Mother owned and ran the small shirt factory for several years near the northeast corner of the square in Moulton, Alabama; even though she did not have a formal education, she was a genius at making designer blouses for women. She knew everything about making blouses and made thousands of the garments for large corporate businesses. She knew how to make patterns, cut dozens of pieces of the material at a time, and finish the final product; she employed some sixty garment workers including her brother Curtis. She knew how to do every job in her sewing plant.

My oldest sister's wedding day was anything but ordinary in terms of the events that took place during and following the wedding ceremony; one thing in particular that occurred during the ceremony was my cousin Carl Welborn was one of the ushers. Carl was determined to have fun at anything that he did and a wedding was a perfect opportunity to have some entertainment. Hansel Black, who was one of my dad's best friends and who dad helped make whiskey, came to the little Methodist Church dressed up like a Philadelphia lawyer in his finest suit with his wife Nell.

Carl Welborn in Korea

Just across the road from the Lebanon Methodist Church was a store that was run by Mr. Charlie Speake; Mr. Charlie was one of the main sugar suppliers for the wildcat whiskey trade in the area and he had supplied many moonshiners including Hansel. Prior to coming on over to the church for the wedding, Hansel and Charlie were having several drinks of whiskey. My dad Brady and my Uncle Cadle Wilburn encouraged Carl to escort Hansel into the church. Carl was anxious to go along with the idea; one of the ushers had already escorted Nell to the very front row of the church to set with the bride's family.

After several drinks with Charlie, Hansel walked across the road to the church and was going to slip into the church unnoticed. However, Carl who was also dressed in his best suit told Hansel that it was his job to escort people into the church. He told Hansel to take his arm and that he would show him to his seat; Hansel was unsure of the ceremony and relented to putting his arm out so that Carl could direct him to his seat. These two grown men dressed like city slicker lawyers came down the aisle of that little country Methodist church arm in arm; Carl gently held Hansel's hand while he was seated by his wife Nell Robbins Black on the very front row of the church. The prank was complete but far from being over; fallout would last another two or more years.

1st Lieutenant Carl Welborn
7th Army, 101st Airborne

Now both Carl and Hansel, who were mixed Celtic Indian men, became decorated war heroes; Carl had been wounded in the Korean War and served 18 months in the U.S. Army Infantry near Soel, South Korea. He had received a battle field commission with President Dwight D. Eisenhower actually penning on his first lieutenant bars during a war ceremony in Korea; for many years, the picture of Carl and the United States President hung in my Wilburn grandparent's home until the old log house burned to the ground. In 1956 while in Germany, First Lieutenant Carl Welborn was selected by his superiors as "Soldier of the Year" beating out other men from all branches of the Armed Forces.

Carl related a story of a near fatal encounter with a Korean maid that I must share; he and the other men were on their bunks in their tent early one morning when one of his buddies just came in off guard duty carrying an automatic grease gun similar to those carried by the mafia. He was sitting on the bunk next to Carl when all of a sudden he opened fire on the Korean maid cutting her body nearly into; in her hand was a live grenade. Carl and his fellow soldiers replaced the pin and pried the grenade from her stiff hand; the quick response of his fellow soldier with the submachine gun was all that saved their lives. Carl eventually resigned his officer's commission when he was discharged from the military and served for several years with the local Lawrence County, Alabama, veteran's office.

Hansel, who was over one quarter Cherokee Indian, had served during World War II; I had heard him say many times about being Cherokee Indian. Hansel talked often about how rough it was fighting those Japanese in some of the most fierce fighting occurring in the Pacific islands especially Okinawa. I will never forget one particular day when my dad and I had gone to the West Flint Creek Bridge on the Alexander Plantation to catch a mess of fish; Hansel pulled his car up on the bridge and stopped; he asked if we had caught anything and about that time I caught a bream. Hansel said, *"Throw me that fish son and I will show you how we survived on those Pacific islands."*

I tossed the fish up on the dirt road where it flopped in the dust and sand. Hansel calmly picked up the dirty flopping fish and stuck the head of that bream in his mouth; as he bit the head completely off, I will never forget that fish's tail flopping wildly. He chewed it up and swallowed it; he stuck the rest of the fish in his mouth and chewed it up and after swallowing the last bite, he said, *"Now son that is the way we beat them Japs!"*

I not only saw Hansel Black eat that fish, but he regularly ate parched peanuts hull and all; he said the hulls were just as good as the peanuts. One day while I sat at Hansel's table watching my dad and the other men drinking fifty cent shots of wildcat, a large number of houseflies had eaten an orange colored sugar looking poison in a tin lard can lid and had died.

One of the men dared Hansel to eat those flies to prove how tough he was; I watched Hansel take his hand wipe up in a pile a large handful of dead houseflies on the table. He picked up that handful of flies and ate them at one time; he followed the flies with a small glass of wildcat and a quick sip of 7-up cola as a chaser. After about two minutes, he puked all the way across that old wood table; I remember the orange crap, flies, and that throwed up whiskey splattering ever where. I thought that Hansel Black was one of the toughest men that I had ever known and everyone, friend and foe, respected his extreme bravery; people knew that he was not afraid of anything.

Now, back to the wedding; with a huge grin on his face of accomplishing the impossible, Carl could not contain himself until he got back to the entrance of the church and an explosion of laughter

Hansel Black

Cadle Wilburn and Mary Lou Hood
Wedding Day

occurred outside the church building. My dad, Uncle Cadle, Carl, and the men on the outside were rolling in laughter; a few sniggers were occurring in the church pews. Mr. Charlie Speake and his wife thought that was the funniest thing that they had ever witnessed; Ms. Speake could not stop laughing about Carl and Hansel coming down the aisle of the church. Carl later said that he had to listen to Hansel cuss him for two years for his stunt at the wedding; Hansel also knew that Brady Walker had instigated the whole thing.

The wedding at the church went off without much more drama but later in the night much more redneck activity was sure to happen and did; my oldest sister Diane Walker became the wife of Ocie Thrasher and they were off to their honeymoon to my Uncle Cadle and Aunt Mary Lou Hood Wilburn's small house about seven or eight miles from the church. Diane and Ocie were only 18 years old and had no money; neither of them had jobs, and they sure did not have the funds to pay for an expensive honeymoon. Several of their friends came to their honeymoon house to help them celebrate their wedding; on that wedding day honeymoon, Diane and Ocie just dreamed they could have a house like my aunt and uncle.

Shortly after the wedding, Ocie got a job helping Grover Welborn plow for five dollars per day; later, Ocie got a job moving furniture for $32.50 per week. Ocie was lucky to land a job at Chemstrand working third shift; however shift work turned into selling vacuum cleaners. Ocie finally retired at Champion Paper Mill in Courtland. Diane eventually retired from General Electric in Decatur, Alabama; today, they have been happily married for 48 years and own two beautiful homes, one in Moulton and one on Smith Lake.

With excitement in the air from the antics of Carl and Brady, Hansel was about ready to kill both men after the wedding, but it was too funny to mar with an all out brawl; however Brady and Carl got the cussing of their lives from Hansel. Shortly thereafter at Hansel's house on the road into the hollow, the wildcat whiskey was broken out for an all night drunk.

After the wedding, many of the male relatives and dad's friends joined in the wildcat celebration that included a moonshine drinking binge that lasted all night and into the early morning hours of the next day. Most of the women folk gathered with mother at our little house in the hollow to endure a long night of hell raising by a pack of drunk men with my dad being the ring leader. My Aunt Mary had to stay with us since my sister and her husband were having their honeymoon at her house.

I will never forget that my mother, aunt, and some of the other ladies who came to our house after the wedding were extremely worried that the men would wind up in jail. The men got out in the dirt road and had a yelling contest; we could stand outside and hear them whooping and hollering for miles through the little hollow.

The drunk bunch went to the nearest phone which was at Rayford Welborn's house a few miles away and called the Lawrence County High Sheriff Office to try to get them to come out; the drunks told the dispatcher that a scuffle and fight was going on in the cow pasture and that they needed help. At the time of the wedding, Mr. Neal Fretwell was sheriff of Lawrence County and knew many of the wildcat whiskey drinking participants; for some reason, the sheriff's office never showed up for the faceoff with a bunch of drunken mountain rednecks.

Today, for many back woods folks, the redneck style of living still survives in the Warrior Mountains. I am sure that many young Celtic Indian boys still relive the life that I had growing up in the hill country of lower Appalachia. Even though things were extremely rough, I still have precious memories of my home and life as a Celtic Indian boy of Appalachia.

Firecracker Fight

My folks had strong family traditions when I was a young boy growing up in the mountains; we had times when all family members would gather at my grandparents' home to celebrate holidays and special events. Besides these occasions, we were expected to be at my Walker grandparents ever Sunday afternoon; whether I wanted to go or not, my parents made me participate in the family gatherings. On certain holidays, we were expected to be at my Wilburn grandparents especially on the Fourth of July.

When we went to my mother's folks for the big gatherings, my dad was always up to his tricks and mischief; however when we were at his parents' home, he always walked a straight line and behaved himself because he knew that his dad would not tolerate foolishness. My Grandpa Dan Walker was a very serious person and he did not say things but one time; he expected you to listen or pay the consequences. Grandpa Dan had the bluff on my dad and kept him in line. Grandpa Walker did not allow any cussing or drinking of alcohol at his place, and my dad would obey the rules or get a very strong reprimand.

When my dad was at my mother's folks for a family gathering, his whole demeanor changed with his drinking wildcat, cussing, getting into loads of trouble; he liked to pick until he got something started that usually wound up in a fight. If a fight was not with a stranger, dad would usually get one started with another member of the family; when my dad was young, it was his nature to want to show out at a family gathering at my mother's folks.

Arthur Wilburn and Hiram Johnson

On one particular Fourth of July event at my Wilburn grandparents, dad had gathered up enough money to buy several packs of firecrackers; most of the time, he was just lighting one firecracker at a time and throwing them at people's feet. My Granddaddy Wilburn's uncle, Hiram Johnson, was getting old and had warned my dad several times about his firecrackers. Uncle Hiram would say, *"I God Brady, you better not throw those damn firecrackers at me."* Of course, that just made Uncle Hiram a target for my dad; since Uncle Hiram wore overalls with those big pockets, Brady could not resist slipping around and dropping an ignited pack of sixteen firecrackers in his back pocket.

After Uncle Hiram danced around cussing to the top of his lungs, he came out with his famous great big ole Case pocket knife and made a slice across my dad's chest just cutting a gash in his shirt. Brady managed to grab Uncle Hiram's arm and with the other hand knocked him to the ground. He had hit Uncle Hiram so hard that he had busted his face and blood was everywhere. Dad got on top of Uncle Hiram and took his knife away and started hitting him in the face.

About that time, my Grandpa Arthur Wilburn jumped on top of my dad and started hitting him as hard as he could. My dad had enough respect for my mother that he would not fight my grandpa; finally, my uncles pulled grandpa off and the fight ended with Uncle Hiram walking home. Of course, the Fourth of July gathering broke up and everyone went their way, but it was an event that I witnessed. I will never forget that particular fight because I thought someone was going to die that day and I was sure it was going to be my dad. My grandpa finally settled down and did not get his gun and shoot my dad; I think the only reason grandpa did not kill my dad was out of respect for my mother and me.

At another one of these Fourth of July gatherings at my Wilburn grandparents, dad and my uncles had gotten into the moonshine and were feeling pretty good. A car came easing down the dirt road and had three McVay men who were also a little drunk. Dad hollered for them to stop and give him a drink of their whiskey. The men stopped the car in the rock road and cussed at my dad. That is all it took for the war to be on; dad run down to the car, jerked the door open, and began pounding the driver in the face with his fist before he could get out of the car.

When the other two men got out of the car, two of my uncles met them head on. One of the men started up the bank and Charles Keeling caught him under the chin with a plow boot and sent him back to the roadbed flat of his back. Before the man could recover, my uncle had his foot on his neck telling him if he moved he would stomp a mud hole in his face. My other uncle, Cadle Wilburn, in the meantime subdued the third member of the car. Nearly all were bloody from the fight but my folks claimed victory and put the men back in the car and told them not to come back.

After the big fight, dad and my uncles cleaned up for the Fourth of July dinner and acted as though things were normal. They talked and laughed about how they had won the fight while eating dinner; of course, me and my cousins were watching all the action and were amazed at such a brawl that occurred just before our meal. However, all of us had grown up in violence and saw our men folks drinking, cussing and fighting before; and this time was no different, we just thought this is how grown men acted when they were about drunk.

My dad was a strong traditionalist like his father; this was an Indian trait that had passed through many generations of the Walker family. They did not like changes to the routine; therefore, each weekend was kind of planned in advance based on years of the same visits, meals, and location. Very little changed in the Sunday afternoon tradition until the death of my Walker grandparents; then my dad started our own family tradition of me and my two sisters being at my parents' home with our kids each Sunday afternoon and that tradition did not change until my mother and daddy died.

As usual every weekend, my dad would prepare his famous pinto beans and corn bread for Sunday dinner. It did not matter what other foods we had for the dinner table, but, you could carve it in stone, we would have pinto beans and corn bread. Everybody was also expected to tell my dad how much they loved his pintos that were soaked in water all night to make them plump and juicy. Today, when I go to my sister's home for

Sunday dinner, you can bet that pinto beans and cornbread will be on the table; some southern traditions never die!

Eating Rocks, Cures, and Cuts

I do not remember going to the doctor when I was growing up except to sew up my cuts. I sliced my right hand open with a butcher knife cutting a water melon. I got my finger caught in the old wringers on our washing machine and nearly tore my index finger off my right hand. I fell off a block wall head first into a pile of metal and a piece of that metal stuck in my head right between my eyes. All these cuts were sewed up by a doctor.

I was playing with my cousins Danny and Sandy Welborn at their house in Gadsden, Alabama; the house was on a steep hill which had a high retaining wall. We were walking on the old block wall when I got off balance and fell. The first thing that hit the metal below about ten feet down was my forehead. A piece of metal stuck into the bone middle ways between my eyes and the top of my head. Today, it is a wonder that I have walking around sense.

I remember my face was covered with blood from that deep gash and mother wrapped a towel around my forehead. That towel did not slow the blood flow and by the time we got to the emergency room that towel was wet with my blood; blood was all over me and my mother's clothes. In addition to stitches in my forehead, I had to have stitches in my right hand to sew up the wounds from the water melon cutting and the wringers of that washing machine.

I remember that the cuts always created an emergency situation; my grandma, my momma, or my sisters would have to find someone to carry me to the doctor to get stitched up. Since very few people had cars in the early days of my youth, it was a problem to find someone who had a car; then they had to be able to take off their work to carry me to the doctor.

I also had to go to the doctor when I got a fish hook so imbedded in my lip that it could not be pulled through or pulled out. I had just got through tying a new hook on my line and had about two inches of extra line that needed to come off. For some reason, I did not have my pocket knife, therefore I was biting that extra loose end of the fishing line from that new hook I had just put on my line. I got a good bite on the line and then jerked it real hard; instead of the line breaking it slipped off my teeth and that hook buried completely up in my upper lip right under my nose. Not having a knife in my pocket, I had to carry that fishing pole to my grandma's house to get help getting that hook out of my lip. Grandma cut me loose from the pole but failed to remove that hook; she said it was stuck in the core of my lip.

Grandma tried to pull the fish hook through the lip and also tried to force the hook out the same way it went in, but no luck getting it out of the hard part of my lip; she pulled my lip nearly off my face, but that hook would not budge. My older sister tried to help grandma but passed out in the process; after pulling on the hook in my lip for an hour, it was finally decided to go to Doctor Price Irwin in Moulton and have him get the hook out. Doctor Price was a small man and usually did not have a lot to say; he thought that hook in my lip was funny and told me that I had caught one that could not get loose. Doctor Price pulled at the hook with no success and finally took a knife and cut the hook out of my lip.

When I got sick and even before I got sick, grandma and momma would come up with all these old timey cures that they swore would prevent me from getting sick or would make me well. One thing that I hated to take was the teaspoon of sugar soaked in coal oil or kerosene; I have no idea what that would cure but it sure did taste bad. I am sure the little pin worms I got occasionally did not like that kerosene.

Mother told me the reason I had those small worms; she said, *"Son you eat too many sweets and I am going to give you some working medicine to clean you out."* Working medicine was something mother gave me all the time to make my bowels move and it was always effective; my dad would say, *"Your mother will make you shit like a tied coon."* I reckon when you put a collar on a coon and tie him to a tree, he will crap all over the place.

I did have a few small pin worms every once in a while but not the big worms my cousin had. My cousin and I were hunting one time and he had to take a crap; after relieving himself, he called me over to his pile and said look at those worms that come out of me. Sure enough he had some worms that were four to six inches long and white round squirming things; looking at his crap of big worms nearly made me sick at my stomach. I told him that he shit worms too big to fish with. Of course, he was a fine example of a boy that my folks would say, *"That person looks wormy"* because he was always skinny.

The other thing that I hated most was wearing one of grandma's homemade poultices. Grandma made pretty poultices on her old foot paddle sewing machine; she would place pieces of cloth together about six inches square and sew tying straps on each of the four corners. She would leave one side open forming a pouch; in the pouch, she would place her potion and add a few hand sewn stitches to hold it shut.

Grandma Ila would fill the poultices with roasted onions, garlic, bear grass, or scraped potatoes; the poultice was then strapped over a boil or risen to make them come to a head. She would then place the poultice over the sore until it got well or came to the surface of the skin; I literally hated to wear one of her poultices that were usually filled with something that did not smell good, but I did because I did not have a choice.

The old folks also used jimson weed poultices to draw up their hemorrhoids or the piles; I will be honest, it would have been very tough for me to wear jimson weed up the crack of my butt and I am glad that I did not have the piles. Most of the time, the jimson weed would be gathered from the garden and mashed up to allow the juices of the jimson weed to come in contact with the piles; I never asked how effective they were in shrinking someone's hemorrhoids and really did not want to know. I am just thankful to the almighty God that this Celtic Indian boy did not have the piles.

Sometimes for an ear ache, daddy or somebody else that smoked would blow smoke in our ears; I have not got the foggiest idea why they did that or what it did to cure the ear ache. My dad also burnt biscuits and made us eat them for an upset stomach; the charcoal on the biscuit was supposed to make our stomach ache just go away. Grandma would soak mint in water and make us drink the water to settle our stomachs. In addition a hornet nest soaked in water was also supposed to settle a sick stomach; the nest would soak in a jar of water for a while, then you would drink the water to cure the sick stomach.

My grandma also had her catnip growing out in the front yard besides the big white oak trees that covered the whole place with a shade; she made sure we were warned not to go near her herbs while we were playing in the yard that was swept clean each week with a brush broom. She made a catnip tea for babies with the colic or belly aches. Also, grandma would take the juice from roasted onions and give to babies to make them rest well.

Grandma also made sassafras tea for us to drink while it was hot; each year, I would go help grandma dig the sassafras roots to be dried for her tea. Grandma would also make a salve from scraped potatoes to pull splinters to the top of the skin; the splinter would easily pop out after it was soaked a few hours in the potato scrapings. She also made a salve out of pig hair that had been scraped off during one of our hog killings; she would heat the hair and add some special concoction to make her hog hair salve. When one of her grandchildren got poison oak, grandma would squeeze the juice out of jewel weed and make a salve to rub on the outbreak of bumps; usually within a week the poison oak would be completely healed.

Both sets of my grandparents believed in spitting snuff or tobacco juice on bee stings; the tobacco would work very quickly in reliving the pain. Folks also used old snake sheds to pull a boil to a head so that it could be mashed out easily; the snake shed would be dampened and placed over the boils or risens; once the shed dried back out the boil was at a head and could be removed.

On a few occasions, I took the bitters tonic which was made with wildcat whiskey, honey, whore hound candy, cod liver oil, glycerin, ginseng, golden seal, and yellow root; this tonic was like drinking something a little thinner than molasses. When you were given three or four ounces in a glass, it was best to swallow as fast as you could; I could feel the mixture burn all the way to my stomach and knew exactly when it reached my belly; I could feel that hot streak of that thick fluid as it made its way down my throat. This was just about one of those tonics that if it did not kill you, it would "chore" you; most of the time you felt better quick because you sure did not want to take another dose of bitters tonic.

**Me and my Mother
Butch and Novel**

My grandpa and I dug ginseng, golden seal, grub root, pink root, and other medicinal plants to make a few dollars and also for a tonic. We would get up early in the morning and pack a lunch for an all day walk through the mountain valleys looking for and digging medicinal plants. All the roots we dug including grub root, ginger, snake root, and others would be placed in whiskey along with ginseng to make a mild tonic that was given for colds and various ailments.

My mother and grandmother also made me drink a lot of store bought elixirs such as geritol, exlax, mineral oil, castor oil, and red liniment for nearly every ailment that I had. Of course I loved the exlax because I thought it was chocolate candy which I craved, but it always made me run to the outhouse; I was always thankful that I made it to that wooden throne before I literally shit on myself. Yes, the Sears and Roebuck catalog was hanging across a board for the wiping paper.

Several afternoons each week after working all day at the shirt factory, momma and I would walk to an old red clay bank of a small ditch or to a red clay bare spot in the yard that would not grow any grass; on top of that red clay would be little round brown pebbles. The small rocks momma picked up were actually hematite and contained lots of iron ore; some even had a rusty color. Mother was very selective in the pebbles that she picked up and showed me how to identify the gravels she wanted me to eat. We would set there several minutes selecting the most desirable pebbles; mother and I would start crunching and eating those rocks. Those little brown pebbles would easily bust when you bite down on them and those rocks really did not taste that bad.

Momma always said, *"Son these rocks are going to improve your blood and give you more iron; you do not want bad blood and get those risens."* Now in those early years, boils, that would come up on the skin then make a big white head, were called "risens." The bad part of that boil was when mother would squeeze out the center that she called the core and that hurt. Mother said that those boils were caused by bad blood; if eating rocks would prevent me from being squeezed to death between her fingernails and also make you strong, then I did not mind eating rocks. Being a young boy, I was ready to be big and strong and if those rocks would make me strong as Tarzan, then I was going to eat them without hesitation.

Unknown Brother

When I was in elementary school, a friend and distant cousin came to me and said, *"I caught our aunt and your dad parked on a dead end log in the forest."* My friend had been riding his new trail bike in the Warrior Mountains and was on the road where my dad and my great aunt had decided to park and have a little fun; however, this was not the first time I knew my dad got around the neighborhood with the lady folks. I knew my mom was aware of the situation, but she would never consider divorce and stayed with my dad until she died.

When I was a young boy, we lived about a fourth of a mile from the great aunt that was having an affair with my dad; one Saturday morning, I looked toward their house and saw a big smoke coming from their home. I ran and told my dad that their house was on fire; dad and I jumped into our family car and tore out to see if we could help. The house was a total loss and burned to the ground; for some reason, and I honestly do not know what I did, when dad and I got back home, he cut a hedge bush switch and gave me a hard beating until that switch broke all to pieces.

I will never forget the house fire or that whipping I got when we got home, but my great aunt had to move from our little neck of the woods to another house. By no means did that fire stop the hot relationship between my great aunt and my dad, but instead just put a little space between the two. I was just a little over eleven years old when my great aunt had a son that looked just like my dad.

Fast forward about seventeen years; I got a coaching and teaching job at Speake High School; as assistant football coach, I became well acquainted with a student who was on the football squad. He was the son of my great aunt who had a long term relationship with my dad. Very rapidly, he and I became the best of friends and developed a close relationship as teacher-student and coach-player. At the time, I had no idea that he was actually my half-brother; he looked more like my dad than I did with his short stature, dark complexion, dark eyes, and long black hair.

He was also a risk taker and a happy go lucky guy like my dad, and at the young age of 19 years old, he died after a terrible car crash. He had been to a concert in Huntsville with a friend and was on the way home in his muscle car that was hopped up for speed. He was challenged by another young driver just prior to reaching Highway 20 coming to Decatur; a car turning from the gas station at the end of I-565 stopped prior to turning. The challenger swerved and he was blocked from the other lane and hit the car at a high rate of speed; thus, ended the life of an unknown brother that I did not know at that time was probably my half-brother.

After my mother's death and the death of my great uncle, my great aunt and my dad had some three years that they were together and enjoyed each other's company prior to my dad's death. My dad and great aunt were happy at last and had each other to themselves for a short period of time; I know that my dad died a happy man with my great aunt by his side in his final minutes of life.

Shortly after my dad died, my great aunt was heartbroken and wanted to talk to me; she made me some of the best fried peach pies that I had eaten and brought them to me, and we had a long talk. She told me that she had been in love with my dad over 40 years, and she also said, *"I have also loved you like a son;"* then, she broke down into a deep painful cry. I also cried like a baby and had no hard feeling toward her or my dad, but only felt compassion for her; that is the last time I remember seeing her alive.

I knew she wanted to tell me as she had told others that her son was my half-brother, but the words would not come from her mouth. My great aunt did tell her two sisters that her deceased son was my half-brother. Many of my distant cousins acknowledged after my dad's death, that indeed he was my half-brother. After looking at his pictures, it is sad to say that he and I did look like brothers; he favors me and my dad.

The fact of having a brother would have been great to know, but some things are just not meant to be.

Hard Love

On a cold dark night, I remember hearing that double barreled shotgun going off in my front yard as my Grandpa Arthur Wilburn stood just outside our front door calling my dad ever kind of son-of-a-bitch he could think of; late that afternoon, grandpa had witnessed my dad giving me a beating. I could have said whipping but that would be an understatement; when my dad was mad and a little drunk, he did not know when to stop using a switch.

Grandpa Arthur putting his cap on my head while my uncle Curtis watches

I truly believe my grandpa loved me more than he did one of his own sons; I know that he would have killed to protect me. Even though my last name was not the same as my grandpa's, the mutual love that my Grandpa Wilburn and I had for each other made no difference in last names. More than one time, my grandpa had tried to protect me; I probably owe my survival while growing up to that man for looking after me.

That particular night, my dad would not let me go to my grandparents after my whipping; therefore, I guess that was the reason my grandpa got drunk and came to my house with his shotgun in hand. Grandpa woke everyone in the house up by repeatedly firing his twelve gauge shotgun into the air and cussing my dad. Mother would not let me go out to my grandpa and my dad certainly was not going out of the house for fear he would get shot; grandpa probably would have killed him if he had gone outside. After about an hour or so of cussing and finally running out of shells, my grandpa went back up the hill to his house; grandpa stayed drunk for about another three days and my dad made sure their paths did not cross for quite a while.

Dad would whip me until he was tired or until the switch broke so short he could not swing it. Twenty to thirty stripes I wore many times from my dad's extreme whipping; even though I always wore blue jeans, that switch would cut through the skin and I would usually have several places that would ooze with blood then scab over. It would take about a week or two for the bruises to go away; the fear, anger, and hate I felt toward my dad when I was growing up did not go away until he was an old man.

After one of these whippings when I was a young boy, I went to my mother who was sitting on the front porch swing; I was still sobbing from the whipping and she began to pet me. I wanted to know why she did not protect me, and she said that I had to mind my dad. I vividly remember looking into her eyes and saying, *"I hate you;"* that was the most regretful statement that I ever made in my life because I loved my mother to the bottom of my heart. I especially loved her thoughtfulness on Friday afternoon after she put in a hard week at the shirt factory; she would bring me a strawberry milk shake and even though it was about melted, I loved that treat. But to this very day, I still regret those words I said out of hurt; that was the first and last time I said something that bad to my mother. Now many years after her death, I still want to talk to my mother.

The last real bad whipping I got was when I was in the eighth grade at Speake School. At that time, I was playing junior varsity basketball and a starter on the junior team. Coach Euel James made us dress out each day and scrimmage with the other teams; however, after my whipping, I looked in the mirror and saw black and blue stripes from my neck down to my ankles. The forty or more stripes were made with a belt; dad finally quit whipping me when the belt buckle slipped from his hand and hit me in the back of the head causing a cut that bled for a while.

The next day after my whipping, I told Coach James a lie; I do not believe in telling something that is not true or even embellishing the facts. One thing that my dad and Grandpa Walker always said was that, *"You can go to hell for lying as quick as you can for anything you do that is not right."* But, I told Coach James that I was sick and did not feel like dressing out; day after day, Coach James would ask what was wrong with me and I kept telling that lie and refused to dress out for basketball practice.

After about a week, I knew that Coach James was wise to my lies; he came over to the bleachers and sat down beside me. He asked me again what was wrong and why all of a sudden that I refused to dress out and practice basketball. Knowing that he knew something was wrong, tears started rolling down my cheeks; he patted me on the knee and said that everything was alright and when I got to feeling better I could get my position back at starting guard. For two long weeks, I did not dress out and Coach James never asked any more questions. Finally those black and brown marks faded; sure enough, Coach James put me right back into my starting guard position.

The next year when I was going into the ninth grade, we moved to C. C. Smith where my parents were to run a garment factory. I played basketball for Mr. Leo Kerby at Mt. Hope School and our junior team won the Lawrence County Championship. In the eleventh grade, we moved back to the Speake Community and I again became a starting guard for Coach Euel James. Because of the kindness that Coach James showed me when I was beaten to a low point in my life, I played my heart out for him. That year of 1967, my varsity team at Speake High School won the Lawrence County Championship by beating the boys I had played with at Mt. Hope High School.

I finally learned to love my daddy before he died. After a near fatal heart attack, he was in the emergency room and I remember looking at him and saying, *"I love you dad and you need to get better so we can go fishing."* That was the first and last time I remember telling my dad that I loved him, but my dad got through that heart attack and lived another ten or so years. We had many more wonderful times on the lake fishing.

Butch and Brady Walker with their catch of bass

On December 29, 2001, my dad and I went to Smith Lake and put our boat in at the Houston Recreational area. We fished all day and had a wonderful time. Toward late afternoon, I told dad lets go to the house and cook us a bunch of these spotted bass to which he agreed. When we got to his house, I cleaned and cooked us a big mess of fish; we had so many that I called my friend Charles Borden to come eat with us. Charles, my dad, and I had a great meal of fresh fish and I left my dad's at six o'clock. About eight o'clock, I got a phone call that my dad had passed away from a heart attack. As I stood in the emergency room looking at his stiff cold body, I felt no fear, anger, or hate, but realized that all things both bad and good must come to an end.

Mother's Church

As a Celtic Indian boy growing up in Appalachia, there were happy times and there were sad times. The following is the most emotionally painful thing that I have ever written, and between the tears I would write some more. My mother, Novel Wilburn Walker, was the light of my life and was there to comfort and protect me through all the struggles that I faced as a young Scots Irish Cherokee child. Before I started to regular school, mother made me go to vacation bible school with my two sisters at Lebanon Methodist Church next to Speake High School. On the last day of that bible school graduation services, my mother went to the church with me and my sisters to be a part of the final activities.

When mom and I were coming out of the church, the preacher asked me would I like to come to church on Sunday; I looked up at him and said, *"Preacher I would come to church every Sunday if my mother would let me."* I had no idea how profound those words were, because my mother told me in front of the preacher, *"Young man you are going to come to church with me every Sunday;"* from that time on, I attended church with my mother on Sundays.

I think I might have been influenced to say what I did to the preacher because of that free red Kool-Aid and cookies we had every day at vacation bible school. But for whatever reason, mother made me go to church with her every Sunday morning; Sunday school did not serve red Kool-Aid or have any more cookies. I did not think it was very fair to lure me to church with the Kool-Aid and cookies and then stop serving them. Therefore, nearly every Sunday, I resisted going to church, but mother did not allow me to decide whether or not I would go; she made me go with her and my sisters.

Me and my mother in front of our car
Butch and Novel Walker

Many years later and a married man with three daughters

of my own, I was standing beside my mother in that same church when the preacher asked her to read the bible verse for the day. She took her bible and stood reading I Corinthians, Chapter 13; she ended the reading with the thirteenth verse, *"And now these three remain: faith, hope, and love. But the greatest of these is love."* After finishing the last verse, her bible fell from her hands and she slumped toward the pew. I caught my mother in my arms, picked her up, carried her to my car, and went to the emergency room. The massive stroke she suffered was her last bible reading, the last time she spoke, and the last time she was in her church until her death.

After this second stroke, mother was left unable to walk without assistance, but it was breast cancer that eventually ended her life three years later. My mother had a co-worker Delaine Moses that had survived breast cancer; mother made us promise that we would not give her radiation or chemotherapy because she did not want to go through what her dear friend had to endure. My family took care of my mother like an infant for those long three years; bathed her, changed her clothes, put nourishment in her body through a feeding tube, and loved her to the best of our abilities.

I was at her side at the Lawrence County Hospital holding her hand when she squeezed my hand and took her last breath. The last words she spoke in her Bible verse is engraved on her tombstone; she was a remarkable Christian woman that was laid to rest in the land of her ancestors. Mother's grave is in her family's old Welborn Cemetery near Pin Hook; she is buried next to her father and mother and my dad.

I loved my mother and will miss her to the end of my life. I can stand at her graveside and see the hills and hollows I roamed as a young boy growing up in the mountains of Appalachia. It is my desire to be buried beside my mother and daddy; the cemetery is within sight of where I experienced the wonderful life of my Celtic Indian childhood.

Maternal Grandparents

Rat Poison Gap

Around 1902, my mixed-blood Scots Irish Cherokee maternal great grandparents, George Curtis (1/8 Cherokee) and Mary Elean Sparks (1/4 Cherokee), moved to the valley of Montgomery Creek in the William B. Bankhead National Forest portion of the Warrior Mountains; this North Georgia family had migrated to Dennison, Texas where they had two daughters, Bessie (born 11/4/1900) and Minnie (born 2/28/1902).

Around 1902, George and Mary Elean Sparks moved east from Texas to North Alabama; George entered a homestead of 160.3 acres near Armstrong Spring on Montgomery Creek. There were two ways to get into the beautiful valley that was part of the larger drainage of Borden Creek. One route was by way of the Oil Well Road that turned south from the Ridge Road and the other way was from the Cheatham Road toward the west along the Rat Poison Gap Road. Both these routes were just dirt paths that had large mud holes which at times were almost impassable. I remember my grandmother telling me, *"Those large mud holes had to be laid with poles to hold up the wagon wheels."*

Most often, George accessed his property from the Cheatham Road by way of Rat Poison Gap. On the 160 acre homestead, my great grandfather built a log cabin and cleared openings in the forest where he planted small patches of cotton, corn, and other crops. He raised hogs and other farm animals in the valley of Montgomery Creek. The yard of their cabin had a

George Baxter Curtis and Mary Elean Sparks

picket fence and was swept clean with brush brooms. The spring was a little distance from the house and was the location where my grandmother's sister Bessie Curtis liked to have been taken by a large timber wolf, but the screams of Bessie and her sister Minnie Curtis frightened the wolf enough for them to make it back to the cabin.

At the little log cabin in the beautiful valley of Montgomery Creek, Mary Elean gave birth to Steven Jonathan Curtis on November 15, 1903, and my maternal grandmother Ila Sarah Curtis Wilburn, who was born on September 1, 1905. A short time after Ila was born, her mother, Mary Elean Sparks Curtis who was born in Fannin County, Georgia, on March 21, 1883, died from complications of childbirth on October 12, 1905.

Ila Curtis Wilburn, Johnny Curtis, Minnie Curtis Welborn, Bessie Curtis Smith
Children of George and Mary Elean Sparks Curtis (little boy Cadle Wilburn)

After her death, Mary Elean's body was taken across Montgomery Creek to the top of the mountain to Fairview Methodist Church which was across the Cheatham Road from the McLemore Cemetery. Her body was transported by a horse drawn wagon along the Rat Poison Gap Road to the funeral and burial site. Shortly after the birth of his fourth child and the death of his wife, my great grandfather George B. Curtis married Mary Ellen Parker, the daughter of James (Jim) Parker. Both George and Mary Ellen were mixed Cherokee and ScotsIrish people.

Today, the Rat Poison Gap Road is an overgrown secondary trail which leads west from the Cheatham Road to alluvial bottomland along Montgomery and Borden Creeks. The trail is deeply worn as it traverses west before proceeding through a deep cut in the sandstone bluffs known as Rat Poison Gap. The trail then winds gently down a long ridge, where it intersects Montgomery Creek. At the creek junction, the first settlers to the area built limestone abutments for a timbered bridge that provided passage of wagons over the creek.

Today, the two stone abutments are still intact with the eastern stone formation containing pieces of long iron rods, that may have been made in my great grandfather's blacksmith shop a short distance up the creek. At one time, it appears the rods secured timbers to the footings; however, the wood has long since rotted away.

After crossing Montgomery Creek, the Rat Poison Gap Road then goes around the end of Oil Well Ridge to the lush Borden Creek Valley. All the small patches of bottomlands my great grandfather farmed along Montgomery Creek have returned to mature hardwood timber with some of his fields containing huge cypress trees that were planted years ago by the United States Forest Service.

In proceeding west from Montgomery Creek, the Rat Poison Gap Road goes through the beautiful lower Borden Cove which still contains some open land. Borden Cove was originally settled by half-blood Cherokee David Borden or his father, Christopher Borden, the namesake of Borden Creek. David's mother was a Cherokee Indian. David married a full-blood Cherokee lady and produced a large family, to which his descendants still proudly trace their Cherokee Indian roots.

The Rat Poison Gap Road traverses west out of Borden Cove where it fords Borden Creek near the old home-site that is thought to be that of Christopher Borden. After passing the old Borden home place on a western knoll of the creek, the old road gently ascends a ridge to a saddle. To the west of the saddle is a well-known cave called the Devil's Well which contains an underground waterfall approximately one hundred feet high.

Proceeding west past the Devil's Well, the Rat Poison Gap Road begins a moderately steep climb up a short ridge to the mountaintop. A few yards north of the road near the edge of the canyon are the remains of another home place. The road gently rises up the ridges and joins the Mountain Springs Road approximately one half mile south of the High Town Path or present-day Ridge Road.

The Rat Poison Gap Trail connected the Sipsey Trail (Cheatham Road) to the High Town Path (Ridge Road) and Old Buffalo Trail (Byler Road). The old road led to alluvial farmlands in the present-day Montgomery Creek and Borden Creek bottomlands. The rich creek bottoms were utilized for growing corn, potatoes, and other crops important to the survival of early Indian people and their families.

Today, all the old fields have reverted to forest, except for the privately owned Borden Cove; Montgomery Creek is now part of the Wild and Scenic Rivers. The old Rat Poison Gap Road has been closed for many years and now overgrown with trees. All that remains is the deep rutted remnants of an early pioneer wagon road that was traveled by my ancestors.

Drunk Ducks and Mattresses

I grew up next to my Wilburn grandparents who lived just uphill from my folks' home on the side of Mull Johnson Mountain and just downhill from Hattie Hogan Spring. I have no idea how Mull Johnson got his named attached to the mountain unless he owned it at one time; however, most of the mountain was owned by the United States Forest Service and was part of William B. Bankhead National Forest.

I do know that Mull Johnson built a house at the base of the mountain in the curve of the old road which headed west toward the old Alexander Plantation. I also know that my grandma and grandpa bought their place from Ms. Hattie and Mr. Moody Hogan. Ms. Hattie told my grandma that she would sell them the forty acre mountain farm if grandma would name the spring on the side of the mountain Hattie Hogan Spring which grandma did.

This story is not about the mountain or spring, but it is about the many nights I spent at my grandpa's sleeping in a feather mattress on the cold winter nights or on a straw mattress during the hot summer nights. Notice that I said I slept in a feather mattress and not on a feather mattress. Once you rolled over one time in a feather mattress, you were just about enveloped in mattress all around you; that was good because that duck feather down kept you warm on the coldest nights of the year.

The feather mattress was especially nice after a chilly night in the woods chasing possums and coons. You could be cold as a chunk of ice and crawl into that feather bed and be toasty in a short period of time. I remember just sinking into those down feathers, getting instantly warm, and having a great night of sound sleep.

The bed was in a room with no source of heat and insulation was unheard of; as a matter of fact, we used to play under the old floor with the dogs and chickens. Both the floor and ceiling was covered with wooden boards; during the winter time, rags were stuck in cracks to keep out the cold air. Initially, the roof was covered with homemade wooden shingles but was eventually replaced with tin. An old saying, that you could count your chickens through the cracks in the floor about sums up the situation.

In the spring of the year, the feathers were taken from a flock of some 15 to 20 ducks that grandma kept on the farm. I would help catch the ducks and grandma would pull the soft down feathers from the duck's under side. These soft down feathers would be placed in pillows and in the mattresses. The insulation properties of the duck down were remarkable; that down would sometimes make you sweat when the ground on the outside was frozen hard as a rock. Now that is what I call warm!

My uncle and cousin, Cadle and Carl, were out by the barn one day drinking on a gallon of wildcat when they decided to play a trick on grandma's ducks. They shelled a lard can lid full of corn and poured it level with the whiskey. The whole flock of some twenty ducks converged on the corn soaked in moonshine. After several lard can lids were repeatedly filled with corn and whiskey, the whole flock of ducks got dog drunk with some of them passing out temporarily. On hearing the racket of all that quacking, my grandpa came around the barn and saw what had happened to the ducks.

Of course grandpa was more concerned with the waste of good corn licker because he loved his whiskey and did not like to see it go to waste. He had to agree that the bunch of drunken ducks was funny until grandma heard the commotion. She came out to the barn lot and told grandpa that her ducks must have got into one of her bee hives because they were going crazy. By that time, grandpa had him a few drinks of licker and told my grandma that the ducks were drunker than he was. After several hours, the ducks sober up and went on their way. Grandpa was just getting drunker; at that time, he did not care about the flock of drunk ducks.

I love a similar story from my Celtic Indian friend Michael Offutt who relates a friend's drunk duck story, *"When I was a little girl, my older brothers had sneaked around and made up a batch of homemade wine. To hide what they had been up to, they dumped the muscadine hulls and seeds that they had strained out of the wine after it had "worked off" into the pond and the ducks we had ate it up. Daddy found the ducks all laid out around the pond, and came up to the house and told Mama that something had killed all the ducks. She told me and the other girls that we couldn't eat them because we didn't know what killed them and it could have been something poison, but we weren't going to let them go to waste. So, they were hauled up to the house in a wheelbarrow and we plucked all their feathers before they were hauled away and dumped in the woods. Right before sundown, there was the strangest thing you ever did see. It was about a dozen naked ducks waddling up towards the barn!"*

Now, I also mentioned that I slept many nights at grandpa's house on a straw mattress which was a whole lot more comfortable than the feather mattress. As a matter of fact, I loved sleeping on the old straw mattresses which were much firmer and had a natural feel to a tired country boy after a long night on the river bank or a long day chopping or picking cotton in the small mountain patches. The straw mattresses were much cooler that the feather beds and were used during the hot summer months.

The best straw was crab grass after it had a good frost; therefore, my grandma, mother, sisters, and I would sometimes help Grandma Ila pull the crab grass from the fields after the crops were gathered. The crab grass would grow like crazy in the hot summer sun and after it was killed by frost made a mighty fine mattress packing.

The straw in the mattresses had to be changed more often than the down because it would eventually flatten out and get real hard to fluff back to where it was soft to sleep on; however, the fresh straw always had such a good smell and seemed to help you sleep and rest. The crab grass also had the benefit of having no stiff stems that could stick you and make you feel uncomfortable. Such was the many nights years ago when I was a young boy who loved sleeping on the feather and straw mattresses that my grandma Ila had made by hand.

Quilt of Love

When I was a young Celtic Indian boy growing up in Appalachia, the house we lived in had no insulation and no central heat; the only heater was a black cast iron potbellied wood burning stove in the living room. Since my small room was just big enough for a bed and in the back corner of the house, the room was extremely cold in the winter time; I usually had several quilts on my bed just to keep warm at night. I loved sleeping under all those quilts that my grandma had handmade to keep me warm even on the coldest winter nights.

Now my grandparents did not have money and were poor, but grandma always found a way to buy us something a little special. For Christmas each year, grandma would always get me a pair of socks and a handkerchief; she may have not had much financially to give to all her grandchildren, but we knew that everything we got was given with lots of her love. I know that my grandma would like to have given us expensive gifts, but she was poor and did not have the money; Grandma Ila had a biblical saying, *"Silver and gold have I none but such as I have I give unto thee."* I let grandma know that I loved my socks and handkerchief; I always give her a big hug for my Christmas gift.

Grandma bought some little something for every one of her grandchildren and all those in her family. A card with a personal note was also included with the Christmas gift; she would tell all her grandchildren that she loved us and wished she could have bought us more. I knew that she loved me because she did things to show me; it was by example and not just empty words. Even though Christmas was a very special time, my grandma lived with the Christmas spirit every day; she took care of us and did things special for her grandchildren each time we were at her house.

Prior to her death, grandma had stitched all of her grandchildren and great grandchildren a quilt; grandma would spend countless hours in dim light sewing her patch work quilts. From the low ceiling in her level room of her old log cabin, a quilt frame hung down at the height that she could set in a straight wooden chair and sew for hours.

The quilting frame was made from four boards about one inch thick and about two inches wide and was attached to the ceiling by fence staples; four heavy strings were tied to the staples and rolled around the ends of the frame. When she wanted to stop quilting, grandma would roll the string around the ends of the frame until it was against the ceiling and out of the way. Even though the quilt frames were hung as high as she could get them, you had to bend over or bump your head every time you passed her quilt frames.

Grandma Ila would take her hard earned money and buy the cloth for the bottoms of her quilts; for the quilt tops, she would spend hours sewing scrap pieces of cloth together to form the pattern she desired. Since my mother worked all her life in the garment business, she would bring grandma boxes of scrap material from the cutting department of the shirt factory; these scraps were used for the quilt tops. From these boxes of scraps, grandma would select the texture and colors she wanted in her quilt and painstakingly sew each little piece of scrap together to get her desired effect. Most of the time, she would use her old Singer sewing machine that she had to run by pushing the pedal with her feet to sew small scraps of material together.

Prior to putting on the quilt tops, grandma would hand card cotton to get the seeds and trash out that she used as the filler material between the top and the bottom of the quilt. The cards were flat pieces of wood about four inches wide by six inches long with handles; the boards had fine metal wires that stuck up about a half inch like the bristles of a hair brush. She would separate and clean the cotton fibers by putting the cotton between the cards and pulling in opposite directions; the cotton would be made into a soft and fluffy layer that would be placed between the quilt top and bottom.

The old home place of my Wilburn grandparents; the old logs were covered with boards and rolled lap siding and a sandstone fireplace was the only source of heat for years.

After placing her cotton layer between the quilt top and bottom, grandma would start the tedious task of hand sewing the three layers together; she loved to make fine close stitches which she thought was prettier. Grandma would usually place her rows of stitches within two to three inches of each other all the way across her quilts; after hours and days of hand stitching, grandma would sell her quilts for thirty to fifty dollars.

One year grandma had saved nearly a thousand dollars from selling her handmade quilts; all her hard work making quilts and her savings made her feel good about having a little money in the bank. At the end of the year since she was on a fixed social security income of less than three hundred dollars each month, she had to report all her income and saving to the retirement folks.

Of course, Grandma Ila never lied about anything and reported the money she made from her quilt sales; immediately, they cut off her SSI checks. My mother took my grandma to the Social Security office to ask about why my grandma had stopped receiving her retirement check; they told her that she was not allowed to save any money and receive the benefits.

In order to get reinstated, my grandma had to close out her savings account and spend all her money on her house; this is the first time I remember my grandma buying her a new couch and chair. After about three months, my grandma got her retirement check renewed. Even though she only got enough money to barely survive in extreme poverty, the government had no regard for her quality of life; therefore, grandma quit selling her quilts and began giving them to her children, grandchildren, and great grandchildren.

I am sure that most all her grandchildren and great grandchildren still have their handmade quilts; I eventually lost mine in the midst of a divorce. My ex-wife Claudia Ann Owens claimed she could not find my quilt; this was one of the times that I had to start life over again from scratch, but my greatest regret was the loss of my handmade quilt that Grandma Ila had given me prior to her death. On each quilt, she had sewed our names in one corner; her personalize attention made each quilt very special.

It was obvious that grandma knew that her time on earth was about completed; she was methodical in completing the task of love that she had chosen. Just before she died, grandma had completed each grandchild and great grandchild their personal quilt which she signed with loving stitches. Such was the time when I was growing up in the hill country of southern Appalachia.

Storyteller

For thousands of years, Celtic and American Indian people had no formal written history of their people; therefore, folks depended on storytelling to pass family information and old legends from one generation to the next. In the Appalachian foothills of the Warrior Mountains where I grew up, things were no different than they had been for hundreds of years; families had storytellers to transfer folk tales from the past to future generations. Usually at least one member of each Celtic Indian family was a storyteller of ancestral customs and traditions; therefore, a lot of written family history was unnecessary because our people entrusted their stories to one who always told the truth.

The very first thing and very last thing I remember about my precious Grandma Ila Wilburn was her telling me stories of my Celtic Indian family; including those stories when she was a small young country girl growing up in poverty. Grandma was born on September 1, 1905, in a log cabin on Montgomery Creek in the Black Warrior Forest, now known as William B. Bankhead National Forest. She was poor all her life in earthly possessions, but she was one of the wealthiest people I ever knew in heavenly treasures. The whole time of growing up I never once heard her say an ugly word, and she always said, *"Son, if you cannot say something good about somebody, just do not say anything at all."*

If only I could have lived by grandma's words, I would have been a much happier person and could have avoided a lot of trouble, but you know that the Celtic Indian boy in me had to experience life for himself. I usually told people what I thought and still do to this day; most of the time people do not want to hear the truth or what I think is true. Many times I let my mouth overload my butt and wound up in a heap of trouble; when I did, grandma had another saying, *"Son remember the golden rule, do unto others as you would have them to do unto you."*

She was still telling me these things at 94 years of age; and all of my life, I witnessed that she lived by her own words. However, I have not yet mastered her skills; even though I tried to mind my grandma and loved her to the bottom of my heart, I failed to accomplish two of her sayings and I have had to pay for my mistakes.

I knew better than disobey grandma and wanted to live by her words; but, I had a temper that was hard for me and grandma to control when people were mean to me. Therefore, here we go with another saying grandma had, *"Sticks and stones can break your bones, but words will never hurt you."* I knew that saying meant no physical harm, but man, I believe I had rather be hit in the face than take some words; of course to think about it, I was hit in the face several times.

After my grandpa died, I would stay at grandma's house real often; I visited her nearly every week after I got older. She was the person that I went to with all my problems and she was always willing to help me resolve my conflicts with words of wisdom. In all situations, grandma always had her stories that she related to every situation; her life experiences were always very uplifting and motivating.

When Grandma Ila shed a tear, you knew she was drawing from her own deepest emotional and hurtful experiences, and I knew to pay close attention. Most all of her advice was based on biblical teachings and her final statement was, *"Let the Lord's will be done."* My biggest problem was not recognizing, knowing, nor accepting the Lord's will; many times I wound up telling people that I disliked, *"I will save you a front row seat in Hell."*

Storytelling did not end with my grandma; my mother and uncles inherited the gift from my Grandma Ila. Mother would tell me stories of her great grandma Elizabeth

Angeline "Betty" Hill Johnson that grew up during the Civil War. Grandma Johnson would tell about folks hiding their stock and supplies in Sugar Camp Hollow; she also had a lot of old sayings that I sadly cannot remember.

Mother's brother, my Uncle Curtis Wilburn, who had no grade school education, had a memory of the storyteller. He could not read or write, but his head was filled with the knowledge of the family and I believe he could tell every event that happened from the time he was a small boy. My uncle could remember the old stories that had passed from generation to generation; I loved to sit and listen to him weave his tales and family folklore.

Now my surviving Uncle Cadle Wilburn was also blessed with the ability to tell stories from the time he was a small child growing up in the Warrior Mountains. He too had the storyteller's memory and is filled with stories of the early history of his family; every time I visit with my Uncle Cadle, he tells me another story, and most of the time, it is one that I have not heard. His stories are captivating and I hang on every word trying not to forget a single detail.

I know now the importance of preserving the oral history of our ancestral landscape. Therefore, I try to glean and record a major portion of the stories I am told so that they will not be lost to the grave; I urge everyone to secure the stories of their family history before it is too late.

Now, storytelling did not only come from my mother's side of the family, but also from my dad's family. I well remember that my oldest uncle, William Roy Walker, though not formally educated, could tell stories of my family history that totally amazed me. Being the oldest son, Uncle Roy was in a long line of William Walkers; his uncle was William Walker who was his dad's oldest brother and so were his great granddaddy and his great, great, granddaddy. Uncle William Roy Walker told me of the death of his grandpa, Sidney Walker, by an accidental shooting prior to a hunting excursion which I have recorded.

In addition, my dad's youngest sister and the only surviving sibling of my dad, Lucille Walker, has such an amazing memory that I plan to do a book of just about her recollections from her early childhood through her 24 years as a career military wife. She experienced some of the most fascinating history of this country. For example, she was induced to give birth to her youngest son Roger who is now 43 in Tripoli, Libya; an American military base that was being overrun by the forces of Dictator Momar Kaddafi. Shortly after giving birth, she and another lady got wheel chairs and diapers; they rolled themselves from the hospital to the air base planes to escape the revolution in Libya. In another event, she was in Berlin, Germany and could see the building of the wall; she lived through the Berlin airlift.

Personally, I feel very blessed that I to can pass stories from all that I have been told by my ancestors over the years of my life. At bedtime when my girls were small children, I would sit on the side of their bed and tell them stories of our family and about growing up as a young Celtic Indian boy in the Warrior Mountains. Nearly every night my girls would say, *"Dad, please tell us a story when you were a little boy."* I hope that my girls will continue to pass the stories to their children and grandchildren in the same tradition as the stories that I was told when I was a small boy.

Back to another story my Grandma Ila told me; when I was a baby just crawling on the floor, I loved to play with my mother's watch and always pulled on it when she had me in her arms. My mother occasionally allowed me to play with her expensive watch that had been a gift of love from my dad. Very few things my folks had in the days of poverty actually cost a lot of money, but my mother's watch was an exception. Actually the watch was probably not worth much in today's world, but back in the day, it was a month's payday.

My grandma said that one day while I was playing with my momma's watch, it went missing; they looked throughout the house but could not find her watch anywhere. For days they looked and tried to get me to show them where I put the "clockem" as they called it in baby talk. Of course, I was way too young to remember, or maybe I wanted to keep my prize as my own personal treasure.

Many years went by and the watch never showed up until some thirty years later; as if fate intervened, I was setting on the step going into the sloping room of grandma's house. The old log house had a level room with a seven foot ceiling where tall men had to duck to avoid busting out the single light bulb that stuck down from a white porcelain fixture. This was the same fixture that had a string to pull the light on and off; it was the same fixture that I saw my uncle by marriage Charles Keeling unscrew the glowing light bulb and stick his finger into the socket then try to grab the closest person in order to give them a big shock.

From the level room, a wooden step down led into the sloping room; the sloping room was used as the main room in the house and had an old black cast iron metal wood burning heater. The room sloped with the ground and served as the master bedroom and living room. If there was not enough room on the single couch, then people were allowed to set on the edge of the bed. The back of the couch was always on the downhill side of the room. There was one door that led to the outside porch where at night I could run outside and take a whizz off the porch; of course, I tried to pee as far as the pressure would allow and not drip on the porch, because during the day, folks would sit on the side of the porch and hang their feet off the edge.

The sloping room had two small windows in the room; it was at one of these windows that I nearly got shot by my grandpa because of my "Lolly Grocker." A "Lolly Grocker" was made from a brown paper Piggly Wiggly grocery bag; we glued big paper ears, paper hair, made an ugly face on the front, stuffed the sack with paper, and placed it on a stick like a "lolly pop." One night, I slipped up to the window and saw grandpa eating popcorn by the heater; I took my "Lolly Grocker" and bumped it on the window several times.

I peeped in to see my Grandpa Arthur grabbing his double barreled shotgun; I threw my "Lolly Grocker" down and went running to the corner of the house yelling to grandpa not to shoot that it was me. I never pulled that trick again; I knew that Grandpa Arthur had already shot at his brother Williard for playing a similar trick on him. Prior to the old house burning down, you could still see where those shotgun pellets made a hole through the door; I am not talking about a flimsy door of today. The heavy door was made out of vertical rough oak boards about an inch thick, and Willard Welborn was lucky to survive and never pulled another trick like that again.

The sloping room ceiling also had the single porcelain fixture with a single bulb; there was no insulation in the house or attic and everyone set close to the heater to keep warm. Anyway I was setting on the step between the level room and the sloping room listening to the discussion going on between my mother, my grandmother, and the other folks that were there that fateful day. While I was enjoying the conversation, I noticed a small gap between two boards that were in the middle of the wall separating the level room from the sloping room; the hole was just big enough for me to stick my finger into.

Even though I was now a grown man, the curiosity of that baby boy many years ago still flowed through my being; I stuck my finger in the hole and pulled. Since only a single nail held the one foot long board in place at the bottom, the board rotated toward me like opening a knife. There to my amazement was mother's watch that I had been told about as a young boy and was lost some thirty years earlier.

I was totally amazed and hollered for everyone to look; to our surprise the watch was exactly like it was when I was a baby and placed it there over thirty years before. The band still had a string that my mother tied it together with after I had broken it as a baby; otherwise the watch was in excellent condition. I wound the watch and it began ticking. My mother replaced the band and wore that watch for the rest of her life. I have no idea where the watch is today, but it would be wonderful if it would turn up again so that I could give it to my granddaughter Myla Marie Weller (Little Turtle), who was born on July 9, 2012, and named after my Grandma Ila.

My Grandma Wilburn told me many stories as I set at her feet watching her bump babies to sleep in her old wooden straight chair that had a woven white oak splint bottom. My Great Grandpa George Curtis made the oak bottoms for my grandma's kitchen chairs and they were stout; he was my grandma's dad. I can still hear the sounds that heavy wooden straight chair made as it bumped from the front legs to the back legs on that dry oak board floor. It must have been a miracle chair because babies would not last very long until they were fast asleep; Grandma Ila told me many times that she rocked me in the same way when I was a baby.

Even though grandma lived the most honorable life that a person could live and had the most caring heart of any woman I have ever known, she was eventually placed in a nursing home a year or so prior to her death. This was the most heart breaking act that I ever witnessed; she had stood by my side and listened to every heart break that I ever had and I was helpless to save her from this throw-away society. If my mother had been alive, I knew that she would have taken care of grandma until she died, but that was not the case.

When she was placed in the nursing home, I made a commitment to see her every Sunday; therefore, on Sunday mornings I would get up, shower, dress, and go visit my grandma. I remember her asking me many times to please take her home; I would tell grandma that her home was sold to pay for her to be here and that I did not have the authority to take her home with me. She would cry and I would cry; I would say, *"Grandma, tell me a story."* She knew I loved her stories and she would begin talking and telling me when she was a little girl with a big smile across her face.

Very late on a Tuesday night my phone rang and I knew that the news would not be good; grandma was found dead in her bed at the nursing home. The last time I saw my grandma alive on the Sunday afternoon before her death, she told me a story. The call was on Tuesday night; I jerked on my clothes and rushed to her bed side knowing I was going to be too late to tell her goodbye. But I wanted to be by her side to insure as much respect as could be had was provided to the lady of my life. I made it to her side before they moved her body from the nursing home and I knew she was in heaven with her maker. Today, I visit her grave often and think of all the wonderful stories she told that made my life complete. I wish she could read the stories that I have written, many of which are in her memory; she was my storyteller!

Horseflies, Candy Bars, and Cotton Poison

One day many years ago when I was a little Celtic Indian boy growing up in the foothills of Appalachia, my grandparents were going to be busy with planting cotton and I was too young to be in school. Therefore, my great Aunt Kate Curtis agreed to watch me while my parents went to work. Since this was the first time that I had to stay with Aunt Kate, everything was new and she wanted me to stay in the house and not explore my surroundings. At the time, I was about five years old and for me to stay in the house, especially one room, would have been a miracle.

After Aunt Kate got busy in the other room, I slipped out the door and made my escape; I went as fast as my legs would carry me to my grandparents who were in the plowed field planting their crops. My Grandmother Ila asked what I was doing; I told her that I did not like staying with Aunt Kate and I decided to come to the field. Now this was not the first time that I had been in the field when my grandparents were working, but it was the first time that I had run away from Aunt Kate to be with my grandparents.

I could walk for hours following that old mule that my grandpa used to till his land; I loved the feel of the fresh plowed soil under my bare feet. My Grandpa Arthur would give me five cents for every horsefly that I would catch while he was plowing; back than five cents was a lot of money for a poor dirt farmer. I would always pinch their heads off to prevent the horseflies escaping because their bodies would add up to a big bar of candy. My grandma sold candy that was delivered in a big white box; those horseflies meant a bar of that candy at the end of a long hot and dusty day.

The big prized chocolate bar cost fifty cents and that meant that I would have to have ten confirmed kills of horseflies to capture my big bar of candy. Grandpa knew I would buy grandma's candy with the horsefly money; I think he did the nickel per horsefly just to keep me busy, and of course, it made his mule happy that I was chasing all the horseflies away. Grandpa would always know where I was when I was following his mule trying to catch me some candy money.

About once every two weeks the candy peddler would come to grandma's house with a whole car load of candy stacked in the big white boxes. Grandma would sell the candy for half the profit and she sometimes took two or three boxes to sell; every kid in the neighborhood and anybody that had a sweet tooth knew that they could buy candy from my grandma.

Today, I understand that grandpa gave me the five cents for each horsefly just to make me happy and show his love toward me; at the time, I did not understand what he was doing. It was a small thing that he did back then, but now I appreciate his gesture of love; therefore, today I try to give my grandkids and my little nieces and nephews a dollar each time I see them. My gesture is not to buy their love but to see them smile and say thank you Paw Paw or Uncle Butch.

One year after the cotton was planted, grandpa got real sick and stayed sick for nearly a year. Doctor Clear said he had an ulcerated stomach, but no one knew for sure what was wrong. During grandpa's sickness, the cotton was about grown up in grass; my grandma had stayed busy taking care of him and could not get the cotton patches hoed by herself. One day several people came to my grandparents' home with their hoes and lunch pails; they all started chopping cotton and before dark they had removed all the grass from the cotton fields.

My Grandma Ila always wanted to provide for her guests but they would have nothing to do with it; they told her that they had their lunch and for her not to fix a thing for them. They had come to help their neighbor and not to be a burden on the family; my folks were stunned at the outpouring of kindness and through the efforts of their neighbors, my grandparents had a successful cotton harvest in the fall from the six to seven acres of cotton.

In the early days, a cotton wagon pulled by mules was used to transport their cotton to the gin; ginning their cotton was about a two day affair by the time everything was completed and the cotton seed was ready in tow sacks. I remember days at the cotton gin watching that big suction pipe, getting the cotton in the five hundred pound bale, loading up cotton seed to feed the cow or for the next year's crop, and finally the smile when the check was handed to my folks. Later, my grandparents got some of the local farmers to haul their cotton to the gin in one of their trucks, but it still took a day to go through the hauling and ginning process.

In addition to planting a garden and small crops of cotton and corn, my grandparents planted sugar cane; the cane was cut near the end of the summer and processed to make sorghum molasses. Uncle Jess Smith, who had married my Grandma Ila's full sister Bessie Curtis, had a molasses mill and a big vat to cook the sugar cane juice into some of the best tasting syrup in the country.

I enjoyed going to the molasses mill to make syrup with my Wilburn grandparents. After getting a load of sugar cane hauled to Uncle Jess and Aunt Bessie, we would spend the whole day going through the process of getting several gallons of sweet tasting molasses which we ate at about every meal especially breakfast with hot homemade biscuits and butter that I helped churn.

Family members gathered at Uncle Jess and Aunt Bessie Curtis Smith's molasses mill which turned grandpa's sugar cane into sweet tasting syrup

On the upper terraces in the crop land, Grandpa Arthur had set out a lot of different kind of peaches that he had ordered from a catalog. Over the years, the peach trees would be loaded down with some of the best peaches that I have ever eaten. I loved climbing up some of the bigger limbs to get the prized peaches. I would literally stuff myself with so many peaches that I would wind up sick and could not eat supper.

Each year, I would anxiously check the ripening of the peaches; I usually was in the peach orchard looking for the first red spot on a peach. Before they got completely ripe, I would eat the peaches that were half green and wind up with diarrhea; home grown fruit seemed to be the best in the world. I also ate strawberries, apples, plums, figs, mulberries, black and tame cherries, black and blue haw berries, huckleberries, wild blueberries, persimmons, blackberries, paw paws, and any kind of wild fruit I could find.

During the first several years, grandpa never had to use any pesticides or poisons to prevent insects from damaging the peach or cotton crops; all the peaches would be perfect and not have a single worm. Later all that would change, the insects would not only infest the peaches but also the trees; the poison that was most commonly used to prevent insects in the peaches and the cotton was DDT. I remember grandpa had to buy this hand held blower that he would have to turn a crank handle and dust his orchard and cotton patch.

I can visualize him walking down the rows and dusting his cotton patch; a white cloud of dust would come out of those pipes in front of him. The two pipes about four feet long come from a "Y" in front of his waist; at the end of the pipes, two flared spreader heads would bend down over the two rows of cotton and would spew the white powder on top of the cotton stalks as grandpa turned the blower handle. The white DDT powder would actually cover him from head to toe and he did not even wear a mask; at the end of the day, the only thing that was not white was his eyes.

Grandpa Arthur also planted his watermelons on some of the terraces in his corn and cotton patches. He grew watermelons so big that I could barely carry them to the house. Many times I would bust a watermelon in the field and eat it all before coming back to the house. One day I brought a big watermelon home for me and my two sisters to eat. My oldest sister Diane wanted to cut the watermelon, but I went to the field to get it and I was not about to let her have the pleasure of cutting that fat watermelon.

I grabbed the butcher knife and not only cut the watermelon but also sliced the palm of my hand to the bone. Of course one of my sisters had to go find someone with a vehicle to carry me to the Doctor Price Irwin's office. After getting some ten to twelve stitches across the palm of my hand, I finally got to go home and eat some of my watermelon.

Today, I still have the very visible scar across the palm of my right hand; even the stitch marks are still visible. The wonderful thing about the scar I carry from trying to cut that big watermelon is the precious memories I have as a young Celtic Indian boy growing up in the Warrior Mountains with my Grandpa Arthur Wilburn; such was the life of the old ways and the ways of the wild of years gone by.

Happy Birthday Grandpa

April 22, 1903, was the date of birth of a very special person in my life, my Grandpa Arthur Pascal Wilburn; and as a tribute on his birthday, I write about his death. The Pascal name came from his dad who was named Pascal Sandy Welborn. My grandpa's dad was named after his grandfather Pascal Sandy Segars who was killed at the Battle of Cedar Run or Slaughter's Mountain in Virginia. At his death, Pascal Sandy Segars was serving under Civil War General Stonewall Jackson with the Confederate States of America; he was buried in a mass grave of Confederate soldiers in Virginia.

However, my grandpa did not like to be called Pascal and preferred to be called Arthur, but to me, he was just grandpa.

It was just about sunrise on a bright and beautiful March morning, but the air was still chilled by the cold that was struggling to break through our clothes as we walked up the hill toward the spring. After I had gotten older, grandpa always allowed me to lead as we talked about the fishing trip he was about to take. I was explaining to grandpa that I had promised my mother that I would go to church with her and could not go with him fishing today. I told him, *"You can have all the minnows that you want for your day of fishing on Smith Lake."*

Little did I know that this would be the last time that I would see my Grandpa Arthur alive or the last time I would get to talk to him; only if I had known the fate of that fatal day, I would have told him how much he meant to me and how much I loved him for being there for me during my darkest days as a young Celtic Indian boy growing up in the Appalachian hill country. This man was my life and I lived to please him because I knew he felt the same about me; we were not only blood but we were from ancestral roots that bound us to each other and to the land that we loved.

For the last week or so I had been checking my minnow traps daily and bringing the pretty creek chubs to a vat grandpa and I had fixed just below the spring on the side of the hill

Arthur Pascal Wilburn

above my grandparents' log house. My minnow baskets were crude but effective; they were made out of old scrap screen wire that occasionally had to be replaced on our screen doors to prevent flies, dogs, and other things from coming in the house during warm weather because we left the doors open to cool the house.

I had set my minnow baskets in the mouth of Sugar Camp Hollow just below the old stock well that my Grandma Ila would haul wash water in the mule sled to the house for cleaning the family's clothes. The stock well was a deep natural sink that would flow with water about seven months a year and the branch that passed the hole was the drainage that flowed by my parents and grandparents homes. In the early spring, minnows would run up the branches to spawn and lay their eggs and were easy pickings for providing excellent fish bait. Since plenty of good bait meant great fishing for grandpa and me, my minnow baskets were the key to a successful day at West Flint Creek or Oakville Pond.

My grandpa loved to fish with the creek chubs that he called steel back minnows. The steel backs were a favorite food for the largemouth bass; my grandpa referred to the bass as green trout which were common in the West Fork of Flint Creek where he and I fished most often with the big minnows. This particular morning, I got grandpa three dozen of the fat minnows; he told me, *"I do not want too many cause they will die and one day next week you and I can catch some trout with them."*

I wished grandpa well on his fishing trip as we walked back down the hill from the spring with his bucket of steel back minnows. Normally, I would have been on that fishing trip, but since it was Sunday, my mother insisted that I go to church with her. Therefore, I told my Grandpa Arthur bye and watched as he got into the old car loaded with other fishing buddies. As the car pulling the little aluminum boat started down the dusty road, I waved bye as the vehicle went out of sight; little did I know how different my life would be in a few hours. From that day on, I would be roaming the woodlands by myself trying to do as my grandpa taught me for some fourteen years.

Since going to Smith Lake was a big deal, everybody in the neighborhood wanted to accompany my dad with his fourteen foot boat equipped with a 25 horsepower wizard motor that he had got from Truman Praytor at Western Auto in Moulton. It was one of those typical redneck fishing trips; my grandpa, dad, uncle, brother-in-law, and family friend were going to the new lake to try their luck for crappie and bass. For a fourteen foot boat, that was just too many people and the boat was going to be overloaded.

After a long day of fishing, the group started toward the boat dock, but about half way back, the boat turned over and dumped the men into the frigid waters of Smith Lake with a temperature of 29 degrees. My uncle circled the capsized boat several times looking for his dad, my Grandpa Arthur, but he never surfaced; after looking around, he realized that grandpa was gone. My grandpa died immediately after hitting the water probably from a heart attack, but the others managed to make it to the safety of the bank.

The survivors were on the verge of dying from the cold water and the cool March air; they turned their attention to swimming to the bank. Not long after making it to the bank, a passing boat recognized the trouble and immediately went for help. Shortly after the men were rescued, search parties and rescue squads started the long task of trying to recover my grandpa's body. His body sank in some 70 feet of water and took the rescue party a few days to find him. After some three days of dragging the deep lake, my grandpa's body was recovered and brought back to his old log home after a short visit to the morgue at the funeral home.

Prior to his body being found, my sister kept telling me that grandpa would probably walk out of the woods one day to the house, but this time, I knew in my heart that it was not going to end like that. I knew that I had lost my best friend in the world and the grandpa I loved more than anything in my life. Gone forever was Grandpa Arthur's presence with me on cold dark nights possum hunting, fishing at our favorite fishing hole, looking for ginseng in the deep hollows, and trapping furbearing animals for a few dollars; all these activities had suddenly come to an end. I was devastated by the loss for I had depended on grandpa to protect me from all that I feared, but now in this last chapter of his life, his love for me transcended death. The love I had for him and his love for me had finally taught me to fear nothing, not even death itself.

Since my Grandma Ila only had a three hundred dollar burial policy, Grandpa Arthur was brought home and placed in the level room in a wood coffin for the wake. Since the other room was built with the incline of the ground and the kitchen was just a lean-to, there was no other place in the log house to put his body except the bedroom with the level floor. Chairs were placed around the room for people to sit in while they were watching the body that night.

During the time period my grandpa died, the deceased would most times be brought to their home where they laid in an open casket until their burial. After dark, people would set up with the dead all night long; therefore, I felt out of love for my grandpa that I wanted sit with the other people who were in the room with grandpa's body. During the wake, I stayed by Grandpa Arthur's side all night and refused to leave him until they placed him in the ground the next day.

From his home, grandpa was taken directly to the burial site where a graveside service was held. The place he was buried was very special to me because grandpa had asked me to go with him a summer before to pick out the place he wanted to be buried; at the time grandpa and I went to pick out where his grave would be, we were picking cotton for Rayford Welborn on the old Welborn home place which was in sight of the Alexander-Welborn Cemetery.

We walked across the cotton patch and looked around the cemetery for a while; grandpa asked me what I thought about a place at the front of the graveyard. From that spot, I told grandpa, *"You can see where we live, where we fish, where we hunt, where we trap, where we dig ginseng, and where we both grew up."* He looked around and agreed that it was a great place to be put to rest; he then told me, *"Go get Ila"* (my grandma). I left grandpa at the cemetery and walked back across the cotton patch and told my grandma that grandpa wanted her to follow me to see something very important.

Grandma was at first a little reluctant because she was busy picking cotton, but on my insistence, she agree to follow me across the cotton patch to the cemetery. When we got to where grandpa was standing, he said, *"Ila, this is where I want to be buried; Butch and I have looked this place over, and we think this is a good resting spot."* Therefore, my Grandpa Arthur was placed in the spot he and I had checked out during that hot day in the cotton patch on the land of his ancestors.

It is at that place where I want to be laid to rest. From that site in the winter time when all the leaves are gone, one can look around and see my ancestral land: to the east are Brushy Mountain, Cedar Mountain, Mull Johnson Mountain, Sugar Camp Hollow, Beech Bottoms, McVay Hollow, and the West Fork of Flint Creek. Then looking south, one can see portions of the old Alexander Plantation, Indian Tomb Hollow, Chestnut Ridge, and the old Welborn home place. Therefore, I will be laid to rest near my Grandpa Arthur, Grandma Ila, and my parents, Brady and Novel Wilburn Walker, where a Celtic Indian boy grew to manhood in the land of his ancestors.

Moonshine and Gambling

Whiskey Thief Shot

Moonshine, wildcat, white lightning, and corn whiskey were the favorite drink of my Grandpa Arthur. I was the only one he trusted to take care of his brew. He showed me how to lean an old hollow log that was made into a beehive to conceal a pint of his liquor. My Grandma Ila had about 40 beehives made out of hollow logs about three feet long and a little over a foot across setting around the hillside. Each year, she harvested honey from hives to sell to the public and also for us to eat with fresh homemade butter and hot biscuits right out of the oven, but the bottom of the hives also concealed many pint bottles of whiskey.

Grandma always kept one old milk cow that she milked every day; many times she would take one of the cow's tits and squirt hot milk right into my mouth as I set there watching grandma milking her dairy cow. I love the taste of fresh milk and she thought it was funny that I would catch nearly every drop. Grandma would allow some of the milk to clabber, and I would get to work the dasher or beater up and down in the clabbered milk to make fresh butter in her big clay churn pot. Not only was the butter good but also the fresh buttermilk. Hot homemade cathead biscuits, freshly churned butter, and mountain honey mashed up together made for a delicious breakfast, but back to hiding the whiskey bottles.

I got real good at picking out a different beehive each time I hid grandpa's whiskey bottle in order to keep the other men from stealing a drink of his wildcat and from finding his stash of shine. Many of grandpa's friends also loved corn liquor and would go to great lengths to have a sip of his brew. When grandpa was in a good mood, he would tell me to go get him and his friends a bottle moonshine.

The trick to my success was never to slap at the wild honey bees that would light on my bare skin, but just move real slow when I tilted their hive and ease the bottle out from under thousands of honey bees. The bees would be coming and going out of the bottom of the hive and would be all over the bottle. Even though some folks would sneak around to see where I put the bottle of whiskey, most were too afraid of getting stung to risk stealing the pint of grandpa's wildcat.

When grandpa came home with five gallons of whiskey, he would let me pour it into his pint bottles. Grandpa always kept a large supply of clean whiskey bottles for the purpose of pouring up the larger container to a size that he could put in his hunting coat and take on our hunting trips. Most of the time if grandpa had on his hunting coat, he had a pint of whiskey in one of the pockets; grandpa wore his hunting coat most all the time unless it was extremely hot weather. He would always tell me not to spill a drop when I made the transfer from the five gallon container to the pint bottles. I got the job because he said I had a real steady nerve and did not waste a drop.

Grandpa Arthur and his brother-in-law Wes Hardin made moonshine whiskey together; Wes had married grandpa's sister Mamie Welborn. Wes and Arthur had made a run of whiskey from their still which was just west of Hartselle, Alabama, near East Flint Creek; my maternal grandparents lived in the area about a half mile west of East Flint Creek for some three years. Prior to pouring up a five gallon container of moonshine into pint bottles, grandpa heard a man that helped him make whiskey and that he drank whiskey with on the back porch. The man was in the process of stealing the five gallons of whiskey grandpa had left on the porch; the man started running across the yard with the whiskey but had to slow up to cross the fence.

Thomas Wesley "Wes" Hardin

As grandpa started out the house to see what was going on, he picked up his double barreled shotgun that was setting by the door and luckily loaded with number eight birdshot. As the man started to make a run to escape with the whiskey, grandpa unloads both barrels into the man's back. The man dropped along with the five gallons of whiskey; he hit the ground like a rock and for a moment grandpa thought he was dead.

Grandma heard all the commotion and ran to the man who was still lying on the ground moaning. Grandma told him to remain still and he would not get shot again; she would go get the neighbor to carry him to the doctor. Before grandma left, grandpa told her that they were going to move for a little while as soon as she got back home and wait for things to settle down; at the time of the shooting, both Wes and grandpa lived west of East Flint Creek in Morgan County where they were making whiskey.

Grandma went and got the neighbor who had an old truck to carry the man to the doctor. Grandma helped get the man into the doctor's place, and the doctor told grandma that she was going to have to help him. She said they took the man's clothes off, and the doctor give grandma some tweezers and told her to help pull out the bird shot from the man's back. Grandma said the shot was just about buried up in the skin, but after what seemed to be a few hours, the doctor and grandma had removed all the visible shot they could find. Grandma said that they had a little dish just about full of bloody birdshot, but some shot were too deep to dig out of the man's back. Grandma also said that the doctor told the man he better thank God that the shotgun was not loaded with buckshot.

Grandpa Arthur was sure he was going to get arrested for the shooting; therefore, grandpa's family and his sister's family of Wes and Mamie Welborn Hardin moved to Fayette County, Alabama. Since Wes and Arthur were working the whiskey still together, my great Uncle Wes and my great Aunt Mamie moved with my Wilburn grandparents to evade the law. Wes and Arthur worked at a saw mill several months prior to moving back to Lawrence County.

For several weeks, my Wilburn grandparents moved to Mull Johnson Mountain in Lawrence County, Alabama; Grandpa Arthur would sneak to the house at night and get something to eat. After a long wait of escaping an arrest, grandpa thought that he was safe from the law, but to his surprise up pulls a strange car to grandpa's house. A man got out of the car and walked up the hill toward the house. My grandparents recognized that the man was the father of the thief that grandpa had shot in the back.

Unsure what was about to happen, grandpa got his shotgun and stayed in the house while my grandma went outside to see what the man wanted. He told my grandma that he wanted to thank my grandpa for what he had done. My grandpa eased out of the house with the shotgun in his hand. The man told grandpa that he was there to thank him and shake his hand. Grandpa was a little curious and asked why. The man proceeded to tell my grandpa that his son was saved and decided to make a preacher after surviving the shooting.

As I stated, grandpa loved his whiskey and did not like thieves who would try to steal his moonshine. He knew I would not tell anyone where I hid his white lightning and that I would bring it to him on request. But after the shooting, most of the whiskey thieves knew not to make the mistake of trying to steal a bottle of grandpa's good old mountain dew!

It was not long after the heat died down and Grandpa Arthur knew he was safe from the law that he and Wes opened up another moonshine still; this time the still was about a half mile from the house at the stock well. The stock well was a natural sink that filled with water from an underground spring; I never remember the stock well going dry, but it would get low during the driest time of the year.

For several months, Wes Hardin and Grandpa Arthur ran the stock well whiskey still until they thought that the law had got wind of their wildcat distillery; they decided to make one last run and then Wes would report the still. After getting the last of their whiskey moved, Wes went to the local sheriff and told that he had found a whiskey still and wanted it moved out of the community; shortly thereafter, the law came to the still and destroyed the illegal moonshine operation.

For years after the moonshine still had been destroyed, I would go with Grandma Ila to the old stock well and fill up barrels of water that she would use to wash clothes for her family and other families for a few dollars. The water would be dipped out of the stock well in buckets and poured into a couple of barrels in grandma's slide; after the barrels were filled with water, grandma would tie an old sheet around the top to prevent all the water from splashing out. Grandma's mule Short would pull the water up the hill to the house; after the law destroyed the still, the old stock well reverted to its name and grandma's cow would again drink water from the hole.

Wildcat, White Lightning

From my early Scots Irish Cherokee ancestors moving into the Warrior Mountains prior to the 1820's, local moonshiners in my family have tried to eke out a living on the poor mountainous soils by converting small patches of corn to the liquid gold of that good old mountain dew, wildcat, or corn whiskey. One limiting factor in the production of moonshine was a good source of sugar which could be obtained from the many local country stores. The size of most whiskey stills were based on a 100 pound sack of sugar; therefore, a six sack still which was the most common size in the Warrior Mountains required six one hundred (100) pound bags of sugar. Some whiskey stills were made as big as 20 sacks.

For each 100 pound sack of sugar, shiners used 100 gallons of water and expected to make around ten gallons of whiskey per sack of sugar. In addition to the sugar, shiners made the mash by using corn, rye, and for some cheap operators, hog shorts. Shiners also used malt syrup and yeast to make the mash ferment. After the mash fermented, it was heated to make the moonshine. The corn and rye whiskey were usually considered the best drinking whiskey.

In the construction of most local Warrior Mountains whiskey stills, the most common material used by my folks was sheet aluminum that was formed into a cylinder with the ends secured by close rows of roofing nails into a poplar board placed on the inside of the pot. The upper and lower heads were also made of poplar boards that would swell tight enough to hold water and steam. The top head was made with a door in the middle that could be covered with a cap that was usually a number two tin wash tub to catch the steam.

The steam containing the alcohol was then sent into the bottom of a thumper and out the top into a copper worm, which was a long coiled piece of copper tubing. The thumper on most Warrior Mountain whiskey stills was just a tin lard bucket. The copper worm was cooled on the outside by water to condense the steam into liquid whiskey; therefore, the mountain whiskey stills had to be built at springs, streams, or creeks. Some moonshiners used a very dangerous method for condensing the steam by using an old car radiator that caused lead poisoning in many cases. My people knew better to use an old car radiator because of the rot gut whiskey it produced.

The main pot was about four feet high and usually a portion of the pot was buried in the side of a bank about one foot deep. The pot had to be heated slowly to prevent scorching the mash and giving a bad taste to the whiskey. The pot was sometimes heated by sour wood which made little smoke, but since smoke was a dead give-away to the law, shiners begin using propane burners to boil their brew. The heat in most Warrior Mountains whiskey stills was directed all around the pot about a foot from the bottom at a uniform rate that was not too hot.

As many other country boys growing up in the Warrior Mountains, I was exposed to moonshine at an early age by seeing some of my folks participating in the moonshine trade or my people being consumers of that mountain dew. I had to many times bear the consequences of my family members that were drunk and placing my life in danger; my dad loved his whiskey and beer, but finally a few years before he died, dad give up his lifelong love of the intoxicating spirits.

I remember on two occasions while I was driving, my dad, who was drunk and riding on the passenger side, reached over and stomped the accelerator to the floor board just to see how fast I could drive. I went through the four way stop at Danville wide open and was scared to death; I'll never know how we survived. My uncles and dad thought that it was funny to see me drive that fast. I thought many times that I would be lucky to make it past my teenage years; therefore, I made a decision at a very early age that I would never drink moonshine or alcohol in any form. Believe it or not, I have maintained that philosophy for my entire life.

During my young days, I would ride with my daddy, uncles, and grandpa to the local bootleggers to pick up moonshine, or to help carry jacket cans, sugar, grain, and other materials to and from their whiskey stills. The jacket cans were army green five gallon containers with handles on top. The cans were fairly easy to carry through the woods and were made of very tough metal; therefore, if some were dropped you did not lose the precious liquid cargo.

Before I was out of elementary school, I knew many bootleggers in Lawrence, Morgan, and Winston County. I sat at many bootlegger tables watching my folks drink fifty cent shots and chase the strong wildcat with a sip of 7-up Cola. I heard my dad tell many people that he drank a six pack of beer and half pint of whiskey every day, and then on the weekends he would get drunk.

I remember one occasion of playing with my cousin Danny Welborn just off the side of the old road while just downhill at the whiskey still a run was being made. We were supposed to warn the men if we saw someone coming toward the still. Even though my cousin and I were just small boys, we were aware of the danger of being caught by the law, but at the time we had no choice as we were told we were too young to go to jail.

Shortly after I got my driver's license, a friend asked if I wanted to make some extra money hauling shine, but by the time I was fourteen years old, I had been the designated driver on the weekends for a bunch of drunks and wanted no part of hauling whiskey. However, many of my high school friends hauled moonshine to make a little extra money and they offered me money to make a run or two which I flatly refused.

Picking cotton was tough but honest work, and the fear of getting put in jail was deterrent enough for me to refuse their moonshine money. Besides, after I got in high school, I could pick over 300 pounds of cotton per day and pull over 600 pounds per day, which was hard work, but I knew it would not put me in jail like the shine.

One of my best friends, and today is still considered one of my dear friends, was making a lot of money hauling to the local bootleggers. Many of the local bootleggers wanted more than just wildcat; therefore, they offered my friend Frank White one dollar for every case of beer delivered to their house. Frank went big time by leasing a huge U-Haul truck and driving to Gadsden, Alabama, to the beer distributers and bringing back a truck load of beer to the Moulton area at a time. During one twenty-four hour period, he delivered two truck-loads of beer to Moulton, Alabama, and was paid one dollar per case, which was a lot of money in the 1960's.

Many of these bootleggers were operating wide open and were giving local police officers a kick back to leave them alone. I knew one local officer in the sheriff's department that would help make wildcat whiskey on his time off patrol. Many of the former sheriffs of Lawrence County were supported by the church people, moonshiners, and bootleggers; the church folks liked the good ole boys and so did the liquor men.

When my dad was young, he loved to box with anyone who would put on boxing gloves; later when he was drinking, he still loved to get into brawls. One such fight while drinking nearly cost my dad his life. My dad, his friend, and my uncle jumped on three men, and in the initial conflict, they seemed to be winning the fight; however, my dad's friend was too drunk to put up a struggle and was knocked unconscious. After my uncle was also knocked out, the three men stomped my dad until they thought he was dead and left him in the middle of the road. After spending considerable time in the hospital, my dad recovered and from that point on was not as quick to pick a fight.

My Uncle Curtis Wilburn had his whiskey still close to the house where I lived and hunted. There was a mountain behind my house with a beautiful bluff facing the southeast that had a spring emerging from the base of the sandstone shelter. My uncle took two by ten boards and dammed up the little valley created by the spring. He then used heavy black plastic on the inside of the boards to make the little pond water tight. His whiskey still was set under the bluff completely out of sight and was used to run whiskey for years. The problem with some of my folks was they would drink up their profits; therefore, none of my people got rich from making moonshine.

The Crap Game

Near the northwestern base of Cedar Mountain about 75 yards west of the road going to the home where I grew up, a limestone rock stands a few feet off the ground; the rock is beautiful, flat, slick, and level as a table top. This limestone rock became a gathering place to roll dice on Friday afternoons for anyone willing to wager their payday in an effort to beat the others out of some of their money.

In addition to one fist with a few dollars and the other shaking the bones, plenty of whiskey and beer could be seen at the site. Excitement was in the air as the dice was rolled across the rock with the roller hollering for a seven or eleven. Such was the scene when I was growing up watching my daddy, uncles, and others gamble on some of their Friday afternoon's paycheck.

Always prior to stopping at the rock, my folks had already made a run to the local bootleggers to stock up on their weekend brew. You could tell that the game was on by seeing all the vehicles lined up along the old road bed. At this site, the old rock road crossed a limestone glade that provides a wide rocky area for ample parking for anyone wanting to gamble.

Even though most of the people rolling dice were drinking, the crap games for the most part were very civil with very few arguments and fights. Most of the poor folks who participated in the crap game did it for fun and usually did not have but a pocket full of change that they did not mind losing.

Many of the men in my family loved to roll dice which went along with their drinking and having a big time with their buddies. Most all the crap games did not involve much money; because my folks did not have a lot of money to use rolling dice when they had to have their smokes, beer, and whiskey. They would gamble with change, watches, and even their shoes, but most wagers were a dollar or less. The gambling was basically a way to fellowship with friends and other relatives that were looking for entertainment.

At one particular gathering, my folks were with a few of the local shiners who had just sold a run of wildcat and made a lot of money; therefore, the wagers got as high as twenty dollars a roll. Usually with the bigger pot, the crap game would get very tense and sometimes end up in a fist fight. This crap game was one that wound up getting out of hand.

One of my great uncles Alvin Curtis and his brother-in-law Hansel Black got into the high stakes game of twenty dollars per roll. It was legal for the one betting to grab the dice as much as three times before they stopped rolling. Since Alvin was on a winning streak, Hansel grabbed his dice on the first roll. Again Alvin picked up the dice and rolled a second time, but again his dice were grabbed before they stopped; this was a technique to put pressure on the roller.

Even though the situation was getting very tense, the third roll ended just like the first two. After a smart remark, the fight was on with two grown men hitting the other in the face like they were going to kill each other. Both men wound up with bloody faces after an intense fist fight that lasted several minutes. With each man bringing a lot of blood and becoming completely worn out, the fight came to a peaceful end with them shaking hands. After getting a bucket of water, both cleaned up their faces and shook hands again. The dice game was over and everyone in attendance went their own way.

My dad had some of his friends that were in law enforcement, but somehow, he would convince them to attend crap and poker games with him in the Warrior Mountains. A house located on top of the mountain was used for several years as gambling place and was well known by most local people in the area. As far as I know, the gambling house was never raided by law enforcement authorities, who probably got a percentage for leaving the place alone.

My dad and uncle would occasionally visit the gambling establishment, but they never had enough money to participate in the high stakes poker games. Some very wealthy folks from all over the country would come to the mountain house to gamble. The man who ran the house would sometimes ask my uncle to go get food for the gamblers.

My uncle said that Mr. Ervin Barrett would walk up to one of the poker tables and reach over into the pot and bring out a handful of money. He would say if this is not enough I will give you the rest when you get back. No one questioned his authority probably because he owned the place and was the only person in the house packing a visible firearm. He also maintained order and never allowed situations to get out of hand.

At a fish fry on top of Wren Mountain, many of the local elected officials including the county sheriff attended the event. My uncle said it was the first time he had ever rolled dice with the elected county leaders. As you entered the house, a fifty five gallon drum was next to the door with beer iced down for anyone wanting to drink. After a large crowd gathered, one of the men hosting the event told the sheriff that they were nearly out of beer.

Sheriff Snooks Ligon sent my cousin and one of his deputies to the evidence room in Moulton; they returned a few minutes later with the sheriff's car loaded down with beer. One of the elected officials asked, *"What about the evidence?"* The sheriff said there was plenty more beer and whiskey that could be used as evidence. Drinking beer, eating fish at a local gambler's house, and shooting craps with elected officials and the high sheriff of the county was a new adventure for my folks.

Rolling dice had a long traditional heritage with some of my Indian and Celtic mixed blood people who settled in the Warrior Mountains. Many of my mountain folks loved their drinking and gambling; my dad, uncles, relatives, and their friends absolutely loved to participate in a crap game. My dad and my maternal uncles carried a set of dice in their pockets along with their keys to their vehicles and a pocket knife; whenever or wherever a few of them gathered a crap game was on.

Short and Slim

When I was a young boy just starting school in 1955, I could not wait until the spring of the year when my grandpa began breaking his cotton and corn ground with his two old mules, Short and Slim. On warm afternoons after getting off the school bus, I would take off my shoes and run through the fresh plowed dirt. I will never forget the cool, soft, and sandy loam soils of that Warrior Mountains farm as I squished the fresh plowed earth between my toes.

I also remember my grandpa yelling gee, haw, and whoa you son-of-bitches as he got aggravated with the way the mules were acting; while breaking ground, his language was mild as compared to plowing the growing crops with a middle buster or scratcher. He would plant five to six acres of cotton to supplement the money he made selling medicinal roots, such as ginseng, and furs that he caught trapping or hunting.

After the fields were broken with the two mules, the ground would be run over with a disk and section harrow in order to smooth the ground for planting the corn and cotton. Then with the mule named Slim, grandpa would use a one row planter to put the seeds in the ground. The other mule Short was used by my grandmother to pull the slide which was loaded with seed, fertilizer, and the other equipment needed to plant the fields.

The wooden slide was made out of oak boards nailed into two runners on the bottom of the slide that were made from six inch poles. These poles would have the outer steel rims of an old wagon nailed to the bottom runners to prevent them from being worn out so fast. The slide was pulled by one mule and could be used to haul anything on the farm from gathered corn, hay, cotton, barrels of water used in washing clothes, and hauling stove wood out of the mountains to the house. My Grandpa and Grandma Wilburn never used a tractor to work their ground, and I never saw them drive a motorized vehicle.

I also loved to be in the fields near the end of the day because Grandma Ila would let me ride Short back to the barn. Short was a calm mule and usually easy to handle and my grandma claimed him as her mule. She refused to use Slim because many times he would go wild and not mind the commands.

One day I asked grandma to let me ride old Short to the Mastengill Hole on the West Fork of Flint Creek. The fishing hole was about two miles from the house and was one of my favorite places to fish, but it was a long walk. Grandma agreed to let me ride the mule to the fishing hole and I thought this would be a piece of cake. I would carry my fishing equipment, tie up Short to a tree, and fish until I got tired. Then hop back on the mule, and head home with a stringer full of fish; I ought to have known that it would not be as simple as I had planned.

I went to the barn and put the bridle on Short; for a moment, everything seemed great and was going as planned. I got on the bare back of the mule, had my fishing gear in one hand, and started down the road on Short who was kind, gentle, and walking a smooth gate. About 100 yards from the barn, I saw this black cloud that was heading straight for Short and me. Too late, grandma had about 40 stands of honey bees; just at the time everything was looking good, the old mule and I were in the middle of a swarm of honey bees.

Instantly, I begin getting stung and so did old Short which caused him to bolt into a wide open gallop that caught me off guard. I quickly lost all the fishing equipment and had to use all my strength to hold on to a mule that was scared to death and on a wild run trying to get away from those bees. Finally, after about a half mile, I decided that scared mule must be stopped; therefore, holding on to the reins as tight as possible, I jumped off Short and dug my heels in the ground. He dragged me about 20 yards before I finally got him calmed down enough I could lead him back to the barn. That was the first and last time I rode that crazy mule.

Occasionally, my dad and I would use Grandpa Arthur's mules to prepare our garden for planting and to bust the middles with a scratcher. Slim was the most aggressive and stubborn mule you could ever imagine. Believe it or not, my dad expected me to plow out the middle of the rows when I could barely hold up the plow. One particular day, I was trying to plow our garden and Slim refused to abide by gee and haw; therefore, it took every ounce of strength I had to keep the mule walking in the middle of the row and prevent tearing up what was already planted.

I was struggling to maintain control of the mule and did not notice my dad coming across the garden with an old two by four board. He walked up besides the mule and hit him up-side the head with that board knocking him into the next few rows. Needless to say Slim bolted and jerked the scratcher out of my hands and tore out across the garden with the plow bouncing along behind him.

My dad was chasing the mule trying to hit the mule again, but Slim was having no part of the lesson. The mule tore out toward the mountains and very soon out run my dad. After about two hours of following the signs left by the bouncing scratcher, we found the mule on the side of the mountain tangled up in some saplings and the scratcher was just about

Uncle Cadle with the mule Slim plowing newground

tore all to pieces.

After my grandpa died, my grandma sold his mule Slim to some shiners who used the mule for illegal purposes. I guess I could take partial blame for Slim getting arrested for making a haul that attracted the attention of federal agents. Here is how the story of my involvement in Slim's arrest goes. I had just got my driver's license and my elderly next door neighbor, Manco White, told me that he would love for me to take him to his old home place in the Warrior Mountains.

Mr. White agreed to show me where my great, great, great grandparents had a grist mill on Rush Creek when he was just a boy. I jumped at the idea of seeing the old mill site of my ancestors; therefore, one Saturday morning, we got in my old 55 ford that my brother-in-law had given me and headed down the Hickory Grove Road to the mountainous home place of old man George Hampton, the father-in-law of Mr. Manco White.

Near the old home site which was located on the county lines of Lawrence and Winston, we stopped and toured the area where Manco had run the grist mill for George Hampton. The last resident of the Hampton home was the family of Columbus Lackey, but it was eventually taken by a paper company and turned into a pine thicket.

But how did this trip wind up in the arrest of my grandpa's old mule Slim? Well, after visiting where Manco was born and then visiting the home place of George Hampton, the father of Manco's wife, we set out to the old grist mill site of my ancestors. This place was only about three miles away near the junction of Rush Creek and Brown's Creek. The old forest service road leading to the mill site was closed; therefore, we decided to hike down Rush Creek to the old grist mill site.

After hiking about 200 yards down Rush Creek through eastern hemlock and mountain laurel, we came to a clear opening on the bank of the creek that had a 20 sack whiskey still. I could smell the aroma of the brew and climbed on top of the head to check it out. After removing the top door, I realized the still was ready to run, but I had no idea that I was being watched. I told Manco that we needed to get out of the area and head back home, which we did in short order.

That afternoon about dark, the moonshiner knocked on the door of my home. My dad told the man that he did not have to worry about me, but he could not speak for anyone else. My dad had tried to keep the bootlegger that the moonshiner worked for in business by being a regular wildcat customer; therefore, the moonshiner was not at all worried about my dad and me. He told dad that they were going to run the whiskey and then move the still. Now, this is where Slim gets involved in the ordeal.

After the successful run of the wildcat was made, the shiners loaded the still in a wagon pulled by my grandpa's old mule Slim. After traveling some distance with the whiskey still in the back of the wagon, a car load of federal agents tried to stop the shiners. Old Slim stopped in the middle of the rock road, but the two moonshiners who knew the woods like the back of their hand managed to out run the revenuers through the woods and make their escape.

The law had been unable to catch the men moving the whiskey still, but nabbed old Slim. One of the agents drove the wagon pulled by Slim to Moulton, Alabama, where the local weekly newspaper, "The Moulton Advertiser", ran the story. There Slim was on the front page of the newspaper with his wagon and his illegal load of a whiskey still.

Paternal Grandparents

Grandma's Huge Biscuits

My Grandma Vady Legg Walker, born August 28, 1891 and died September 9, 1967, was a strong woman to give birth to fourteen children; two of those babies were born dead; two died at a very young age, and ten children lived to old age and had grandchildren of their own. I have no idea how she managed to have so many kids, take care to them, keep them clothed, and to feed the whole bunch. My Aunt Lucille Walker is the sole survivor of my grandma's large number of offspring. Lucille was the youngest Walker of fourteen children, and she married a Walker and kept her last name.

Shortly after my Walker Grandparents were married conflicts started between Dan and Vady over his job of making moonshine. My Grandpa Walker, who was born on June 18, 1888, in Georgia, and died on October 2, 1969, was a little Scots Irish and over half Cherokee and Creek Indian. Grandpa Dan made whiskey with other family members in Tar Springs Hollow.

Eventually Grandpa Dan got caught by federal revenuers while working at the whiskey still on Capsey Creek in the mountains. They loaded grandpa in their wagon and started down the mountain along the old Jasper Road; my grandpa always wore overalls and boots. While making moonshine Grandpa Dan kept a pistol inside his boot; when the wagon got to the bottom of the mountain, Grandpa Walker reached into his boot and pulled out his handgun.

The first thing the federal men heard was the cocking of the hammer on grandpa's handgun; he told the men that he would get out of the wagon and for them not to turn around and look back. Grandpa told the men that he was going to follow them for a while, and if the men looked back before he decided to quit following them that he would kill them.

Prior to the men leaving, grandpa told the agents that he would be in Huntsville the next Monday and if he saw them they would be dead men. As promised, my grandpa made the long trip to Huntsville on his horse and the federal men that arrested him did not show up. This ended the conflict with federal agents, but started a more personal battle for control of the Walker household which my Grandma Vady eventually won.

Vady, Dan, Roy, Thurman, Paul, Oliver
Kenneth, Ida, Lodine, Violine, Lucille, Brady

    The arrest incident increased the whiskey making tension between Grandpa Dan and Grandma Vady to the point that a severe confrontation occurred. According to my aunt, Grandpa Dan got his shotgun, and at one point, he held the gun on my Grandma Vady. My aunt said that Grandma Vady with complete resolve stood in front of the gun with her two young boys William Roy Walker and Thurman Walker; she told Grandpa Dan to do what he had to, but she was not going to let a shotgun change her mind about his involvement in the moon shining activities. Grandpa knew he could not win the whiskey standoff and went back into the house and put his gun up.

    It was this intense confrontation that ended the moonshine career of my Grandpa Walker, and from that point, he never participated in the making of whiskey. Instead my

Grandpa made a complete turnaround in life; shortly after he quit making moon shine, Grandpa Walker begins a career as a hell fire and brimstone Baptist preacher and even helped establish churches in the surrounding area. As far as I know, my two Walker grandparents never had another severe confrontation to the point that someone's life was threatened.

Brady Walker

My dad Brady Walker had nine other siblings to live to adulthood and was born May 2, 1925, near Addison in Winston County, Alabama; he died December 29, 2001, and is buried in the Welborn Cemetery next to my mother near Pin Hook in Lawrence County, Alabama. Brady lived through the great depression and told me about taking big biscuits to Danville School in a tin pail for lunch. Brady also said that during the worst time of the depression that they would eat cornbread and molasses for breakfast; during the severe economic times of the 1930's, Brady wore brogans (plow boots) that got too small for his older brothers.

Brady Walker told about the day he quit school; he and other boys wanted to shoot some basketball. The coach told the boys not to get on his basketball court without tennis shoes; my dad did not have any shoes except plow boots and his parents could not afford shoes just to play basketball. Since the urge to shoot the basketball was so strong, Brady ran out on the court with his plow shoes; the coach grabbed a paddle and started for my dad with the intend of giving him a whipping. When Brady saw the coach coming after him, he took off running out the door and toward home; he never returned to school.

The thing I remember about my Grandma Walker is her extra-large biscuits which were about four inches high by four inches across; it was nearly all one could do to consume one of those biscuits. Grandma's huge biscuits tasted real good and believe it or not she managed to cook them all the way through; I always tore mine apart and eat the tops and bottoms which were the size of a regular biscuit. I would throw the center of the biscuit away after I made a dough ball out of the middle.

I never allowed anyone to see my dough ball for fear that they would make me eat the mashed up center of that biscuit. I stuck the dough ball in my pocket and when I got outside I would feed it to the chickens or dogs. The reason I hid the middle of my biscuit was simple, my parents and grandparents always made me clean my plate; they did not believe in wasting food.

If I left a little food on my plate, they would say, *"Boy you better clean that plate before you leave the table;"* or, *"Boy, was your eyes bigger than your belly? You clean that plate so the next time you only get what you will eat."* I understand not wasting food, but it is a miracle that I am not very fat because most times my eyes were bigger than my belly. I endured the plate cleaning without a lot of adverse effects of being too fat.

When I was a baby, my mother told me that she would chew my food and roll it into little balls; she would place the balls of food on the edge of the table. Mother told me that I would walk around the table and grab those little balls of food and eat them as fast as she could make them. Of course, my folks did not have baby food; they could not have afforded the baby food if they could have bought it.

I really enjoyed helping my Grandma Walker make peanut butter; she also allowed me to turn the old meat grinder to make the peanuts into a paste. I loved my grandma's homemade peanut butter and it was always of the chunky variety. She would parch the peanuts until they were cooked to perfection; then we would shell the parched peanuts, and grind in the meat grinder. I am not sure what grandma would add to the peanut butter except molasses to make it taste so good, but I thought her homemade peanut butter was the best I ever ate.

My grandma also made regular butter in her churn and I got to plunge the dasher up and down in the clabbered milk until the butter was formed. Grandma always had plenty of butter, fresh butter milk, and regular cow's milk. My Grandma Walker also cooked some big pones of cornbread about four inches thick; cornbread and butter milk was a staple part of the Walker diet, but I liked cutting up fresh tomatoes, green onions, and then putting lots of pepper and salt in my butter milk and cornbread. I guess having so many kids was the reason everything Grandma Walker cooked was real big; therefore, she did not worry if one of her biscuits or piece of her cornbread was enough for one person.

My Walker grandparents had some forty head of milk cows and sold milk in four or five big metal cans; the milk cans had to be set out beside the old Jasper Road (present-day Highway 41) every morning for the milk truck. When I was a young Celtic Indian boy growing up in the Warrior Mountains, the old Jasper or Danville Road was just wide enough for two vehicles to pass and was basically a dirt surface with big mud holes every time it rained a lot. The Carnation Milk truck was high off the ground containing two racks one above the other to hold the milk cans. The truck had side doors and the heavy cans full of milk had to be lifted all the way to the second rack. I still wonder how stout the man had to be to lift all those cans full of milk every day.

All forty of the cows were hand milked and I watched my Grandma Walker milk the old cows many times. My grandma and her children, including my dad, helped with the milking activities; every morning before my dad and his siblings went to school they had to hand milk the forty head of cows. They carried a bucket of clean water to wash the cow's teats, a stool to set on, and a bucket to hold the fresh milk.

Grandma Vady, Diane, June, Novel (Mom), Butch

After they milked a cow, they would pour the bucket of milk through a big wire strainer lined with a clean flour sack into the milk can; grandma and her kids strain all the fresh milk prior to putting in the metal milk cans. After school, the Walker children were again at the barn milking the old cows, but the milk in the afternoon was placed in gallon jugs, and the jugs of milk were place in lard buckets that were set in the pond to keep cool. During the next morning, the afternoon milk would be placed in the big metal milk cans. During all the milking activities, I never saw my Grandpa Walker milk the cows; I believe he thought that was a job for women and children.

After my mother and daddy got married, they lived in an old share cropper's house on my Grandpa Walker's farm. My parents were living in the old clap board house just up the road on my grandparent's home when I was born; my dad carried my mom to the Hartselle Clinic which was just off the north side of Main Street in an upstairs room where I was born. My dad worked as a farm hand for my granddad and helped milk the cows and farm for some years until we moved up north to pick fruit for a season.

My Grandma Walker also made clothes for her children from flour sacks and fertilizer (guanner or guano) sacks. All the children's underwear were made from the softer flour sacks and usually had some pretty print, but the boy's drawers were made with plain white flour sacks. When I was small, I too had the privilege of wearing flour sack drawers. Since the fertilizer sacks were a little tougher they were used to make work shirts, dresses, and other garments. Fertilizer sacks were also used to make mattresses, sheets, towels, and about anything made from cloth. My Aunt Lucille said my grandma lined her high school prom dress with flour sacks.

My Grandma Walker never had modern conveniences, and even when I was a good size boy, I remember her building a fire under the old cast iron wash pot and using a rub board to wash and clean every ones clothes. She would rinse off the clothes in a big tin tub and then hang them on an outside clothes line to dry. All the water used in the house and to wash and rinse clothes had to be drawn from the well; a long water bucket was let down into the well and pulled back up with the use of a pulley that hung on a beam above the well hole.

In order to take a bath during the warmer months, the kids usually filled tubs of water in the morning before school in order for the water to warm in the sun. My aunt told me that my dad would promise her a quarter to draw his bath water, but she said he never paid. In the winter time, a small pan of water was set on the stove to heat for a bath; I was in the ninth grade before we had a bathroom with a regular indoor bath tub.

Grandma Walker's house was heated with a big pot-bellied stove that set in the middle of the living room. A large bucket containing coal was kept close by the heater in order to add coal to the fire when it got low. About one time per year, a large coal truck would deliver a huge load of coal to last through the winter time. Usually everything in the house smelled like coal smoke during the winter months.

In the kitchen was a smaller cook stove where Grandma Vady spent most of her time preparing meals for a big family. Every Sunday it was expected that all the Walker children and grandchildren be at Grandpa and Grandma Walker's home for dinner; I have no idea how my grandma fed that bunch of people. But I do know that we all had to gather to listen to my Grandpa Dan talk for several hours, mostly about religion. When we finally got to go home, my dad would give Grandpa fifty cents for a gallon of milk; after we got home, we always had cornbread and milk for supper on Sunday night.

After my Grandma Vady died, my Grandpa Walker married another lady and he took her out to eat at restaurants; my aunt told me that she never remembered that Grandpa Dan ever took my Grandma Vady Walker out to eat. Such was the life and times of a Celtic-Indian boy growing up in the Warrior Mountains of North Alabama.

Shotgun Wedding

Many times to write from the heart, one has to bear their soul and open themselves up to criticism that otherwise they would never face; such is the true account of my family and the trials and struggles they had to bear. People in the old days were familiar with the phrase shotgun wedding, and my family was no different than other families that had to face very similar problems including the literal shotgun wedding; a shotgun was useful in the marriage of my mother and daddy.

One day four of my daddy's siblings, Oliver, Violine, Kenneth, and Lucille Walker, were in the field in my granddaddy Dan Walker's peanut patch shocking the peanut vines, in order for the green peanuts to dry in the field prior to pulling the peanuts off the vines. Shocks were stacks of peanut vines similar to a haystack; the stacks of peanut vines would be piled up above waste high. After the peanuts dried out completely, the nuts were picked off the vines and the vines were fed to the cows.

The siblings were not far up the hill from my Walker grandparent's home when a fellow carrying a shotgun came up into the field and asked to see Mr. Dan Walker. My aunts and uncle were surprised to see a man in a long sleeve shirt, overalls, and wearing a hat carrying a double barreled shotgun looking for their daddy. My Aunt Violine asked the man who he was and why he wanted to see their daddy. The man said that his name was Arthur Wilburn and that he was really looking for Brady Walker who was seeing his daughter. All my daddy's siblings knew that their brother was in a field not far away using a turning plow with a set of mules, but not one of them acknowledged that they knew where Brady was at that time.

At supper that night, my Grandpa Walker and his family were at the table ready to eat supper, and my Aunt Violine told my grandpa that Mr. Arthur Wilburn came by with a double barrel shotgun looking for you and Brady. My grandpa said that is enough said and we will not discuss this at the table; my Aunt Lucille said you could hear a pin drop for the rest of the supper, and from that point, not one word was spoken.

My Grandpa Walker was a very strict man and only told his kids one time what he required; the second time meant serious consequences for the one who violated his rules. His girls were never allowed to wear shorts or pants; even when the girls helped in the fields with plowing or picking cotton, they were required to wear dresses. Even after my aunts were married, they were not allowed at Grandpa Walker's house in shorts. I guess growing up in that culture is the reason I feel uncomfortable wearing shorts today.

My Aunt Lucille Walker told me that she was married and had two children when she came home from Germany with her husband who was a career soldier in the military. One morning, she was at Grandpa Walker's washing clothes in her shorts when her dad saw her and told her that he did not allow women at his house to go naked. He pointed out that the school bus would be passing his house in a few minutes and he expected her to be dressed. My aunt quickly honored my Grandpa Walker's wishes and went in the house and put on a skirt over her shorts even though the shorts were down to her knees.

Back to the shotgun wedding, my aunt told me that my dad came in early one morning drunk and was lying on the front porch when she went out to go to school. She was unaware that my dad had been drinking and thought that he was sick because he was throwing up; therefore, she went back into the house and told my Grandpa Dan Walker who came out to see what was going on. Grandpa said something to my dad who replied with a smart remark; my aunt said grandpa picked up a brush broom and beat the tar out of my dad even though he was twenty years old.

A brush broom was a bunch of saplings tied together to sweep the yard; in my early days, both sets of my grandparents did not allow grass to grow in their yard. They used the brush broom to sweep the sand in the yard clean of all debris. I love to play in my grandparent's yard after we swept it clean of chicken droppings, limbs, leaves and other rubbish.

After Grandpa Walker and my dad had a come to Jesus meeting, my dad was married to my mother by Probate Judge Isaac Johnson, Jr. on October 30, 1945, at Lawrence County Courthouse in Moulton, Alabama. Believe it or not, my Grandpa Wilburn did not shoot my dad, even though he confronted my dad on more than one occasion with that old double barreled shotgun. My parents stayed married until their deaths, and as other families, they endured many hardships raising three children on low wages.

Even though my siblings and I were not sure that my dad would make it through life without killing someone, to our surprise he went to his grave before sending someone else to their final resting place. My dad was the wild one of his family, and he was not afraid to mix it up with anyone that confronted him. In other words, he had several fights while out with his drinking buddies; sometimes he got the worst end of a fight and many times the other fellows received a few bruises.

It is hard for some folks to believe the country and mountain culture that a Celtic Indian boy grew to manhood has change from a very reserved lifestyle to the very loose lifestyle of today. My grandparents would have never allowed their children to be in public in the swimsuits that people wear to the beach this day and time; they did not even allow their children to wear shorts or pants. Today, I very seldom wear shorts because of the culture that dominated my life in the Warrior Mountains of North Alabama.

Outhouse

I was in the ninth grade before my parents ever lived in a house with indoor plumbing. Prior to that time, my house at the edge of forest service property had a little one hole outhouse that was located on the bank of a large branch which would wash away the dung during rainy weather. During drier times, I still did not have to worry about a pile of crap building up because my chickens could not wait for a fresh meal, and we still ate the eggs. Many times the dogs would beat the chickens and clean up the mess shortly after it fell; therefore, we did not have to worry so much about the smell.

Of course, outhouses were very common across the Warrior Mountains of North Alabama because most homes when I was growing up did not have indoor plumbing. Some folks kept a slop jar in their bed rooms that they would use if they had to pee or take a crap especially if it was extremely cold at night. The slop jar had a lid that kept the smell down, but in the morning, it was necessary to empty the contents and clean the container. I would always go outside because we did not have containers to use inside, and I sure did not like the idea of using a little pot that would have to be cleaned at daylight.

Cleaning the pot first thing in the morning would not be a job that I would look forward to, but sometimes, grandma would ask me to empty and clean her slop jar while she cooked breakfast. Now that was not an appetizing chore that I wanted to do; that fresh breakfast was reward enough.

I must relate the following story; one night my cousin was at my house and had to make a solid removal of his bowels. He said he was a little scared to go to the outhouse by himself; therefore, he asked me to go outside with him because it was extremely dark. Being the good person I am, I agreed to accompany him along the narrow trail leading to our little one hole outhouse about 300 yards toward the forest property.

Upon arriving at the outhouse, my cousin Don Welborn said it was too dark to see how to use the hole and wanted to take his dump in the woods. Not wanting to step on his deposit the next day, I got him to accompany me another 200 yards into the forest. Since we did not have a flashlight, we just had to creep up the hill until I felt it was safe for him to do his business out of harm's way.

He squatted by a big white oak tree and about the time he started to strain; my dog came running off the hill in the dry leaves. Being in the late fall, the leaves were extremely dry and noisy; he anxiously asked what is that, at which I screamed, *"Bear, bear,"* and tore out running downhill. As I stopped after a short distance, I could hear him rolling my direction in the leaves with his pants down around his ankles; I had the best laugh and the worst cussing at the same time. Needless to say, he was a mess more ways than one.

The outhouse that my Walker grandparents used was some 100 yards away from their house to keep the smell from causing problems. The Walker outhouse was one that accommodated three people at one time and was wide open on the inside; in other words, the big outhouse for the large extended family had three seats or holes to set over; you could take a crap next to two of your uncles or two other people who were in a strain and need a place to relieve themselves before you got finished.

I hated it when other people came to the outhouse while I was using it; I remember one large Walker family gathering at my grandparents when I was setting over a hole doing my business. Prior to completing my bowel job, a lady came into the outhouse and said, *"I am sorry son but I really got to go;"* therefore, she plopped down on the far hole. I was glad there was at least one hole between us.

This reminds me of a friend of mine whose grandma evidently did not wear any drawers. When she wanted to pee, the lady would simply just reach and pull her dress out in front, spread her legs slightly, and urinate while talking to other people; when she moved, a large wet spot was left on the ground. What was exceptional about this activity was that she could continue her conservation while doing her business and not miss a word like nothing was happening.

I also hated the smell of my Walker grandparent's huge outhouse and the big old worms that ate all that mess in a big pit below the seats; I had this great fear of falling in that hole of crap and being eaten by those worms because it was always working alive in big brown hairy maggot like worms. In addition, I always had a fear that something was hiding just under where you had to sit; many times I would peep through the hole while holding my breath to see if a wasp nest or spiders were lurking in wait for an unsuspected stinky thunder, yellow shower, or brown hell.

The toilet paper used in the outhouse was the John Wayne version; *"Rough and tough and did not take any shit off of anybody!"* Literally, if you did not rough that catalog paper up real good, it would only smear brown streaks all over your bottom. The wiping paper consisted of a Sears and Roebuck catalog usually hung over a wire coat hanger; I usually entertained myself by looking at the toys and pretty girls before selecting a page to wad up and rub between my hands to soften up prior to use.

Grandma Vady and Grandpa Dan Walker

Instead of using all that slick rough catalog paper, we would keep the corn cobs to use as wiping material; the technique was to use the red cobs first then follow up with a white cob to insure all below was clean. Both sets of my grandparents had corn shellers that worked similar to a meat grinder, but the ears of corn were placed in the top and when you turned the handle all the corn kernels would fall into the box below. Of course all the cobs were saved to be used like toilet paper.

Prior to my Grandma Walker's death, my Aunt Lucille Walker had an indoor bathroom installed in their house. My Grandpa Walker told my aunt that Ms. Vady could use the indoor outhouse, but he intended to keep using the outhouse on the outside. Old habits are hard to break, especially with a streak of Walker stubbornness, but such was the life of a young Celtic Indian boy growing up in the 1950s and 1960s.

Tobacco Plugs and Snuff

Our cabinets were stocked with plenty of drinking glasses from grandma's snuff jars, and from the jelly jars that were filled with great tasting jellies and jams that were delicious on fresh hot biscuits. The snuff that my grandma dipped was packaged in pretty little glasses that would hold some eight to ten ounces; my mother bought jelly in larger glasses that would hold twelve to sixteen ounces. Therefore, we always had a set of small drinking glasses from the snuff jars or the larger drinking glasses from the jelly jars.

My Grandma Walker loved her Bruton snuff and most of the time she had a dip in her mouth. Now grandma was a good spitter and she used the finger style by placing her first two fingers into a "V" against her lips, and after a good breath, she could spit some ten yards. I never could master her technique, and only one time is all it took me to know that I never wanted to dip snuff for the rest of my life. In addition, Grandma Vady probably knew that I would be broke from snuff dipping if I swallowed enough to make me sick; sure enough I got a near fatal dip. Shortly thereafter, I got sick as a dog after sucking some of the dust down my lungs and drinking some of the snuff sauce.

Most of the early settlers had a small tobacco patch for their own use, and my grandpa was no different. I well remember my great grandpa rolling his own twists of home grown tobacco that would turn nearly black after a while. He would roll the leaves into a long tight cylinder about one inch around and two feet long; then he would then fold the cylinder and twist the long piece of rolled tobacco around each other with a loop on one end and the two tag ends twisted as tight as he could get it. After all this twisting, he allowed the chewing tobacco to dry; after which he would take his pocket knife and cut a large plug that he would place in his jaw.

One time is all it took for him to cut me a small plug to chew. After a little of that juice started to flow, it was the worst tasting stuff that I ever put into my mouth; immediately I got dizzy and sick at my stomach. I could not spit enough to get the taste out of my mouth, and grandpa thought that was so funny. Through the efforts of my grandma and my grandpa, I never desired to chew or dip tobacco; to this day, I have never used tobacco in any form.

I must share another story from my Celtic Indian friend Michael Offutt, *"I always get amused at kids getting sick off of tobacco. It seems like that while growing up in rural north-central Alabama that trying and using various forms of tobacco was a Rite of Passage. We tried every brand of snuff and chewing tobacco we could get our hands on. You really had to "work your way up" to say, to Taylor's Natural Plug, Brown's Mule, or Natural Twist. They even had grape flavored snuff for the novices. After that, most kids could learn how to handle Red Man or Levi Garrett chewing tobacco. We would entertain ourselves and show off our prowess with spitting and chewing contests."*

"One such contest we had, the contenders got to choose the other one's brands and combinations to be dipped and/or chewed until spitting clear. My challenger set the stakes and I had to go first. After I had succeeded with the combo of a lip full of Bruton's Scotch Snuff and a big cut off of a plug of Brown's Mule, I laid down the gauntlet for my younger contestant to survive dipping the grape flavored snuff and a cut off a plug of Bloodhound Brand. It came real close to a tie and a rematch, until he right at the end, began pukeing his guts up. Back home, his mother almost took him to the ER. He was a pale green and running a fever, and couldn't get out of bed except to go dry heave. His elderly great-aunt took one look at him and knew, saying, "Aw, that boy's just sick off of ta-backy", and laughed!"

However, tobacco was used on a regular basis to get rid of intestinal worms. When I was young, most people had some kinds of intestinal worms that would wiggle around in their feces, and tobacco was very effective in killing the internal parasites. It did not take but a little swallow of the nicotine in the dip or chew to kill the round worms and tapeworms; therefore, it was not uncommon for young children to be allowed to chew or dip tobacco.

I well remember my grandma telling of a small child in our family that got real sick from a worm infestation and died, and for a day or two later before the child was buried, grandma said you could see his belly area move because he was full of the intestinal parasites. I am sure it did not take but one or two deaths like that for parents to allow their children to dip or chew tobacco in order to kill the worms.

Dan and Vady

Most of the tobacco grown in the Deep South was used for personal use and was not sold widespread except in the hill country of Tennessee and farther north. Our area of the Warrior Mountains was plagued with tobacco worms which had to be plucked off the growing plants or they would eat up the small tobacco crop. It was one of jobs of the children to keep the tobacco worms off the growing plants, and each day, the kids checked the plants and pulled the worms that could destroy the tobacco.

I remember my grandparents telling about removing the worms from the plants that their parents depended on for their source of tobacco. Both Grandpa Dan and Grandma Vady used tobacco; Ms. Vady loved her Bruton snuff and Dan loved his cigarettes.

My great grandparents were users of tobacco, and I remember some of them setting in their rocking chairs near the fireplace with their chew or dip of tobacco. Most of the men seemed to be partial to cutting their plug of tobacco directly off their twists; while the women loved to dip their snuff with a black gum twig that was made into a snuff brush. I remember cutting black gum twigs for snuff brushes for my grandma.

Also, my dad told me many times about his Indian Grandma Vicey Stevens Walker loving her tobacco; she chewed, dipped, and smoked her old corn cob pipe. After her husband died, she stayed a lot with my daddy's folks Dan and Vady who helped take care of her. She died at my dad's house and laid a corpse at their home until the burial, but dad told me many times that the white neighbors never came to the house while they were waiting for my grandpa Dan to get home. My dad told me that he always believed the white neighbors stayed away because she was Indian. Such was the times of a Celtic Indian boy growing up in the foothills of the southern Appalachian Mountains.

Death Calls and Body Bag

As a young child, I was not blessed to have any brothers; my double cousins Danny and Sandy Welborn were as close to brothers as any boy could hope. We were kin by blood on both the Walker and Wilburn sides of our family; my daddy's sister Violine Walker was their mother and my mother's uncle Willard Welborn was their daddy. Danny, Sandy, and I grew up around one another from a young age, and even though I was not a brother, I felt a very close and personal relationship to these two boys. We spent many nights together either at my Walker Grandparents or at my Wilburn Grandparents. We were poor and did not realize it until we were much older and saw what other kids had at our age.

In school, the three of us, Danny, Sandy, and I, were very competitive and played basketball against each other. Danny and Sandy went to Danville High School and lived next door to my Walker grandparents. I played basketball at Speake High School during my junior and senior years. The two schools were some seven miles apart. Danny and Sandy started on their basketball team and I was a starter on the Speake Varsity Basketball Team. We faced each other on our yard courts and also on the basketball hardwood at both schools; we played our hearts out trying to beat each other at the game we all three loved.

Prior to reaching that high school level of playing basketball, Danny, Sandy, and I were the best buddies who fished, hunted, and roamed the woods together. Since we were blood kin on both sides of our families, we attended funerals and family gatherings together. Danny and I did everything that brothers could have done with each other; my first double date was with Danny and his girlfriend Brenda Sapp.

I had earlier met Donna Jean Hayes at a Beta Club Convention in Birmingham at the Thomas Jefferson Hotel. Donna Jean also attended Danville High School with Danny and we planned a double date. During another double date, I fixed Danny up with Yolanda Morgan who went to Speake High School. Yolanda kept telling Danny that she had another boyfriend; therefore, his blind double date did not go beyond that one night at the movies.

Prior to my first date with Donna Jean Hayes, I will never forget that Danny and I had just eaten a hamburger all the way which included onions. After eating that burger, Danny called and got a date with Brenda and the double was on. I was very upset that my first double date may be my last because of my stinky onion breath; Danny fired up a cigarette and told me to take several puffs and that would neutralize the onion smell. After about three deep draws off that smoke, I got so sick that I thought the date would have to be called off. After a glass of water and several deep breaths of fresh air, my dizzy head and nauseated stomach settled down and I was good to go. To go on the date, I had to borrow a car from my oldest sister Diane and her husband Ocie; I drove the car to the Thunderbird Drive-in Theater in Decatur.

I had met Donna Jean Hayes, but had not had an official date. When I saw her beautiful face and smile, it was love at first sight. I later wound up marrying that beautiful black haired girl, who became the light of my life for three short years. We went to the University of North Alabama together and lived in an apartment in Florence. Even though we both attended classes and worked part time jobs, there were good times and struggles that we faced together as husband and wife, but it was a life that was not meant to be permanent.

Two days after I graduated from UNA, I signed our divorce papers in her lawyers' office of Ralph Slate in Decatur. Two days later, I was drafted into the U.S. Army and was off to Fort Jackson, South Carolina. Since the day I signed our divorce papers many years ago, I have not talked to Donna Jean but one time. I learned that she got her doctorate and was a professor at the University of Alabama in Birmingham.

Willard Welborn and Violine Walker were the parents of Danny, Sandy, and Ronnie Welborn. When my Uncle Willard died in 1954, he left three young boys with my daddy's sister Violine; Danny was five, Sandy was three, and Ronnie was six months old. Not long after the death of my Uncle Willard, Aunt Violine married Charles Keeling; Violine and Charles had another son who was my first cousin Larry Joe Keeling. Even though we faced some difficult times, Danny, Sandy, Ronnie, and I found our way through life to become somewhat successful and struggled to become members of the middle income class of folks, but Larry Joe somehow fell through the cracks of society partly through trying to rise above poverty by means that were considered illegal.

After my Aunt Violine and Charles divorced, Larry Joe Keeling did not have the fiscal stability to live up to the standards of other kids his age. Larry Joe had the dark complexion and dark hair of our Walker Indian ancestors; he was a handsome young man who looked much more mature than his age would suggest. Larry Joe could not accept the slow gradual crawl from the depths of poverty to compete with his friends and girls much older. By the time he was fourteen, he was dating beautiful girls several years older than he was. To support his recreation and dating, Larry Joe began petty theft and experimenting with drugs. He was now on the path of desperation and despair and it seemed that no amount of encouragement from his folks could turn his life in a different direction.

I know that Larry Joe wanted to escape the poverty ridden life that we all faced as teenagers. I always had to borrow a car to take a girl out on a date and so did my cousins but Larry Joe started dating too young to drive. I well remember the first time he got into trouble; my dad was cussing mad that Larry Joe was poor and did not have the proper legal representation to get a slap on the wrist as two of the other boys who had been caught with him. My dad said they got off scot free while Larry Joe had to pay the price of the crime for all three. Larry Joe would eventually pay the supreme sacrifice for the situation he got caught up in with the legal system because of his poverty. The mold was set and Larry Joe would continuously fall outside the acceptable behavior of a teenager. At fifteen years old when my aunt was in the hospital, Larry Joe took the car keys from Aunt Violine's purse and picked up two of his friends to party.

Larry Joe and his friends collected all their parents' medications and pain relievers; all three boys took a hand full of these prescription drugs at one time. For two days, the boys were missing until the car was found outside of Hartselle upside down in a ravine near the road; at the initial inspection of the car by law enforcement authorities, the boys were pronounced dead.

The coroner come to the scene and upon removing the bodies realized the boys were actually alive; the large amount of drugs had slowed their heart rate to the point a pulse could not be detected. After their stomachs were pumped, Larry Joe and his two friends spent two days in the hospital recuperating from their near fatal overdose of drugs that could have easily been the end of their lives. This was the first, but not the last time that Larry Joe would face a near death encounter.

Eventually at about fifteen years old, Larry Joe was sent to reform school at Four Spot Reformatory. Our judicial and legal system was attempting to force a change in his behavior but he already had a taste of freedom. Larry Joe told my folks that he had a child on the way and had to get out of the facility. At the reformatory, Larry Joe was enrolled in a vocational program to become a barber; one day while cutting a clients' hair, Larry Joe managed to get the man's car keys and run from the building. He jumped in the car and attempted to escape but was caught by the authorities before getting out of the parking lot; the young teenager Larry Joe was in for a rude awakening.

Because of the attempted car theft and escape from the reformatory at the young age of sixteen, Larry Joe was caught and placed in Draper Prison. At Draper, Larry Joe was trained as a wheel vehicle mechanic and got very good at his job, but the urge to leave and see his young wife and child became overwhelming. His young wife would visit Larry Joe with my Aunt Violine and his brothers, but he was determined to have his freedom once again. Larry Joe and a friend he had made at Draper Prison decided that life was not worth living without freedom; therefore, the two of them planned a daring escape that they knew might cost them their lives. I must admit that Larry Joe had a surplus of the bravery of our family's Indian lineage, and he was willing to sacrifice his life for another quick taste of freedom.

One day Larry Joe and his friend were working on an old Draper Prison truck that was not running; after figuring out and repairing the problem, Larry Joe and his friend jumped in the truck and started for the main gate. Through a hail of machine gun fire, they crashed the truck through the gate at the main entrance and made it two miles down the road before having to abandon the old bullet hole ridden prison truck; neither of the boys was wounded as they made their daring escape from Draper Prison. Larry Joe's friend was caught almost immediately but Larry Joe's athletic abilities and Indian instincts kept him a free kid for some four days. He was eventually caught under an interstate overpass; his clothes were in shreds and he had not eaten during the time he was on the loose.

After this second vehicle theft and escape from a correctional institution, Larry Joe was placed in the Mt. Meigs Correctional Facility which contained hardened criminals; it was here that the sixteen year old boy faced a hell on earth. When family members would visit, Larry Joe would cry and beg for help; he would tell about being raped repeatedly and being force to perform oral sex acts for the older and bigger male prisoners. After several weeks of sexual abuse and being a whore to the other prisoners, Larry Joe ratted on the men who were making his life a living hell; again he was ready to die rather than face the continued abuse.

Shortly after reporting the male prisoners that were sexually abusive to him, the family was called and told that Larry Joe was on his death bed. He had been stabbed repeatedly in the stomach and chest with a shank made from a pair of scissors; this was the second near fatal encounter with death that Larry Joe faced in his short life. Miraculously after several days in intensive care, Larry Joe survived the horrible ordeal but was transferred to Atmore Prison as soon as he was well enough to be released from the hospital.

At the maximum security Atmore Prison, Larry Joe was confined with death row inmates; he told about having to pass the electric chair every day when going to eat. Atmore was tough, but by this time so was Larry Joe. He had faced two near death encounters and somehow managed to control his behavior long enough for prison officials to consider parole.

One key element of his parole was that Larry Joe must have a job prior to his release from Atmore Prison; at the time of his parole consideration, my mother was running a small shirt factory in Moulton, Alabama. Mother had earlier employed my Aunt Violine, who was Larry Joe's mother, and my Aunt Lucille; the three of them could keep an eye on Larry Joe. Prison officials agreed that Larry Joe would be released since he had a job working for my mother.

For a few months, Larry Joe made an excellent employee at mother's little shirt factory. During this time, he met a girl from Tennessee. Larry Joe brought the young Tennessee girl to Alabama and claimed that they were married. His first marriage had ended during his prison terms but that marriage was blessed with a beautiful daughter. The Tennessee girl was also pregnant with his child but wanted to return home.

Larry Joe made another near fatal mistake when he carried the girl he called his wife back home. Supposedly her father and her brothers thought that they had beaten Larry Joe to death and threw his body in a ditch off the highway. After being found by passersby, Larry Joe would spend another several days in intensive care; he was unrecognizable by his mother, his brothers, and kinfolks. Somehow, Larry Joe survived the third near death experience.

After recuperating from his injuries, Larry Joe returned to work at the shirt factory; within a few weeks, Larry Joe just disappeared and was not heard from for over two and a half years. This time, everyone though that Larry Joe was dead, but one day his mother's phone rang and on the other end was Larry Joe; he was alive and well. Larry Joe was living in San Antonia, Texas; he ran a thriving prostitution business with over ten whores for which he was pimping.

Larry Joe was also into the drug trade; he told his brother Danny that he was making meth and the law had not figured out what the drug was, but he said it sold better than heroin. At last Larry Joe had moved out of poverty to have anything that money could buy; he had a yacht, motor home, Cadillacs, and a big fine home. Eventually, the drug cartel that Larry Joe worked for wound up with everything that he owned and his family received none of his money or possessions.

The last time my cousin Larry Joe was seen alive by his family was not long before his death; he was driving a brand new Cadillac that he had paid cash for and in the car he had several weapons including a machine gun. He had come to Danny's house for a visit and had brought one of his beautiful whores to keep him company; Danny said that Larry Joe introduced the very attractive girl as one of his prostitutes. The girl admitted to the family that she was indeed a prostitute, but she was extremely nice and catered to Larry Joe's every command while they were at Danny's home; he visited my dad before returning to Texas.

On April 8, Larry Joe was bringing his new motor home to Alabama to visit his mother on her birthday. He and two of his body guards were to have a drug payoff of $10,000.00 at a rest stop, but the guy did not show. They went to the nearby motel where the drug dealer was to pay the money. Larry Joe was standing by the side of his motor home in the parking lot while his two body guards went up opposite stairs to the second floor room that the dealer was using. When they knocked on the door, a hail of gunfire came through the door with one shot hitting Larry Joe dead center of the backbone killing him almost instantly; this time was not a close encounter with death but the real thing.

My two cousins Danny and Sandy went to Texas to claim the body of their brother; an autopsy had been performed and the remains of his nude body were in a plastic body bag with a tag tied to his big toe. Larry Joe's brothers asked the sheriff about his money and possessions. The sheriff informed them that they better be happy to just get his body and forget about trying to claim his possessions at the risk of their lives.

Our family made up money to cover the expenses for bringing the twenty six year old body of Larry Joe home and for his burial. Larry Joe is buried next to his mother, my Aunt Violine, and my Uncle Willard Welborn at the Aldridge Grove Cemetery. Larry Joe Keeling was given a proper burial by his people and many members of his family attended the funeral; also in attendance to the funeral were two of his body guards and one of his beautiful young prostitutes.

As a sad note, Larry Joe's dad Charles Keeling came to visitation at the funeral home, but he left before the graveside service and burial. Later Charles Keeling would be buried by the county services; my cousin Danny and Charles' wife at the time were the only people that attended the funeral services other than the ones burying him in a plain wooden box. Danny told me that the lid to Charles' wooden casket was one piece; four red bricks were placed in the bottom of the hole where he was buried in order to remove the straps from the wood coffin that held Charles' body. After the straps that lowered the box were removed, Danny grabbed a shovel and helped county workers bury the body of his deceased brother's dad.

Some of my poor Celtic Indian cousins, my sisters, and I were able to rise above a poverty stricken life. We move beyond a hand to mouth style of living into the middle income class of people without getting into crime, but being very poor in the southern hill country of lower Appalachia during the 1950s and 1960s increased the burdens that we had to overcome.

For some kids such as Larry Joe who had committed nothing other than petty theft before being sent to reform school, our criminal justice system, our educational facilities, and our economic institutions failed miserably to address the needs of the poverty ridden children found throughout Appalachia. As society discarded kids such as Larry Joe to reformatories and prisons, our society of taxpayers had to bear the financial burden of incarceration and reform without receiving desired results. With my first cousin Larry Joe, the reverse occurred by assisting in turning him into a harden criminal, whose life was very short and painful. Such was the tragic life of another Celtic Indian boy from the Warrior Mountains of the lower foothills of the Appalachian Mountains.

Ways of the Wild

Walks in my Home Land

As a young country boy growing up in the foothills of the Warrior Mountains, I became very familiar with the creek bottoms and woodlands of the northeastern portion of the Black Warrior Forest, now known as William B. Bankhead National Forest which was named after a white politician. I grew up next to forest service property and was introduced to the forested mountains by my granddaddy Arthur Wilburn.

Along the banks of West Flint Creek, I learned at an early age to hunt and harvest wild game from the woods, catch fish from the clear deep holes, gig suckers during their spring run, and probe for mud turtles on sandbars in the creek bed during the late summer. I was taught how to find and dig ginseng including other medicinal plants from the rich hillsides; trap furbearing animals during the winter months; to follow a pack of hounds on dark dreary winter nights for possums and coons.

All these activities taught me a way of survival that my grandfather and other ancestors followed by living off what mother-nature provided. My grandpa would always half the money from the night's catch after the furs were stretched, dried, and sold. If I assisted him with the trap line, he would always give me an equal share of the profits from the sale of the furs. Many memories have lasted a lifetime were instilled within my heart and gave me a love for the great outdoors that I still have to this day. It is my hope that I too can teach my grandchildren the ways of the wild and a love for the great outdoors.

During the early years of my life, the adventures and activities with my grandpa occurred in the area of West Flint Creek drainage which was the central place of focus during my boyhood days. Brushy Mountain, Sugar Camp Hollow, Indian Tomb, Beech Bottoms, McVay Hollow, Thompson Creek, Indian Creek, Oakville Pond, and the Mastengill Hole were just a few places that were the regular stomping grounds of grandpa and me. These places were etched into my memory by day and also during the nighttime hunts.

When I was too young to drive, the main area of my adventures were always within walking distance and were associated with that slow meandering creek, known as the West Fork of Flint Creek which split the old Alexander Plantation. During my youth, we lived for a while in an old clapboard house on the old plantation site where my father was a work hand on the land that was farmed by Mr. Joe Jacobs, who was the son-in-law of Mr. Jake Alexander. Jake, the son of Thomas Jefferson Alexander and Sally Fitzgerald, managed to control the huge estate, even though he had a lot of siblings who also had a claim to the big farm.

After the Alexander Place was sold to Mr. Dallas Yeager, my Uncle Curtis Wilburn and his wife Dean lived in the old plantation house while he worked for Yeager. I remember spending many days playing with my cousins Joan and Mike Wilburn in the big house and exploring the farm. Curtis built fences, cleared land, plowed the crop land, took care of the cattle, and did all the farm work for Mr. Yeager; while Curtis worked as a farm hand he and his family lived in the old Alexander Plantation house.

The Alexander family built three other big plantation houses besides the one that Mr. Jake Alexander lived in that was just alike. One was near the south end of the Drag Strip Road and was built for a daughter of Thomas Jefferson Alexander who married Captain Warren. The other was built for Henry Alexander the half-brother of Jake and it is the only one still standing and is the home of Mr. Don Alexander. The home still standing is about one mile east of Flint Creek Bridge on Highway 36 on the north side of the highway. The third big house was built just southeast of the intersection of Alabama Highway 36 and Highway 33 near Wren.

Curtis, Joan, Mike, Dean Wilburn

West Flint Creek not only flowed through the Alexander Plantation, but also formed the hollows and bottoms in the foothills of the Warrior Mountains. A lot of the land surrounding the upper drainage of the creek was at one time privately owned and farmed by the early settlers of Poplar Log Cove. Later in the early 1900's, the area became the Black Warrior Forest; today it is now part of the William B. Bankhead National Forest.

The West Fork of Flint Creek began in the southeastern part of Lawrence County in Poplar Log Cove. The limestone spring in the upper portion of the Poplar Log Cove was the source of a steady stream of water and was the beginning of the West Fork of Flint Creek. The main tributaries near the southeastern beginnings of the creek were Wiggins Creek, Indian Creek, Thompson Creek, and Elam Creek.

Thompson Creek also had two important tributaries that included Gillespie Creek that flows through the center of Indian Tomb Hollow and Lee Creek that starts at Shiloh Church on the Leola Road. It was along these creeks and hollows of West Flint that my boyhood life was formed in the tradition of my ancestors who depended upon the area for survival. Not only did these woodlands provide my grandpa and I many wonderful meals of fish and wild game, but also provided my grandfather the major portion of his income during the winter and spring months.

The ways of the wild sometimes seemed harsh but the rewards, even though small by today's standards, were great in the eyes of a young boy following his grandpa through the woods. I knew that the animals taken would be a tasty meal after being prepared by my grandmother on the old wood cook stove. She would help prepare and cook rabbits, squirrels, opossums, coons, muskrats, beavers, groundhogs, turtles, and fish for many daily meals.

In addition, my grandparents knew that the sale of medicinal roots, honey, wild meat, and hides would supplement their fall harvest of three to four bales of cotton grown on the poor hillsides. Such was a way of life and the focal point of a lifelong adventure into a world not far removed from the old creek of a boyhood memory.

Today, I still hunt and roam the forest service property in the drainage of West Flint Creek and it always feels like it is my homeland. Indian Tomb Hollow is still a very special place to me which I visit and hunt on a regular basis. Each visit to Indian Tomb recharges my inner being and refreshes my spirit because I know I am walking the trails my ancestors walked for many generations.

Fiddle Worms and Rattlesnakes

Years ago when I was just a young boy, my daddy, uncles, and grandpa would decide that we were going to the Tennessee River for a weekend fishing trip. We fished, slept, and ate on the river bank while trying to catch fish for the table. My grandma, Ila Wilburn, would make up a bunch of dough balls that would be used to catch carp, drum, and buffalo fish. My Grandpa Arthur and I would get the old handsaw and head to the woods to find fiddle worms for catching catfish.

Occasionally, we would get our ten foot minnow seine and go to Tonnical Branch that ran from a hole on the side of the Alexander Motorway known as the Suck. When using the minnow seine, we would keep crawfish, minnows of all kinds, and small bream to use as bait on our overnight fishing trips. On one particular seining expedition to Tonnical Branch, my dad, Brady Walker, was wearing hip boots and carrying two buckets of minnows and crawfish that we had just caught; his boots were about half way down and just flopping from side to side as we were heading back to the car.

My Uncle Willard Welborn, who was my daddy's brother-in-law and my mother's uncle, was always up to mischief. As Willard was following behind Brady, he grabbed a long stick that he stuck between Brady's legs. Of course about the same time that my dad felt the stick, Willard hollered snake; my dad jumped into the air but managed to hold on to the minnow buckets. Shortly afterwards, Willard, who was laughing uncontrollably, got a good cussing from Brady Walker; even after the cussing, we managed to go to the river for one of our weekend fishing trips.

Now back to fiddling worms; to get fiddle worms, we would cut a sapling about two inches in diameter about one foot above the ground. The best saplings to fiddle worms would be those with long tap roots. The sapling we chose to fiddle would be in a rich damp portion of mature hardwoods usually around limestone outcroppings. We had special spots where we could get fiddle worms on a regular basis. Sometimes when a sapling was not in the spot we wanted to find fiddle worms, we would drive a stake deep into the ground; then we would take a flat rock or old board and rub across the top of the stake to create vibrations that would cause the fiddle worms to come to the top of the ground.

Willard Welborn

Fiddle worms could be found only in moist, heavily shaded, woodland areas that usually had limestone rock close to the surface. Most of the fiddle worms were white, about a foot long, and would secrete a sticky slime when you picked them up. By the time you got your bucket filled with the worms, your hands would be black and sticky. Fiddle worms were much messier when you tried to bait your fishing hook; the second you stuck the worm with the hook, it would give off the sticky yellowish slime. Most of the time, we would have a bunch of rags to clean our hands after baiting the hook, but fiddle worms were excellent catfish bait.

Sawing with a dull handsaw down through the middle of the sapling would cause the sapling stump to vibrate as we pulled the saw across the cut end of the stump. As the ground vibrated from the sawing, fiddle worms would start coming to the top of the ground and crawling around on the leaves. One of us would start picking up the fiddle worms while the other kept the fiddle music going with the old handsaw.

I would take the old five gallon bucket and place leaf litter in the bottom including moist leaves. We would place hundreds of fiddle worms in the bucket for the all night fishing trip on the weekend. Usually within a short period of time, we would have all the catfish bait we needed for our fishing trip. Most of the time, fiddle worms would not last more than two or three days; therefore, we would have to fiddle for the worms the day before the planned fishing trip to the Tennessee River.

My dad, Brady, would have two or three hooks on his line. He would place the biggest gob of fiddle worms he could get on one of the hooks and on the other he would put a small bream or big minnow. Brady had tied on the end of his line a large chunk of lead; he used one old casting reel with heavy braided line. Brady always swung the bait and lead round and round before letting it fly across the water. I guess dad thought he could throw his rig much farther if he would swing it in circles before releasing the line.

My uncles and Grandpa Arthur used fishing poles that were creek canes. When we went to the river everyone had two to three canes each which were tied on top of our car. We had cut the green fishing canes on West Flint Creek; the canes were always dried before they were used as fishing poles. The green canes were tied at the little end on a high limb and a rock as a weight on the big end so they would dry straight. After several weeks of drying, the canes would be ready to rig with line, cork, lead, and hook for fishing poles.

Grandpa Arthur always tried to get the biggest and longest creek canes he could find for his fishing poles. He would stick the pole into the bank which had a heavy line slightly longer than the fishing cane. Grandpa usually had at least two hooks on his line that he baited with dough balls or fiddle worms. After his line was baited, grandpa would throw the baited hooks with a big lead sinker on the end of the line as far as he could into the river and wait for a buffalo, carp, drum, or catfish to bite.

We kept every kind of fish that we caught; Grandma Ila would pressure cook and can in mason jars all our catch in order to keep fish for the winter. After being pressured cooked and canned, the fish would be made into patties and fried on the old wood burning stove. Fish patties were some great eating on cold winter days. Usually we would have fresh homemade biscuits and milk gravy with our fish patties. I loved the way my grandma cooked her canned fish which I always said were better than salmon patties.

We not only kept all the fish we caught on our overnight fishing trips, but we also went to the dewatering area at Swan Creek and grabbled all kinds of fish which we could catch with our hands. Every spring the state conservation department would drain the water off the wetlands to plant grain for waterfowl. They would allow people to come to the area for salvaging the fish that were trapped in shallow water and small ponds. We would wade and feel around the stumps and other structures until we felt a big fish that we would catch by hand. Sometimes I would carry my bow and shoot many carp and buffalo. All the fish we got would be carried home to be pressure cooked and canned for our winter food supply.

A few times during fiddling worms, some other things would be coming out of nearby holes. On one occasion, my uncle and cousin were fiddling worms when a large timber rattlesnake came out from under a nearby limestone outcropping. The rattlesnake had ten rattlers and a button; of course, my uncle killed the unwanted guest to the fiddling for worms. Rattlesnakes were quite common and usually seen on our fishing trips to our favorite fishing spot called the Mastengill Hole on West Flint Creek. On one trip to the hole, my uncle had carried his 22 rifle to kill a young squirrel for dinner. Many times we would carry a frying pan and cook our dinner of fresh fish on the creek bank; those were some of the fondest memories I have of growing up in the foothills of lower Appalachia.

On the trail to our fishing spot was a large mulberry tree that had fresh fruit which attracted squirrels, but this particular day, something else had made the tree home. After seeing a large snake in the tree, my uncle shot and killed a huge rattlesnake that had somehow climbed the tree. The rattlesnake had caught and swallowed a whole squirrel.

On another fishing trip, my grandpa and cousin were on the way back from the Mastengill Hole when they spotted a huge rattlesnake and king snake in a fight. The king snake would twist around the rattlesnake forming tight coils which eventually killed the big timber rattler. Grandpa removed twelve rattlers off the snake after it was killed; the king snake just crawled off after killing the rattler.

On another occasion my sister June and I went over to the creek to look for arrowheads. On our way to the mound field, I stepped across a huge rattlesnake. I told June that a big rattlesnake was between the two of us and she went wild and started screaming. June took off running and went right by the snake again. I normally killed dangerous snakes that were in the area that I hunted or walked on a regular basis. Most of the time, my dog Pee Wee would kill a snake before I would have time to do the job.

Back to catching fish for canning; my great uncle Wes Hardin worked for the state at a nearby rock quarry. Wes had married my grandpa's sister that I called Aunt Mamie; prior to my Aunt Mamie's death, she lived next door to us for many years. Uncle Wes would bring sticks of dynamite home from work; he would take some to the creek to fish. We would go to the deep holes on the creek where Wes would throw a stick of dynamite into the water; after the explosion many fish would come to the surface for easy pickings.

Wes Hardin

On a particular dynamite fishing trip, the family dog Truddle which loved to fetch sticks followed Wes, my Uncle Cadle, and the other fishermen to the creek. On a high bank just downstream from the swimming hole, Uncle Wes threw the stick of dynamite into the hole of water and the dog jumped in to retrieve the object. As the dynamite fizzled under water Truddle swam around to find what he thought was the stick. When the dynamite went off, the dog went several feet in the air. As quick as Truddle hit the water again, he headed back to the bank and appeared unhurt. Needless to say, the dog did not get in a hurry to get back into the water.

In the late summer and early fall, walnuts begin falling from the huge black walnut trees that grew in the rich alluvial creek bottoms. The walnuts would still have their green covering that could easily be peeled off the nut. Each year at the time walnuts started falling during the driest season of late summer and early fall, West Flint Creek would quit running and dry up except for the deep holes. Grandpa would take a bunch of green hulls of the walnuts, stomp the green hulls into a pulp, and throw them into one of deep holes of water found along the dried up creek bed. After a few minutes, the fish in that hole would start coming to the surface gulping for air and were easy to catch with your hands.

Catching fish was a way of obtaining food for winter survival; to get fish, we had to find bait, especially if dynamite or green walnut hulls were in short supply. Grandpa and I would spend countless hours securing enough fish bait for our fishing trips to the creek. A particular bait that I loved to use to catch bream was ragweed grubs; in the late summer, we would look for tall ragweeds that would have knots on the main stem. After cutting the ragweed, we would split the stem and remove a nice grub about one to two inches long. These grubs made excellent fish bait for catching bream and mud cats.

We would also get other worms for fish bait that we called leaf worms, wood wigglers, or what we called jumping worms. These worms could be found just below the leaf litter in certain spots in the forest. One of our favorite places to gather the leaf worms which were like giant red wigglers was near the lake at Grayson which was in the middle of the forest.

From Grayson, we transported a lot of the big wigglers to the banks of West Flint Creek near our home and the worms took off multiplying at a rapid rate. In a few years, the big wigglers were all along the creek banks. These worms were about three to six inches long and were very active; they would flop and jump around when you tried to pick them up and we started calling them jumping worms. These big wigglers were also very messy and would secrete slime like the fiddle worms.

At times, Grandpa Arthur and I would dig for regular red worms with a shovel around the hog pen or around the barn. These red worms preferred to be around manure from the mules and hogs. I liked to use the red worms found around the barn because they would not cause your hands to become nasty and sticky, but the digging was a job to find a can of red worms. For a young boy who loved to fish, finding good fish bait meant a fresh meal of fried fish. During my early years, we did not run to the grocery store every time we needed something to eat; we usually caught, killed, or raised our food. Such was the life of a young Celtic Indian boy growing up in the southern foothills of the Warrior Mountains in lower Appalachia.

Quail Trap

Many times, I was amazed at the skills of my Grandpa Arthur to provide food for his family. In the fall, he could go to his corn patch and bring back eight or more bobwhite quail for supper; his method was simple but very effective. He showed me things that I would have never dreamed of doing. After the corn stalks had dried and weathered, grandpa would look for a small drain cut through the field by a hard rain; the drain would be of particular size which was about three to four inches deep and about the same width.

Grandpa would cut the dry hard corn stalks and clean them up a little; he would then construct a pyramid about three to four feet square at the bottom with the small washed out drain in the middle of one or both sides. The corn stalks would have a space between each row that was only the width of the stalks used in construction; this space was too small for the quail to escape through. As he went up with the bird trap, the stalks got shorter and shorter for each preceding row until a perfect pyramid was formed. On top of the pyramid, a field stone was place on the last row of stalks to hold the structure together and keep it in place.

After completion of the trap, Grandpa Wilburn would take an ear of corn and shell a row of grains into the little natural ditch that went under the quail trap and also throw a lot of shelled corn inside the trap. As the quail fed on the trail of corn into the trap, they would not go back down into the drain to escape and would continually try to get through the cracks between the corn stalks. The quail trap was simple, but it was effective in catching a mess of quail without firing a shot.

Prior to the invasion of fire ants and coyotes, bobwhite quail in north Alabama were very abundant. Several coveys of quail could be found on each forty acre block of property that had open ground such as row crops or pasture land. Today, the quail struggle to survive with the fire ants attacking the young chicks just prior to emerging from their eggs. Once the babies pip the shell and create a small breathing opening, the fire ants attack and kill many of the baby quail just prior to them hatching. In addition, coyotes also kill and eat the young quail and their parents if they can catch them. The fire ant and coyote invaders have only impacted the quail population over the last some forty years, but the impact on this beautiful and tasty bird has been devastating.

In the past and prior to my grandpa's death, he loved to shoot every hawk that he had the opportunity. Since I loved to raise my bantam chickens, I took up the fight to down every hawk that would prey on my egg producers. Of course all our chickens roamed on free range, but they usually stayed within close distance to where they were fed and at night would roost in the nearby trees.

As most farmers trying to protect their property, grandpa, me, and others kept the population of hawks in check. Thereby, we inadvertently helped our local quail population reach its maximum carrying capacity by eliminating their predators. Today, hawks and other birds of prey are protected by federal laws; their increased population probably has also had an impact on the quail population.

Back to the quail trapping; after a few years, grandpa built quail traps out of wire. We trapped quail any time we wanted a fresh mess of those birds. The wire traps were just a large cage about four feet square and about a foot high. Two runways that were about three inches by three inches extended inside the trap approximately six inches. They were baited the same as the corn stalk traps, but once the birds walked in that square funnel like entrance, they would not go back out the way they came in and would try to get through the wire.

In addition, every time grandpa and I would go hunting, we would take each opportunity to shoot quail whether it was in season or not because we knew how good those birds were on the table. My Grandma Ila would pepper and salt the birds prior to rolling in flour and then cook them until they were golden brown. She would also make a batch of homemade biscuits and have a large bowl of milk gravy; this was a meal we could eat at breakfast, dinner, or supper.

Even though the methods we used to catch bobwhite quail were illegal, it was a matter of having something to eat. In my early years, times were hard on my parents and especially my grandparents who would always got commodities. The wild game we caught and ate supplemented the powered milk, boxes of cheese, bags of flour, bags of rice, and other items that the government provided to my folks and other poor people. I was honored as a Celtic Indian boy growing up in the Warrior Mountains to get to help pass out commodities to all the poor folks in our county. It was a job, but one that I knew would help a lot of poor people including my own.

Turtle and Wild Meat

I helped my Grandpa Arthur probe for mud turtles in the creek beds during the late summer. A nice big turtle meant a great meal of fresh meat. Sometimes grandpa would probe with a fishing cane if he did not have his metal turtle probe. If a cane was used, the turtle would have to be dug out of the mud by hand. The turtle probe was a rod about four feet long with a t-handle on one end and a sharpened arrowhead type point on the other end. On the sand bars, grandpa would punch the probe into the sand and listen for the hollow sound it made when it hit a turtle's hull.

During the hot, dry, late summer, mud turtles bury themselves on the sand bars like a type of hibernation. Most of the time, small air bubble holes can be seen on top of the sand bar or the area will look freshly disturbed. When grandpa hit the turtle hull, he would jam the arrow point through the hull and make a half turn. When he lifted up, the turtle could be pulled out of the mud with the probe imbedded through its hard shell. We would then get the turtle to bite a stick so we could cut the turtle's head off without getting bit and let him bleed out.

I have cleaned many mud turtles to eat; you would take the skin off then cut off each leg as close to the hull as possible. Each leg would make two pieces of meat; then you would cut the tail and neck portion as close to the hull as possible. A seven to ten pound turtle would produce a large meal of fresh meat for four or five people.

My grandma always told me that the mud turtles had seven types of meat. Some of the meat tasted like chicken, some like pork, some like beef, and I have no idea what the rest tasted like, but it was all delicious to eat. The turtle's front legs was one type of meat, the neck was another, the tail portion another type of meat, and the back legs another meat, but that does not add up to the seven different flavors of meat. Only the good Lord and Grandma Ila knew what was the seven different tastes of turtle meat and where they were located.

Grandma Ila would stew the big turtles real slowly on her wood burning stove for several hours; then she would pour the water off the meat after it was real tender. Grandma would salt and pepper the meat prior to rolling it in flour before it was fried golden brown. She always told me to never use the stew water from a turtle to make gravy, but always discard the turtle stew water because it was no good for anything. She never told me why you could not use turtle stew water for gravy, but it must have been bad. We usually made gravy out of the stew water from rabbits and squirrels. My favorite was squirrel gravy with hot biscuits.

We ate ever kind of wild meat; let me think of the different wild meat we consumed. Besides turtle, we ate squirrel, rabbit, ground hog, coon, possum, beaver, muskrat, quail, dove, wood cock, snipe, duck, goose, turkey, deer, bull frog legs, fish of all kinds, and small birds of all kinds. Of course about the only domesticated meat we ate were the hogs we killed every fall and the yard chickens we ate on special occasions. My Grandma Ila knew how to cook all the wild meat we brought to the house and it was delicious.

Most of the time, we would kill the small birds at night with 22 rifle and carbide light from the cedar trees where they roosted. We would clean and keep the breasts of all the small birds for grandma to make us a bird pie; just like chicken pot pie, but we used all kinds of small birds. Bird thrashing is what we called our night time killing of the small birds. We would go from cedar tree to cedar tree and shine the roosting birds and then shoot them in the head with a 22 rifle.

Another way to have bird pie was to kill several blackbirds with a shotgun when they that would gather in a large flock during the winter time. Sometimes starlings, black birds, cow birds and other types of birds would be so thick that several could be killed with one load of number eight shot from our shotguns. In addition, we would bait our homemade bird traps especially during real cold weather or snow and catch all kinds of birds to eat.

If we killed it while hunting, caught it while fishing, or trapped it on our trap line, we ate it, except for mink, skunks, bobcats, and foxes, but grandma would stew the meat of those animals for the dogs and they would eat every bite. Once the animal carcasses that we did not eat were cooked, the dogs seemed to love the meat and any internal parasite would be killed during the cooking process.

On one occasion, my cousin and I came in from hunting and were real hungry; grandma had a pot of meat stewing on the stove. We looked the animal over which smelled delicious and were sure it was coon; therefore, we ate a big meal of the tender meat before grandma come into the house. She said, *"Boys what in the world are you doing eating that red fox I am cooking for the dogs?"* Well, we had no idea we were eating a fox, but it tasted very good and we had our bellies full. I understood then why the dogs would eat every bite of wild meat. Grandpa always wanted his dogs fed very well, but he wanted the meat cooked so they would not chase after anything but possums and coons.

When I was a young Celtic Indian boy growing up in the Warrior Mountains, wild meat was a staple portion of our food supply and we always had some type of meat to eat at every meal. Sometimes we ate fried quail and squirrel for breakfast, fish for dinner at noon, and coon or possum for supper at night. I thought my grandma was the best cook in the world, and if she cooked it, I love to eat it.

Fresh Possum

During the cold winter days, a fresh baked possum would be consumed by Grandpa Arthur and me in one sitting, but I am sure that would not have been possible if it had not been for the expertise of my Grandma Ila's cooking skills. She had an ability to turn any wild game into a delicious meal by using her old wood burning cook stove.

Most of the time when the cook stove was hot, a big stew pot that held some wild animal carcass was on the stove slowly simmering until it was tender enough to either roll in flour and fry or to place in the oven to bake. Grandma usually had salt, peppers, sage, and some of her herbs giving the whole kitchen an aroma that would make the mouth water.

The possum would be stewed until just the right tenderness was achieved; then grandma would take the possum out and place the animal on a baking pan. She would baste the possum in peppers, sage, ketchup, a little honey, and I have no idea what the rest of her concoction included, but I know that the animal was as tasty as any meat that I have ever eaten. Sometimes she would place sweet potatoes, onions, carrots, or other items around the possum as it baked until it had a golden brownish color.

The preparation of the possum required more than just cooking and eating the animal. First, we had to catch the possum and that usually required a little bit of monkey skills which I had when I was a young boy. I used to practice my tree climbing skills near our old outhouse which was surrounded by young saplings twenty to thirty feet high.

I could go from the outhouse to my chicken coops which were about 100 yards away by swinging from one tree to the next and never put a foot on the ground until I ran out of the small trees. I would climb to the top of one of the trees and then swing out. As the tree bent toward the ground, I would grab on to another tree and start the same process over again and again until I had reached the end of our thicket.

Most of the time, a possum would not jump out of the tree once the dogs had him bayed. The possum would usually not put up a lot of effort in trying to avoid being caught by the tail. Therefore, if our dogs treed a possum in a small tree, I would climb the tree; grab the possum by the tail; and drop him into a tow sack. Only one time, I had a possum to tear a hole in the tow sack and try to escape, but it did not take a long time for our dogs to put him back up a tree; the second time he did not get away.

I would bring the possum home in a tow sack and place them in a special pen for fattening them until Grandpa Arthur and I were ready for fresh cooked possum. My possum pen was next to the hog pasture; when I fed the hogs, I would feed my possums. When Grandpa and Grandma Wilburn were ready for fresh possum, I would get one out of the coop and break his neck which was a quick and humane way of getting the possum ready for the dinner table.

My Grandpa Arthur had showed me many times how to kill a possum which was fairly simple. To kill my possums, I would just place one hand on the back of the neck close to the head and hold tightly. Then I would place the other hand under his lower jaw and snap the lower jaw over my wrist which was behind the possum's head. The possum's neck would break instantly and he would immediately defecate or crap just prior to death. I always held the possum out until it had done its business. I only remember getting bit real bad by a big boar possum, and he put a big canine tooth through my thumb. The bite hurt, but I was able to get that possum to finally turn loose of my thumb which bled for a while. I had sweet revenge when I helped eat the critter.

After killing the possum, I would begin the skinning from the back legs and pull his skin toward the head. After the possum was skinned, the animal's carcass was gutted and washed real clean. Grandma would usually place the freshly killed possum into a pan of water and allow it to soak overnight in the refrigerator to remove all the blood from the meat.

After taking care of the carcass, the skin was stretched over a board, dried, and later sold to Mr. Earl Martin who lived near Mt. Hope. Mr. Martin would come by about every two weeks during trapping season to buy the furs Grandpa Wilburn and I had collected. Many times Mr. Charlie Nance would ride with Mr. Martin. I always felt that Mr. Martin gave us a fair price for our furs.

Earl Martin buying furs from Grandpa Arthur Wilburn

I remember that life was good growing up eating possums and other wild meat as the staple food at my grandpa's house. Besides the chickens we ate and the hogs we killed each fall and occasionally a can of sardines or canned oysters, wild game was the only other meat I remember eating as a young Celtic Indian boy growing up in the Warrior Mountains of North Alabama. Such was the back country life that I loved prior to the death of my grandpa in 1964.

Hunting Dogs

Squirrel Dogs

I grew up in the edge of the Warrior Mountains where hunting dogs were a part of everyday life. During those early years, a good squirrel dog was worth a lot of money and helped provide much of the meat that went on our table. I loved the way my grandma stewed the squirrels until they were real tender, rolled them in flour after applying a generous sprinkling of black pepper, and then fried in hog lard until they were cooked to perfection. Along with squirrel gravy and fresh biscuits, the meal could not be beat, but to be able to eat a regular diet of squirrel meat, you had to have a good squirrel dog.

Two of the best squirrel dogs I ever owned were Shelp and Pee Wee; Shelp was a mix of a little Shepard and Fiest and Pee Wee was a mix of a Fiest and Jack Russell. Shelp was the first squirrel dog that I trained from the time he was a puppy. I would do as my grandpa and I had done with his coon dogs; I put my squirrel dog in his pen. I would drag a squirrel hide all over the wooded hillside; after dragging it several yards, I hung the skin up a small sapling. I then turned my puppy loose and got him to track down the squirrel. I am not sure if he was following my scent or the scent of that squirrel hide, but it did not take him long to catch on to the game. He would set at the tree for a long time barking and looking up for a squirrel to move; every time he saw the squirrel, his barking would increase to an excited yelp.

Shelp became an outstanding squirrel dog and nearly every afternoon when I got home from school, Shelp would be up in the woods treed. He knew exactly what time that big yellow bus would be coming down the road; grandpa said about ten minutes before I got off the bus that dog would go to the woods and tree a squirrel. Shelp would stay at that tree until I got my gun and went up the mountainside and killed that squirrel; then the hunt was on until it got dark. Dark usually did not stop Shelp from hunting. When he treed after dark, I would take my flashlight and join him on the hill side where he would have a big fat possum treed. Before I got back home, he would be treed again; I do not know of another dog that loved to hunt more than Shelp unless it was Pee Wee.

Everyone in the family wanted to use Shelp when they went squirrel hunting because he could find the squirrels. I would let Grandpa Arthur and others use my dog when I was at school. One day, a cousin of mine carried Shelp hunting. He shot a squirrel out of the tree, but the squirrel was much alive and started running away. Just about the time Shelp caught the squirrel, my cousin shot; he killed both the squirrel and my dog. Of course, I cried for several days every time I thought about my wonderful squirrel dog; however, my dog had not been dead long until my daddy brought home a black and white short haired puppy that I named Pee Wee.

It did not take Pee Wee long to become a squirrel dog. He just loved chasing squirrels or any animal he could run up a tree from possums to coons. Pee Wee also hated snakes and tested his skills every time he found a snake. He would dip and dart around a snake so fast before grabbing and shaking the snake time and time again until it was dead. I never saw or knew of Pee Wee getting bit by a snake. It did not matter to him if it was a timber rattler or copperhead; when he saw a snake, the fight was on.

Butch and Pee Wee

Pee Wee also became an outstanding squirrel dog; people would come from miles around just to hunt with my dog. I remember on one occasion where four or five men came to hunt with me and Pee Wee. That particular day, we killed some thirty squirrels between all of us hunting. Mr. Earl Martin from Mt. Hope offered me $150.00 for Pee Wee, but he was not for sell. Pee Wee was like a part of my family and I loved that dog.

Pee Wee also got to doing the same tricks as Shelp; in the afternoons about the time I would get off the school bus, Pee Wee would be on the side of the mountain treed. As with Shelp, I would grab my gun and head to the woods for an afternoon squirrel hunt with Pee Wee. I loved to hunt and so did my dog, but on one hunt, we almost got caught by the law. This was the only time that I ever got chased through the woods by a game warden. I think Pee Wee knew what was going on, because he stayed up with me and followed me all the way to my house.

Each year prior to the fall hunting season, Pee Wee and I would kill some 80 squirrels before the opening day. One afternoon not far from the rock road, I shot a squirrel and a few seconds later I hear a car door slam. I got real still and in a few minutes I could see and hear a game warden coming through the woods looking for me. I did not hesitate any longer and headed to the top of the mountain as fast as my legs would go. I was about a mile and half from home and I ran all the way over the mountain and down to my house.

In those days, I could run up and down the mountains and hollows with ease. I waited around in the yard of our house for what seemed about an hour. Finally, I hear a vehicle coming from the direction and sure enough it was the game warden. I was scared he would stop at my house, but he kept going down the road while I peeped through the hedge bushes watching his truck slowly go out of sight.

When we moved from my mountainside home to the flat woods north of Mt. Hope, Pee Wee went with me to our new home at C. C. Smith School. We actually lived in the principal's house located next to the school; now Pee Wee and I had a whole new area to explore, but it was much different. The area was flat as a pancake and you did not have hills and hollows like the area where I grew up and hunted. At first, I hated the area and missed roaming in the mountains near my former home.

Every day the bus ride was a little over an hour long and by the time I got home, Pee Wee and I did not have but a short period of daylight to hunt. After sunset in the flat woods, there were no terrain features to guide you toward home. Therefore, the afternoon squirrel hunts ended earlier than either Pee Wee or I wanted, but we did kill a bunch of big fox squirrels in those flat wooded bottoms.

On the mountain where we came from, I did not tie Pee Wee, but allowed him to run loose. Therefore, I never kept Pee Wee penned up when we moved except to check my trap line. When I run my trap line, I usually put Pee Wee in the barn stable, and on two occasions, Pee Wee got out of his pen and tracked me down. Both times I would hear Pee Wee howl when he got caught in one of my steel traps. He let me know that the trap hurt, but he would be patient while I got his foot freed.

After a about a year at C. C. Smith, Pee Wee went missing. A friend of mine, Don Johnson, and I hunted all over the area for my missing squirrel dog. After several days, Don brought Pee Wee's dog collar to my house. He said it appeared that some bird hunters had shot the dog in the side and killed him. Pee Wee loved to hunt and would join any hunters that would be in the area; however, quail hunters were the wrong group for Pee Wee to try to hunt with and it cost him his life.

I was heartbroken over the loss of my prized squirrel dog. Both my dogs had died doing what they loved the most which was hunting. I did not get to see either of my squirrel dogs after they were killed; therefore, I got to give neither of my beloved dogs a proper burial. In addition, I never got to see where either one had died. They may have not been registered dogs, but were the best of the best squirrel dogs. Such was the way of life when I was a young Celtic Indian boy growing up in the back woods of Lawrence County, Alabama.

Blue John

In the 1950's, life in the Warrior Mountains was difficult at its best for my grandparents. They were trying to make a living and survive on a forty acre tract of the poor mountain soils; therefore, feeding and taking care of another animal was not taken lightly. All the game chickens, tame ducks, genie fowl, fattening hogs, pair of mules, and even the old milk cow had a vital function in the mountain farm, and hunting dogs were no different.

The hunting dogs were expected to be productive and carry their responsibility of being a beneficial farm animal that provided subsistence to the family; therefore, if the dog would not tree or chase game animals, it was not needed on the farm. It was in this light that my grandpa got this beautiful blue tick hound pup that we named Blue John.

My grandma took on the responsibility of taking care of Blue John, but never bought the dog commercial food. As a puppy, Blue John was fed table scraps, and if that was not enough, grandma would bake him some corn bread from freshly ground meal. In addition to the corn bread, grandma would take all the foxes, bobcats, and other carcasses of the animals that we did not eat and cook them for Blue John. For some reason, grandma would never feed the dog raw meat. Anyway, Blue John grew up very fast within a few months and grandpa said that we must train the dog to be a good coon and possum dog.

After trapping some coons, we took one of the smaller coons and sacrificed the meat and hide of the animal to train Blue John. Very seldom was the meat of a coon not eaten or sold to make a dollar and neither was the hide which would bring several dollars after it was stretched and dried; however, this coon was a special training tool for Blue John. We let Blue John get a good smell of the coon and then put the dog back into his pen.

After taking a rope and tying it tight around the coon's neck, I began dragging the coon through the woods for several hundred yards. I would then throw the loose end of the rope through a fork of a tree and pull the coon up the tree beyond the reach of the dog. I would go back to grandpa and we would get Blue John out of his pen and set him on the coon's scent. After a few pulls of the coon, the route got much longer and Blue John would get much faster finding that coon. It was wonderful to hear that long deep howling bark of that blue tick hound as he was trailing the coon to the tree; it was much better to hear him baying as he treed the coon.

The next step in our training of Blue John was to turn a live coon loose and let Blue John track it until he treed. Blue John struck out after that coon and it was not long until he had treed. Blue John had at last become a coon dog and was ready to take with other hounds on a big coon hunt. My grandpa's two double first cousins, Biddie Johnson and Omie Johnson were willing to let us take Blue John with their coon hounds on an all-night coon hunt.

After treeing several coons, Blue John would join right in with the rest of the hounds and fight to get his bite on the coon after it was shot out of the tree. Finally, Blue John was ready for grandpa and me to take him to the creek bottoms of West Flint on his first solo coon hunt. Blue John did not let us down and treed a coon in Beech Bottoms next to a swamp. After I shot the coon, it fell in the edge of the swamp and Blue John bailed into the water and brought out that coon. After that first solo night with Blue John, Grandpa Arthur and I had us a coon dog.

One night grandpa and I coon and possum hunted our way down the creek toward Beech Bottoms and I had several possums in my tow sack. From Beech Bottoms, we circled around the northeast end of Brushy Mountain toward Cedar Mountain. Suddenly, Blue John struck a hot trail with a loud excited howl that shut off very quickly. We had no idea what happened to the dog or the animal he was chasing; therefore, we started up toward the point of the mountain where we had heard the last bark.

We hollered for Blue John, but had no response from the dog. As we neared the point of the mountain, I heard a faint bark that sounded a long way off. I told grandpa that we should go toward the weak sound and he agreed. As we walked the sound got closer and we finally could hear the sound coming from a deep hole on the side of the mountain.

After examining the hole, we realized that a big rock had fallen in behind Blue John and had him trapped. I climbed down into the hole, but the rock was too big for me to lift. The hole was too tight for me to move enough to get the rock out of the way. I could shine my light on the other side of the rock blocking the hole and could see Blue John trying to get out. Since grandpa could not get in the hole and I could barely climb out, we decided to go home and come back after daylight.

The next morning, we got up early and gathered some tools we would need. Grandma had this old steel axle that she used to make holes in the garden to plant tomatoes, and she suggested we could use it to break the rock into smaller pieces.

Therefore, after breakfast, grandpa, grandma, and I headed to the hole on the mountainside with a bunch of tools to rescue Blue John.

      Of course grandma was correct about the steel axle which made smaller pieces of the big rock. I climbed back into the hole and handed out pieces of the rock until finally Blue John was able to escape. I do not think I have ever seen a happier dog. After that memorable event, grandpa and I had many more wonderful coon and possum hunts with that big blue tick hound, Blue John.

Backwoods Fun

Grapevines and Saplings

When I was growing up on the side of Larrymore Mountain or Mull Johnson Mountain located on the northern edge of the Black Warrior Forest, my play ground was the woods behind my house. Not only did I hunt and explore the mountainous area, but I also used the place to have adventure and fun. My swings were grapevines that I found attached to the limbs of the highest trees. I would search the entire mountainside to find the most desirable vines to swing on.

The best vines for swings were those big high straight ones; I would work on the base of the vine for a long time cutting it into with my pocket knife. I loved the real long vines that grew on the steepest side of the mountain. It was on these vines that you could swing out to great heights over the sloping forest floor. Sometimes I would find vines growing close to rock outcroppings; you could hold the cut end of your vine, climb up the rock wall, and jump off with only the vine between you and your maker.

Some of my back problems of today are probably attributed to the falls I took when my grapevines swings would eventually break from overuse. I had one fall in particular that left me breathless for what seemed a long time. I remember seeing stars and gasping for breath; my grapevine broke at the mid-height of the swing and I went crashing through brush before finally landing flat on my back.

It was a good thing that I fell from the broken vine with the slope on the leaf cover forest floor and not on a pile of rocks; of course, I was skinned up all over my back, the breath was knocked out of me, and I was by myself. I slid down the hill for a long time before finally coming to a stop. I had to lay there for several minutes before I could get to my feet and walk out of the woods. From that day on, the first thing I would do was to jerk on the grapevine swing as hard as I could to see if it would break before attempting a ride.

One other ride that the forest would provide was the very tall and slender saplings or small trees that grew along the face of short bluffs some fifteen to twenty feet high. It was from these low bluffs, that I would jump out, grab hold to a young tree in the top, and swing to the ground below. I never had a green sapling or tree to break and I could usually tell if the small tree would bend correctly to prevent me from being hurt real bad.

I well remember that the bluff jumping was the greatest adrenaline rush that I had in my forest playground and was probably one of the most dangerous. Sometimes the tree would be ten or more feet from the edge of the bluff and in midair you had to grab hold of the limbs and hold on tight. I have no idea how I survived without getting hurt real bad; of course, I never told my parents or grandparents about the dangerous playground toys I used in the forest.

I know the reason I did the stupid things of swinging on grapevines and jumping off cliffs; if Tarzan could do it, I could to. I loved those Tarzan shows on our old black and white television. Man, when we got that old Raytheon television, I thought we had done got rich, but the thing was snowy, usually rolling with black lines, and always made a grinding sound that was louder than the voices of the people on the shows. The reception was so poor you could barely see the show. My dad would make me go out on some of the coldest nights to turn the antenna pole until he hollered that he could see the show better.

Since Tarzan lived in a tree, I built my own tree house in the edge of our woods. The floor of my tree house was about fifteen feet above the ground. I had scoured the area around grandpa's place and our house looking for dry oak boards to construct my tree house. Most of the nails that were used in the construction of my treetop hideout were used nails that I would pull from old boards. Trying to drive those bent rusty nails into oak boards were next to impossible and I would wind up with several black finger nails.

Grandpa told me that I needed to let those finger nails bleed by drilling a hole in them; therefore, I would take the point of my knife and drill a hole in my finger nail after I busted it with a hammer. Of course in those days, I had many choice words that were said every time I hit the wrong nail; to think about it, I still do not like to bust my finger with a hammer. After many days of work and several hurting fingernails, I had a tree top hideout. I spent many hours improving and maintaining my boyhood tree house.

I would retreat to my tree house to contemplate my next adventure or just think about the rat race that was going on around me. I also would go to my favorite spot on a high bluff that was covered with a thick layer of soft moss to resolve my problems. I remember setting and lying in my tree house or on that high moss covered perch for hours trying to solve any conflict that I might have that was bothering me.

From my mountaintop view, I watched the cars some two miles away going up and down the distant highway like small ants. It was at this site that I felt a bond to my creator and where I could give up all my problems and feel at ease. Everyone needs their secret place to be at peace and clear their minds of all the clutter that builds up with the daily stresses of life. Such was the days when I was a young Celtic Indian boy growing up on my ancestral mountainside.

Truck Wagon

Years ago, a two by ten oak board with four wagon wheels and a lot of guts was all it took for a young Celtic Indian boy to be skinned up from head to toe. My first truck wagon was high class with a steering wheel but no brakes. On downhill rides from the mountain side, I would reach a top speed that could have been the death of me, but somehow, I managed to survive with only a few scars.

The thrill of riding a truck wagon down a steep mountain road without any brakes cannot be explained, but once reaching the bottom of the mountain trail, it was an exhausting push to get the truck wagon back up the mountainside for another well-earned ride that was repeated several times in one day. Even though my truck wagon was made from scrap materials, it provided me with many hours of fun.

The base of my truck wagon was made from a wide oak board that had two upright boards about two feet high that held my steering pole mechanism. A round wooden barrel top was my steering wheel which was attached to a heavy broom pole that set in grooves on the very front and in the middle upright boards. A plow rope was wrapped around the middle of the broom stick or steering shaft; then the rope went down to the base board around two grooved thread spools; then the ends of the rope went forward where they were attached to each side of the front axle.

The two wooden empty thread spools were attached to the base board by putting a sixteen penny nail through the center hole of the spool; the nails were then driven into the side of the base board. The spools were grooved with a "V" shape in the middle of the thread spools to keep the rope in place. When the steering wheel was turned, the front wheels would guide the truck wagon to the left or right. The back axle of the truck wagon was fixed, but the front axle board was attached to the base board with a single large bolt in the middle that would allow the truck wagon to be turned. My Uncle Cadle was the one that came up with the simple but ingenious steering mechanism.

Eventually after numerous high speed crashes coming off the mountainside, the steering mechanism was completely broken off my truck wagon. Instead of making the repairs, I just moved my seat forward so I could guide my truck wagon with my feet. I would place one foot on each side of the front axle board and push the axle to the left or right toward the direction I wanted to go. The truck wagon was not a fancy gasoline go cart, but it provided many hours of fun and entertainment to a young Celtic Indian boy growing up on the side of Mull Johnson Mountain.

After an extremely hard crash that broke my axles and left me without any breath after running off a high bank, the truck wagon was retired and never ridden again. The truck wagon was soon replaced with a much more sophisticated ride which was my first bicycle. My dad and I went to Moulton to the Western Auto to get something that my dad needed for a repair. Dad had been drinking a little moonshine prior to arriving at the store and was in a good mood. When we got to the store, I spied a beautiful red bicycle and asked my dad would he get it for me because my truck wagon was torn up.

Since my dad had been doing business with Mr. Truman Praytor of the Western Auto for years, Mr. Praytor said, *"Brady you ought to buy your boy that bicycle."* My dad then told Mr. Praytor if he would sell it on credit that he would; Mr. Praytor said, *"Son your dad just bought you that bicycle and you just roll it on out and take it home with you."* I had not dreamed that the trip to the Western Auto would end up with me having a new set of wheels, but I was tickled to death with the first fancy toy I remember getting.

Riding a bicycle for me seemed very natural, and it was not long that every mountain logging trail within a few miles of my house became my playground. If hillsides were too steep for me to pedal up, I simply got off and pushed my new bike to the top of the hills which was much easier than pushing my old heavy truck wagon. The ride down those mountainsides was not near as dangerous because my new bicycle had brakes where I could slow down when I needed. I was riding my bicycle along the old mountain log roads long before I ever heard of a mountain bike. I would grab my fishing pole and ride my bicycle to the creek to fish; that bicycle was a dream come true.

Corn Cobs and Cotton Bolls

When I was a young boy growing up in the mountains of North Alabama, we did not have television or the video games that young kids play with today. My folks did not get electricity until the day after I was born. The only thing we had for a long time that used electricity other than one light bulb in each room was a refrigerator. Before I completed elementary school, my parents managed to buy a black and white television that was snowy and always rolled with the least interference. Therefore, the games my cousins and I played were entirely different than they are today.

One of the favorite games we played was throwing corn cobs at each other. Each person would pick up old corn cobs around the barn and stock pile them in a tow sack or lard bucket. When each person got a good supply of cob ammunition, the corn cob war was on. I always wanted the wet and muddy cobs from the hog pen. The wet cobs could be thrown much more accurately because they were much heavier than dry cobs. An additional benefit was that the wet and muddy cobs hurt much more than a dry cob; if the wet cobs hit our clothes, they would leave a big muddy spot. Based on the muddy spots on each other's clothing, you could tell who got the worst end of the corn cob battle.

During corn cob battles, we would attack each other with a vengeance, and it always felt good to make the first strike to the head of an opponent. I loved to see the wet muddy cob splatter across the head or face of your enemy. Most corn cob battles would usually end with one person getting hit extremely hard and breaking down crying running for help from our parents or grandparents.

I well remember one scary corn cob fight that could have turned out to be bad, but I was lucky. My friends and I had been involved in a very aggressive corn cob battle, and I had made some great hits on one of the new guys playing with us. After he had been hit several times with wet cobs, he went missing from the battlefield around the barn.

After a few minutes of intense battle, I peeped around the corner of the barn just in time to see the boy with a BB gun aimed right at me. I was too slow to move back around the corner when I felt the BB hit me nearly right between the eyes. The BB nearly buried up in the skin of my forehead. Needless to say, the corn cob battle ended very quickly and my friends were able to remove the BB. I still remember the sting of that BB hitting me about an inch from each eye, and from that day forward, I never got into another corn cob battle with that boy.

Another game which had to be played when the adults were out of sight was a cotton boll battle. My cousins and I would sneak into grandpa's cotton patch and pull a lot of green cotton bolls for our ammunition. The green bolls were slightly larger than a golf ball, but they would raise a knot when a direct hit was made on the head. We would run into high cotton and try to make surprise attacks on our opponents. It was every man for himself and everyone in the cotton patch was fair game.

One day, we had got into an intense cotton boll battle and failed to notice what was going on behind us. Suddenly to our surprise, my dad and my grandpa were coming across the cotton field wide open with stalk switches in their hands. We were caught and all of us got wore out with those cotton stalks. Needless to say, the whippings ended that particular cotton boll battle.

As two of my cousins and I got older, we loved to play basketball out in the yard. Most of our games would end up in a fist fight, but knowing the ultimate outcome of our games, we would still compete against each other. All three of us went on to start on our high school basketball teams and were competitors on the basketball court.

My two cousins Danny Welborn and Sandy Welborn played for Danville High School and I played for Speake High School and I always dreaded for our two teams to meet on the court. It was all about bragging rights, and I thought about all our fist fights to settle the score; on the school basketball court, we could not settle the outcome with our fists and had to endure the bragging until we met again. Many times for poor country boys, life was not easy, but we had our fun without ever using video games for entertainment. I guess you could say that those were the good old days when corn cobs and cotton bolls provided hours of fun.

Hill Country Recreation

Skinny Dipping Plowboys

If you walked up to the bank of the Kelly Hole on the West Fork of Flint Creek just about 200 yards north of Highway 36 in the late summer afternoons of the 1950's through the 1960's, you would think there was a male nudist convention going on in that cold community swimming hole. But no, for sure there were no nudist colony, at least that I knew about; just a lot of naked full blooded redneck grown country boys who had been on the farm all day long wanting to cool off in the creek's very cold water. It was well known that the Kelly Hole was not a place for women; everyone in the surrounding area knew that a bunch of naked semi-drunk men would be frolicking at that hole every afternoon during the hot summer months.

I have no idea how the old swimming hole became known as the Kelly Hole, but if law enforcement saw such a group naked men today, they would probably all be arrested for indecent exposure. Believe me, it was indecent exposure at that swimming hole and I never saw anyone with swim trunks on. At that time, all the naked hillbilly rednecks at the Kelly Hole would laugh someone with swim shorts out of the county; or think he was too high society to be a part of their group. There was no shame with this bunch of naked country rednecks who just wanted a break from a day of hard dusty farm work.

Most of the plowboys would come to the swimming hole in overalls and plow boots; they would be covered with dust and dirt from setting on an old tractor or walking behind a pair of mules plowing crops all day long. After arriving at the swimming hole, the men would strip down buck naked and throw their clothes in a certain pile on the bank of the creek.

A dip in the creek was a lot easier than drawing a number two wash tub of water out of one of the local wells. Many would also bring a bar of soap to the swimming hole and first wash off the grit and grime of a hard day's work in the fields. My dad and uncles were no different and participated in the community bath at the Kelly Hole, but many times my dad and uncles would have to take a big swig from a pint of whiskey before they dove into the cold water.

To a young Celtic Indian boy growing up in the area, this was a sight to behold when all these naked men started playing trout and the minnow. Everyone was expected to participate in the wild water game except us kids and we just played in the shallow water. We watched while all these hillbilly redneck adult men chased each other through the woods around the swimming hole and diving off the high banks to avoid a tag by the trout.

All the men would be the minnows except the one that was the trout; the man minnow that was finally tagged trying to escape the trout had to become the trout until he could catch another minnow. This had to be the craziest and funniest game that I ever witnessed a bunch of naked men playing in a public waterway within sight of the highway with their private parts swinging in the breeze, but back then, no one seemed to care.

As some ten or more naked men were running in and out of the water, the creek banks would become very wet and slippery; therefore, accidents were bound to happen and they did. One afternoon while my wild dad was the trout trying to catch one of the minnows that he had chased up on the bank; he was making a crazy dive from one of the high banks. Just about the time his feet left the ground, a grape vine caught his foot and he slapped the bank of the creek so hard that it knocked him out. He proceeded to slide down the steep bank into the water, but a bunch of his naked friends grabbed him under the arms and dragged him back to the top of the bank.

After two or three big gulps of wildcat, my dad was good as new, except for being skinned up on his belly and chest. I witnessed the feat and thought for a second my dad was dead, but the Indian in him would not allow him to be out done and within a few minutes he was back in the game with all his scrapes and bruises.

Another game that was played in the late summer was what I call watermelon polo. A large watermelon that would just barely float would be taken to the swimming hole. The watermelon would stay under water for a long time before it rose to the surface very slowly. One man would shove the water melon at the other men trying to do damage to his family jewels; of course, a twenty pound water melon traveling even at a slow speed could make a big man fold over if it hit him in the gonads.

The water melon would travel a long distance under water before it resurfaced. The man who found the melon first got a free shot at his naked companions. It appeared that the water melon game was enjoyed by all because of the mystery of where the melon would wind up after its trip under the muddy water. Leave it to a bunch of naked redneck plowboys to come up with some ridiculous water games in the swimming hole after a hard day's work and several drinks of moonshine.

The swimming hole, just north of the Alexander Bridge on the West Fork of Flint Creek, was not as heavily used as the Kelly Hole downstream some five miles, but the

Alexander swimming hole was used by men, women, and children with swim suits. Most swim suits were cutoff britches or wore out clothes that were used for bathing in the creek. The Alexander Hole was used by a bunch of sharecroppers that lived on the old Alexander Plantation.

At one time, there were as many as eighteen clapboard sharecropper houses on the old farm and families lived in every house, and sometimes extended families lived in the same home. Most of the farm hands and their families preferred to go to the Alexander swimming hole to take a bath instead of trying to get a wash tub of water to bathe in. I remember many times that my whole family enjoyed our bath in the old Alexander Hole when I was a young Celtic Indian boy growing up on the banks of West Flint Creek.

Cow Pasture Baseball

When I was a small boy in the 1950's and early 1960's, most country folks like mine did not have a television, very few had radios, and many were without electricity or could not afford the cost; therefore, cow pasture baseball was a local sport that many people enjoyed watching to pass the time. The baseball teams were not allowed to play on crop land, but most folks would allow the teams to play in their pastures. During these years, each small community had a baseball team; most of the time, the players would play ball in overalls and plow boots or barefooted.

People would gather at the home field pasture where their baseball team would play and have a big picnic. Some folks would donate chickens and garden vegetables for the big stew pot and ice down drinks in number three wash tubs. Some communities would have a fish fry at their baseball games; these baseball picnics were to raise money for their team to travel or to buy only necessary equipment. All the items donated by the families were used to raise money for the home team.

I enjoyed going with my folks to the cow pasture baseball fields and watch my Uncle Cadle Wilburn pitch. All the players were trying to get a win and took the sport very serious. At a very early age, I loved to catch ball for my Uncle Cadle who had just returned from a tour in the U.S. Air Force; it made me feel big and important to catch baseball for the pitcher of the team. My uncle wanted me to catch while he practiced his cow pasture pitching skills. I squatted barefooted in the yard without any protective equipment and tried to catch every curve, drop, fastball, and changeup he would throw.

Cadle Wilburn and friend Jerry Richardson leaving for duty with me, Harm Johnson, Curtis Wilburn, and Wendell Logan to the left. The car is a new 1957 Chevy owned Carl Welborn.

After a while, I got to be a pretty good hind catcher, but his fast balls would burn my hand, make me mad, and he would beg me not to quit catching. The old catcher's mitt I used was round as a dinner plate and about three inches thick with a spot in the middle just the size of a baseball. The mitt had no flexibility at all; you had to get the ball in the right spot to make the catch. I have never seen another catcher's mitt like the old one I used to catch for my uncle.

My Uncle Cadle Wilburn was a member of some of the cow pasture baseball teams; he played for Speake, Wren, and Pin Hook. He spent most of his amateur baseball playing with the Pin Hook team that, for a long time, had their home field in the pasture of Mr. Ben McMillan of the Pin Hook Community. He said, *"One of the best baseball teams that I ever played against was the black team from Oakville; Babe Ruth (Buddy Taylor) would knock a homerun nearly every time the ball went over home plate."*

Oakville was a black community not far from my home and had a black league that played most of their games in P.B. (Bryant) Lowery's cow pasture or across the road where the church now stands. I remember Mr. Jimmy Speake who was an attorney in Moulton for years telling me that a black man from Oakville who was called Babe Ruth could knock a baseball over 500 feet on a regular basis. Mr. Speake said that the black

Babe Ruth from Oakville could have been a major league baseball player; the Babe Ruth of Oakville was James Andrew Taylor, also known as Buddy Taylor.

Babe Ruth Taylor played catcher and doubled for many years as a coach for the team; he could throw a runner out at second base without even standing up. His son Rayford Taylor told me if a man was on first base that his dad would say to the pitcher, *"Let him run, I got him;"* seldom did a runner ever steal second base when Taylor was catcher. At the time that Buddy Taylor was catching baseballs, it was legal for the catcher to chatter, and he was constantly chattering to the batter. Buddy would say, *"You can't hit what you can't see; the bat must have a hole in it."* I loved to hear Buddy Taylor chatter at a baseball game.

Also, Buddy Taylor had a feel for the baseball; he would tell the players this ball is dead and we are not going to play with it anymore. Buddy's son said that he went up north one time to try out for professional baseball, but did not want to leave home. From all that people have said about Babe Ruth Taylor, you could tell that he loved the game of baseball. After he got too old to play baseball, Babe Ruth Taylor coached a girls' softball team that was also very good.

Buddy Taylor and many of the other black players from the Oakville team did farm work for Mr. John Wiley, Mr. John McCay, and Bryant Lowery. Buddy Taylor was definitely one of the best baseball players to ever play the game in North Alabama. Today, years after his death, everyone in the area of the Warrior Mountains has heard of the baseball exploits of Buddy "Babe Ruth" Taylor. It was an honor for me as a young boy to watch the legendary Babe Ruth Taylor play baseball at Oakville.

James Andrew "Babe Ruth" Taylor also had a son that was also a great baseball pitcher; his name was Hosey Lee Taylor. Hosey would usually start the game pitching left handed, and about half way through the game, he would switch to pitching right handed. At one time, the Oakville team had five good pitchers: Johnny Stover, Floyd Lee Stover, Lonzo Griffin, Denny Orr, and Hosey Lee Taylor. Besides Hosey Lee Taylor, Babe Ruth Taylor had other sons that played baseball: Wyman Taylor, Wayne Taylor, and Rayford.

Charlie Pointer, who is Babe Ruth Taylor's first cousin, told me he grew up on the C. P. "Clebe" Preuit farm. Clebe Preuit would give Charlie's daddy and the other farm hands tickets that were good at the four stores at Wren. Mr. Pointer would get in the wagon pulled by a pair of mules and go to Wren and swap the tickets for lard, meal, flour, and other food items.

Charlie Pointer, who is now 88 years old, said, *"I also worked for Mr. Clebe Preuit; he told me one day to get in his car that we were going to Moulton. Mr. Preuit bought me my first pair of shoes and two pair of overalls from Howard Delashaw's store in Moulton. Before that day, I went barefooted and wore clothes made from flour or guano (fertilizer) sacks."*

After Mr. Clebe died, Charlie worked for his son John Preuit; he said, *"If John Preuit told you something, he would do it. I was at their home when both Mr. Clebe and Mr. John Preuit died."* After Mr. John Preuit died, Charlie Pointer began working for Tass Jacobs; after Mr. Jacobs died, Charlie worked for Ms. Willie Jacobs for ten years. Ms. Willie gave Charlie cash money to pay for his place.

When Charlie started playing baseball, he played in his overalls and went barefooted. He and his four brothers played for the Oakville baseball team which was made up entirely of black players. Charlie said, *"My older brothers Robert and Louie Pointer played ball before I was old enough; but at sixteen years of age, I got to play with my other two brothers Aaron and Dee Pointer. Aaron would steal second base as soon as the pitcher stepped on the pad on the pitcher's mound; me and Aaron stole every base on the field including home plate."*

Charlie played shortstop for over ten years, Aaron Pointer played second base, and his other brother Dee Pointer played first base. During the some fifteen to twenty years that he played baseball with the Oakville team, Charlie Pointer said, *"I do not ever remember us losing a single game of baseball; we had two teams, when the first team got so far ahead, we would let the second team finish the game. Athens was the roughest team we played, but we still beat them. We went to Tuscaloosa and played four games in two days and won all of them. Bryant Lowery had a ton and half Chevrolet truck and he would drive for twenty-five cents per player and would watch us play ball. When we stayed overnight, we would stay with the other teams' players."*

Charlie said, *"A baseball scout came down from the New York Yankees and watched the our team play four or five games; the scout stayed for two weeks trying to get Buddy 'Babe Ruth' Taylor, me, and my brothers Aaron and Dee Pointer to try out for the New York Yankees, but we were not about to move to New York City. He tried to get us to go north to play professional baseball, but we all refused to go."*

Mr. Charlie Pointer said, *"When I started playing baseball, we would go to the games in wagons pulled by mules. One game we played Moulton and did not have the wagon; therefore, we walked from Oakville to Moulton, played the game, and walked back to Oakville. Now, all the players I started playing baseball with are now dead."*

Mr. Rayford Taylor, the son of Babe Ruth Taylor, told me that the Oakville team finally raised enough money to buy uniforms and equipment. The team would get together and seine Oakville Pond; the fish they caught would be cooked and sold at the baseball game to make enough money for the team's expenses. They would fry the fish, and then sell fish sandwiches and cold drinks to the spectators that came to watch the home games.

Charlie Pointer said he remembered Mr. Earl Aldridge, a long time barber in Moulton playing for the Pin Hook baseball team and my grandpa Arthur Wilburn pitching for Pin Hook. Charlie said the Oakville team played the Pin Hook team in a pasture about one quarter mile west of Elam Creek; the Pin Hook baseball field at that time was just west of the Preuit farm that Charlie grew up on and that the pasture land was later bought by a Mr. King from Moulton. Later, the Pin Hook team played in another pasture near the old Pin Hook Church.

My grandpa was pitcher for the Pin Hook team and referred to the game day as a big picnic. A bunch of teams would get together and meet for all day games; during his day, most of the people would come to the game in a horse and buggy. Stew would be cooked in big black cast iron pots and sold during the game. During one of the early Pin Hook games, Mr. Floyd Hill got into a fight with another man from the opposing team. Hill whipped out his pocket knife and gave the person a pretty bad cutting. Many times the game would get so heated that the fans would wind up in fist fights.

Jimmy Speake also loved the sport of baseball and was coach of the independent Speake Baseball Team until he went to college to become a lawyer. My uncle played for Mr. Speake for a short period of time. The Speake baseball field was located on the north side of the school property where the old agriculture building was built. The field was also used by the school and the Speake independent baseball team.

My uncle left the Speake team and did most of his pitching for the Pin Hook team; besides Cadle Wilburn the team consisted of brothers Don McCay and Aubrey McCay, Raymond Smith, twins Foy Hall and Hoy Hall, brothers Wade Long and Kenneth Long, Lynn Wiley, Hoyt Hill, Hoover Legg, and the coaches were Tom Hall and Floyd Hill. Mr. Tom Hall would use his ton and half flatbed farm truck to transport his team to their games all around North Alabama; Tom Hall and Floyd Hill carried the entire team to Mooresville in the back of the truck to play ball.

Besides playing Oakville, the Pin Hook team played all the independent teams in the area and won most of their games. The Piney Grove team was a very tough opponent; most of the guys who played with Piney Grove were barefooted and would have their britches legs rolled up nearly to their knees. The Piney Grove baseball field was in a cow pasture in front of Glen Luker's old home place; the pasture belonged to Carl York. Some of the Piney Grove players included Rethal Hightower, brothers Cranford York and Donnver York, Conrad Bell, twins Reford Jarrett and Raford Jarrett, Jerry Carter, and brothers Phillip Bryant and Ted Bryant; my uncle said the twins would fight at the drop of a hat and if you fought one, you had to fight both.

Rethal Hightower was the catcher for the Piney Grove team and always caught with his britches legs rolled up and barefooted. All he had for protection was a wire face mask; Rethal would get close enough to the batter to bump his glove against the bat causing the hitter to miss the ball by a foot or more. Since the umpire did not have any protective equipment, he called behind the pitcher and could not see the bump by the catcher's mitt. My uncle warned Hightower that he better quit bumping his bat, but Hightower ignored the warning. Just prior to the swing, my uncle took a half step back and knocked the catcher's mitt all the way to the pitcher's mound. He said Hightower never bumped his bat again.

The baseball team would start each game with a new ball and had two extra practice balls. If something happened to the new ball before the game was over, they would finish the game with the old practice balls. The catcher only had a wire mask; later the team earned enough money to purchase a chest protector. The team would sell chicken stew at the home game to generate funds to pay for some of the equipment. Grady Sanderson would start the stew in a big black pot early in the morning of the game. Sanderson used a boat paddle to stir the stew until it was done. The Pin Hook team never was fully equipped, but they love the game of cow pasture baseball.

I have fond memories of going to the independent league baseball games to watch the men play, and I was proud that my uncle wanted me to catch as he tried to become the best pitcher in the area. However, today the old community baseball teams have faded from the country scene, but I will forever cherish the memories of cow pasture baseball when I was a Celtic Indian boy growing up catching ball for my uncle.

County Fair

When I was a young Celtic Indian boy growing up in the country, I would spend hours in the cotton patch thinking of the fall fair that would come to Moulton each year. My thoughts were on winning a big ole stuffed teddy bear. For some reason, a big fair teddy bear was my holy grail; I spent precious cotton picking money to try and beat the system with the crooks that ran the booths. On two occasions, I beat the odds and did what I was supposed to in order to win one of those pretty teddy bears; however, I never got a bear.

On one occasion, I won by tossing little round rings around the tops of coke-a-cola bottles, but the guys running the booth told me that I cheated and leaned over crossing their imaginary line. Therefore, they did not give me my bear even though I knew that I had won. I thought about going and getting the law when I knew I was cheated out of that bear that I so desperately wanted to win, but my folks, especially my dad and uncles, had no use for the law of any kind so I just sucked up the loss. Since every year I planned on winning me a teddy bear, it hurt that the booth operators cheated me out of my bear at our county fair.

I did come home and tell my Grandpa Arthur Wilburn that I was cheated out of a beautiful stuffed teddy bear. Then he told me a story about his experience with the same kind of county fair folks when he was a young man trying to win a teddy bear for my grandmother. Grandpa was throwing soft baseballs at a man that would move his head from hole to hole in a cut out board; if grandpa would hit the man three times with the soft balls he would win a bear. According to grandpa, he won a bear but they claimed he missed one ball and refused to give him his prize.

After getting into a confrontation with the crook running the fair booth, grandpa left the fair and got a real baseball. In his younger days, grandpa loved to play cow pasture baseball and was a great pitcher for the Pin Hook team. He played baseball with Mr. Earl Aldridge who used to cut my hair at his place on the south side of the square in Moulton when I was growing up. Mr. Aldridge would talk while he burred or flat topped my head and always pulled out a bit of my hair. When he hung up his clippers in my hair, he would tell my dad, *"Brady your boy has the coarsest and toughest hair for a little kid."*

Mr. Earl Aldridge tried to explain why he jerked out clumps of my hair, but it always hurt and I would always holler out in pain. Man, I dreaded to sit in his barber chair, but I loved listening to his stories and he told a bunch of them. Mr. Earl would also tell about my Grandpa Wilburn pitching cow pasture baseball; he said, *"Arthur Wilburn was the most accurate pitcher with a baseball than anyone I have ever seen or played against. He could pick up a rock and kill a bird setting on a fence, and I seen him do it."*

Back to grandpa and the county fair story; grandpa had a drink of wildcat and returned to the fair booth where he had been cheated. Grandpa paid for three more of the soft baseballs and made very accurate throws the first two soft balls, but the third ball, he swapped for the real baseball that he had brought to the booth. He threw the third ball and busted the man's face; grandpa said he saw the blood fly just before he took off running out of the area. Grandpa was very satisfied getting even with the crook that cheated him out of his stuffed teddy bear.

Grandpa also had another story about one of the big teddy bears at the fair. He knew a fellow by the last name Aldridge that the owner of the booth tried to cheat. After getting into an argument with the crook that was running the booth, the Aldridge man just climbed over the rail and picked up his bear and started to leave. The situation got into a physical confrontation that ended when Aldridge jerked out a pocket knife and began cutting the booth operator. Grandpa said that Aldridge got his bear and the cheating booth operator got cut up. Grandpa never did say if the Aldridge man got arrested for the cutting, but Aldridge did keep his teddy bear.

The fair also had some amazing rides, but I had a big problem with motion sickness when I was young. Therefore, every time I tried to ride one of those wild fast rides, I would get sick as a dog that had eaten a rotten possum. When I got off the ride, my head would keep spinning and I could not walk straight. I would have to set down on the ground, try to quit throwing up, and wait till the earth stopped moving. My head would spin several minutes after I managed to crawl off those rides. Ever since I was a little boy, I have gotten sick on every fast ride that I have tried to enjoy.

After my several series of motion sickness at the fair, I settled for a ride on the big tall Ferris Wheel. I even quit that ride, because I did not like real high places. Every time I rode, the conductor would stop my seat at the top of the wheel and it would rock; of course, being on a little wooden bench fifty feet off the ground swinging back and forth was not very much fun to me.

One thing that I looked forward to each year at the fair was getting a big blob of cotton candy. I took my time eating the stuff because I knew it would be a year before I could get another one. The caramel cover apples were also a treat, but both the cotton candy and apple covered with all that sticky sweet covering made a mess. I usually wound up getting the mess all over me no matter how hard I tried to eat it without getting sticky.

Exhibits were one thing most of us kids did not care a whole lot about, but we looked at them because we were expected to. We would walk around and view the exhibits of various schools and community clubs. Sometimes animals would be on display such as deer from the conservation department. Most of us boys would spend a lot of time looking at the game animals we would chase during our hunting days. Back then it was difficult to see a deer track much less to stand so close to a big live buck deer that we would all love to kill.

Farm exhibits would include canning, cooking, or decoration competitions. Farmers would sometimes have competitions for their hogs, sheep, cattle, and even chickens. Now, I liked the animals a whole lot more than I did all those patch work quilts and country art work.

When I was young, the county fair was like going to Disney World; it was the biggest event that my sisters and I got to attend for the entire year. We would plan to go to the fair with our school friends who were just as excited to be a part of the big yearly event. Most of us kids had got out of school for six weeks in the fall to pick cotton and were anxious to spend a little of our hard earned money to have some fun. Such were the times in the Warrior Mountains during the late 1950s and early 1960s when the fall county fair would come to town.

Coon on the Log

An old southern tradition that I enjoyed as a youngster was the "Coon on the Log" events that was sponsored by many coon hunting associations throughout the Warrior Mountains of North Alabama. All the coon hunters had to have to put on the coon and hound attraction was a big pond or lake, plenty of parking space, lots of food and barbecue, all kinds of liquids to drink, a place for people to relieve themselves, a bunch of live coons, all kinds of four wheel drive trucks with dog boxes loaded with hundreds of coon hounds, and several cameras to take pictures of all those winning coon hound dogs.

With the correct combination of facilities, hunters and spectators of all kinds would flock to the coon on the log activity by the truck loads. It was just interesting to look at all the different trucks from the rusty and muddy beat up models that had plowed through thousands of miles of log roads chasing coons to the big wheeled trucks that were spit shined. But there was one thing all the trucks had in common; the truck bed was outfitted with a box or cage to haul their coon hounds. The coon hounds were as different as the trucks from redbone, Walker, black and tan, blue tick, and many other various breeds.

Since both my grandpas and I love to coon hunt, we were very interested in seeing a great coon hound dog in action taking on a mean boar coon. Some of the big old boar coons could whip a young inexperienced coon dog and give an experienced hound a tough fight. Big bad boar coons were known to drown some very outstanding coon hounds and could put up a fierce fight against a single coon dog.

My Grandpa Wilburn had a way of testing the metal of the "bad to the bone coon hounds" that his friends claimed was tough enough to whip any coon. Grandpa had this big old ground hog that he had fitted with a collar. He would place the ground hog in a wooden nail keg and challenge any of his coon hunting friends to let their bad coon dogs get the ground hog out of the keg. The ground hog would lie on his back when the dog's head came into the keg, and that ground hog would scratch and bite the hound's head until dog would come out of the keg bloody. The ground hog always won the fight and my grandpa would laugh at his coon hunting friends and their dogs; the ground hog never lost a fight in the wooden nail keg.

Back to the coon on the log; this was a sight to behold just to witness all those beautiful breeds of coon hounds showing their skills at removing the coon from the log in the middle of the lake or pond. The coon hunters and coon hounds seemed to get real excited about the challenge, but the poor coon probably had rather been in a den tree sleeping instead of fighting a big old coon hound in the middle of a lake with hundreds of spectators cheering for their favorite dog. Every so often, fresh coons would replace the coon on the log if it got injured badly or if it refused to fight the coon hounds.

The coon on the log was a challenge for the hunters as well as the coon hounds. From a designated starting point, the coon dog had to swim out toward the middle of the lake and physically remove the coon from his log or perch. The coon was equipped with a collar and a long leash that was threaded through a hollow cane or section of pipe about six feet long; the leash through the hollow tube allowed the handler to stay away from the coon and prevented him from being bit. The hollow tube also allowed the coon handler to pull the leash tight and shove both the coon and dog under the water once the hound dragged the coon off his log.

Once under the water, the coon dog would turn loose of the coon and swim back to the surface and go toward the bank. The handler would then lift the coon out of the water and place him back on his perch. Shoving the coon under water would prevent severe injuries to the animal, and the coon could fight several more hounds before he would be replaced with a new coon. Changing coons was done often in order to make sure the coon was in good enough shape to give the hounds a good fight and to keep the event fair to both the dogs and their owners.

Locally, a former Alabama State Representative Bruce Dodd from Lawrence County, Alabama, would host a coon on the log for local hunters and the public at his pond on Highway 36. Hunters from all parts of the Warrior Mountains would bring their dogs to test their coon catching skills, but the largest coon on the log event that I ever attended was at Zip City north of Florence. The Zip City activity attracted coon hunters from all over the country and had hundreds of spectators watching the coon on the log all day long.

Some coon hunters had paid top dollar for their hounds, and the hunters wanted everyone to know that they had a great coon dog. Many times the dog would refuse to go after the coon because they did not want to get wet or swim the distance to get to the coon. Often the frustrated and aggravated coon hunter would throw their dogs into the lake just to have them turn around and swim back to the bank. Inexperienced coon hounds would sometimes refused to swim to the coon, and if the young dog swam to the coon, he would not challenge the coon on the log and head back to the bank. Once their dogs were disqualified, some owners would give their dogs a good tongue lashing.

Sometimes the coon hounds would make the swim all the way to the coon. When faced with a ferocious coon setting on his perch, the hound would refuse to fight and swim back to the bank embarrassing their owners. However, some coon hounds would make the swim at break neck speeds, grab the fighting coon, and drag him into the water in short order; of course, the hound that accomplished this feat in the shortest period of time was the winner. The hounds winning the coon on the log would instantly increase their monetary value with the other coon hunters watching the coon hound's performance. Of course, the winning coon hound would get his picture taken with his owner and many times wind up in the local newspaper.

If a person did not like to hear the baying of coon dogs during the entire event, they had better not come to the coon on the log. Besides baying, many of the dogs would wind up in fights if their owners did not keep close watch on their hounds; therefore, people who did not want to see a few dog fights also needed to stay away from the coonhound activity. Of course the worst part of the coon on the log was that some people did not like seeing that poor old coon getting in a fight with a big coon hound in the middle of the lake. This is probably the reason you never hear of the coon on the log anymore.

The Humane Society, PETA, Friends of Animals, and other animal rights organizations have protested coon on the log activities because it was viewed as animal cruelty. After involvement of animal rights people, the coon on the log events started putting the coons in wire cages to prevent the coon from being harmed; however, the changes just about put a stop to the coon on a log which was an old southern tradition that got caught up in political movements and anti-hunter campaigns.

A lot of the old southeastern Appalachian mountain entertainment involving the use of an animal has been banned, but events like coon on the log brought a lot of people with similar interests together to enjoy their coon hounds and to have a good time participating in the hunting sport they loved. Coon hunters are not as numerous as in the days when I was a Celtic Indian boy following my grandpa and a pack of hounds through the hills and hollows of the mountains all night long. Today, coon hunters still cherish their coon hounds and are honored to have one of their prized coon dogs buried in the Coon Dog Cemetery in the Freedom Hills of the Warrior Mountains.

Fighting Game Cocks

My Grandpa Arthur Wilburn loved his gamecock chickens and his fighting roosters which were brilliant colors with gray, red, black, silver, golden, or multicolored capes cascading from their heads down to their shoulders. Grandpa's gamecock roosters were some of the most beautiful yard chickens that ever roamed around his barn lot, pasture, hog pens, and yard of the old log house. He never cooped up his beautifully colored roosters and they claimed different territories around the farm. If a mistake was made by an invading rooster from another territory, the fight was on until one was chased back to his domain or until one was dead. The victor always claimed his harem of the prized gamecock hens.

On one occasion, Grandpa Arthur and I were at the chicken house trying to separate two of his beautiful roosters that were fighting; a big red caped rooster had finally killed a beautiful golden caped gamecock. The spurs were so imbedded in the rooster that they had to be physically separated. Once grandpa separated the live rooster from the dead one, the big red cock spurred grandpa through the ear and I saw the blood start pouring from the side of grandpa's head. The red caped rooster got a cussing of his life, but grandpa was so proud of his fighting chickens that he allowed the rooster to live.

Grandpa would seldom have chickens other than gamecocks, but Grandma Ila had her chickens that were for egg laying or strictly for the dinner or supper table. When grandpa's folks would come, they would stay two or three nights at a time and everybody slept on pallets in the floor or anywhere they could find an empty spot. It was very common when I was a young boy for the whole family of kinfolks to stay all night when they came to see my grandparents on the weekends or holidays. Grandma was expected to feed everyone in the family regardless of how long they stayed, and every time grandma would tell me to go catch us a frying size chicken to cook for dinner or supper.

Now I had several ways of catching chickens to feed the family during their stay. One way to catch a chicken was to get in the barn loft and place a loop of a trotline fishing cord on the ground in a circle in which I dropped some grains of corn. Then when the right chicken stepped into the circle I would jerk up on the cord and snare a chicken in the slip loop. This was a very effective method of catching a chicken and one I practiced quite often; even when my grandparents did not even want a chicken for supper. Since I loved setting in the barn loft snaring chickens, grandma would have to tell me to leave the chickens along until she wanted one to eat.

Another way to catch a chicken required very quick reflexes, I would call the chickens and start shelling corn around my feet; when the chicken was eating the corn I would grab it before it would escape. The third way I caught a chicken for the dinner table was just to chase it down by running it until it give up. If I had cousins that were staying all night, grandma would say, *"You boys go out there and catch us a frying size chicken for supper."* With that command, only one method was used to catch a chicken; two or three boys would be running chickens all over the mountainside to see which one would be the first to catch a chicken for supper.

Now I knew the fine art of killing a chicken and it was my job to do the dirty deed regardless of who caught the chicken. Grandma had taught me at an early age how to wring the neck of a chicken. I would grab the chicken by the head and whirl him around and around until his body separated from his head I held in my hand. Even though my grandma was a real devoted Christian woman, she told me, *"Do not to hold the chicken's head and pickup his body while the chicken was dying."* Grandma never fully explained exactly what would happen to me if I held a dying chicken, but I knew it was not good.

I wanted to understand why I could not hold a dying chicken, and I believed it was something to do with mysterious things happening to you if you did. To test the theory, I held some chickens by their legs while they were dying and all I got was blood splattered all over my clothes while they were flopping around in the last dying moments. I did not tell grandma about my deed of holding a dying chicken. When questioned about all the blood stains on my clothes, I told her as the headless chicken was jumping around that it slung blood everywhere, and that was the truth.

The only problem with chicken for supper when a bunch of kinfolks were staying all night at my grandparents' home is that all the adults got to eat first. It did not matter how much I wanted fried chicken for supper, most of the times the adults ate every bite. I along with the other kids was left sopping up the grease and crumbs with a biscuit, or if I was fortunate, I got a wing or neck.

I helped Grandpa Wilburn work on his chicken house for his game chickens. The shed was covered with wooden shingles and had built in roosting racks for the birds to rest on at night. Also, the chicken house had nest boxes attached to the walls all around the house. I loved to go to the nest boxes to gather the eggs that were eaten at every breakfast with gravy and biscuits. We always left a fake egg or an old real egg in the boxes in order to attract the hens. The nests were always filled with fresh hay every so often in order to keep the hens happy and to keep them laying eggs. Sometimes when eggs were plentiful, we would leave a nest of eggs so that the hen would hatch a new bunch of chicks.

My cousins Johnny Proctor and Donald Proctor always loved to challenge my grandpa's gamecocks with their fighting roosters, but we did not use steel spurs in our rooster fights. The roosters had the natural spurs that Mother Nature had given them to beat their opponents. Donald and Johnny were about my age and were the sons of my Grandpa Wilburn's sister, Williemuryl Welborn Proctor. They loved to watch a rooster fight as much as I did, and nearly every time they came to visit my grandpa, they would bring some of their fighting roosters.

On one occasion, Donald and Johnny brought a big yard grown white leggeron chicken to fight one of grandpa's gamecock roosters. The big white rooster was twice as big as the gamecock and was willing to fight to the death. After both roosters fought to exhaustion, the fight was just about stale mate, but because of his size, that big white rooster, even though he was extremely tired, completely wore out the fighting gamecock finally winning the match. The game rooster decided he had enough of his big opponent and decided to run; the fight was over with Donald and Johnny claiming victory with their big white rooster.

Fighting gamecock roosters was a way of life in the Warrior Mountains when very few people had televisions and no electronic entertainment. Some folks fought chickens for entertainment while other people fought their roosters in order to sell their breed of gamecocks for a high price or just to gamble on the outcome. Some of the spectators just came to watch the cock fights, drink moonshine, bet a little money, and have a good time. Even though it was illegal, my men folks loved their whiskey and liked to watch a good cock fight. Most of the time, they did not have any money to bet on the fight's outcome, but they still loved the entertainment.

In the nearby community of Oakville, the gamecock ring or fighting pit was very simple; people stood around the ring or brought chairs to watch the cock fights. Doc Whitson was a black man from Oakville; he ran the local cock fighting ring every Saturday and Sunday afternoon. People would gather from all around the area bringing their fighting cocks to the ring to test their skills with the steel spurs. Sometimes thirty to forty fighting roosters would be brought to the cock fight event. Lynn Wiley was one of those Oakville cock fighters that loved to see his roosters perform; he also liked to win the money from his victorious chicken fighters.

There was always a little wildcat whiskey for those who wanted to have a few drinks and get wound up for the fight. During those days, you seldom heard of anyone smoking pot or being on drugs, but most of the men drank corn whiskey. At the cock fight, one person was responsible for the whiskey sales and making sure that everyone was served all the moonshine that they wanted as long as they paid for their drinks. Fighting gamecocks was a way for local bootleggers to sell more corn licker and make a little extra money gambling while being entertained watching a good cock fight.

Usually there was one man in charge of taking the bets prior to each of the cock fights; from twenty to two hundred dollars would be bet on the outcome of some of the fights. Each afternoon, bets might be placed on fifteen to twenty different cock fights. Half of the men participating with their roosters would go away with a few dollars less and a gamecock rooster for their stew pot. At least, the next day they would have chicken for dinner or supper. Even some of the men who had winning roosters went away with a combatant gamecock so cut up that they too would be eating chicken for the next day or two.

The opposing gamecock roosters would be fitted for battle with razor sharp spurs. The roosters would be faced toward each other to size up their opponent and to stir up their fighting instincts. The gamecocks would then be placed on the ground which was sometimes covered with sawdust and shavings; in short order, the fight was on. Most fights did not last a long time until one of the roosters was mortally wounded or dead. I watched many roosters bite the dust; a rooster that lost his life fighting would wind up in the stew pot and feed a family. A loss for the rooster was a meal for the kids at home; the rooster's life sure was not a waste during the hard times of survival in the area of the Warrior Mountains.

Back to my grandparents' farm; I was scared of the gamecock hens that would throw their spurs at you when you got near their bunch of baby chicks. You had to be careful around a game hen that just hatched off a lot of little furry chicks because she was very protective of her brood. Grandma would want me to help gather the newly hatched chicks so they could be put up in a pen until they were big enough to escape from the possums, snakes, hawks, stray cats and dogs, and other varmints. After the chicks were big enough to take care of themselves, they and the mother hen were let out to roam over the farm to find their own food. At dusk and late afternoon, the mother hen would teach her chicks to fly up in the surrounding trees as protection from predators.

Many of the chickens claimed the highest limbs of the white oak trees that were scattered all over the yard, barn lot, and pastures. I loved to be out at dusk and watch all those chickens choose their favorite roosting spot. Most of the time, the dominate gamecock rooster would chase other males from his favorite perch next to his swooning females. I would watch until the birds got settled into the trees at night and I would know that they would be ready to wake everyone at the first light of dawn in the early morning hours. It was great to awaken to the sounds of many roosters trying to out crow the others in the bunch. You could tell when it was about to get daylight by the crowing of the gamecock roosters in the trees around my grandparents' home. Today, when I hear a rooster crowing in the early morning hours, the sounds bring back sweet memories when I was a young Celtic Indian boy watching gamecock roosters fight.

Mountain Work and Survival

Hog Killing

When the weather got cold in November, it was time for killing the fattening hogs for the winter's meat supply. We would remove the testicles on all the boar pigs in the spring of the year which we called cutting hogs. While one of the men would hold the hog by the back legs, I got to use a razor blade to castrate the animal by making small slits on the scrotum, and then squeezing the balls out to be removed.

After the job was done, we would take coal oil or kerosene mixed with lard and rub in the wound. It would usually be a week or so and the cuts would be healed and the pigs would be fine. The larger boar testicles would usually be taken by someone wanting some good ole mountain oysters. The balls would be pealed and sometimes cut into slices or at least halved; then the gonads would be rolled in flour and fried. Some folks were wild about the mountain oysters and considered them a delicacy, but for some reason, I never could get into eating a hog's gonads.

After the pigs got pretty big during the summer, one or more of the better looking shoats were remove from the hog pen. We always put the fattening hogs in a stable where they were fed a diet of corn, supplements, and slop made with a sack of shorts. Special attention was given to insure by fall that we would have a nice fat hog to kill for the winter's meat. Fresh pork was delicious and would provide a supply of protein during the harsh winter months. On a cold November day, a large number of family members and neighbors would gather at grandpa's house for the hog killing event.

I sometimes got to kill the hog by placing a 22 caliber rifle right between the eyes and pulling the trigger at point blank range. We would then take a single tree to hang the hog and cut its throat so it could bleed out real good. The hog's carcass was then laid out on boards; boiling water from the big cast iron pot that had been setting on the fire for a long time was poured over the freshly killed hog to scald the hide enough to loosen the hair. Several people with butcher knives begin scraping the hair off the hog's hide immediately after the scalding water was poured on the hog's skin. All the hair was removed and the outer surface of the hog was cleaned prior to butchering the animal.

The big black pot was first used to boil the scalding water that loosens the hair on the hog's skin, and later, the pot would be used to render the lard in making cracklings and pork skins. Now, I loved fresh cracklings and crispy fried hog skins and would anxiously wait for them to get cooked. Some folks would also make chit-lings from the hog's guts. I could eat fresh chit-lings, but after they were cold, they tasted just like hog guts to me; therefore, I was never a big fan of eating cold chit-lings.

Later, the same pot would be used to make lye soap from some of the lard. I loved to watch my grandma making her lye soap. She would take the rain water that had gone through the ash hopper which concentrated lye. She poured the lye water into the pot with the liquid hog lard in order to make her soap. She would stir the lye water and liquid animal fat in the hot pot; then she let the mixture stand until the pot cooled and the soap hardened. She would then take one of the big butcher knives and slice the lye soap into hand size blocks.

The thing I hated about the lye soap was all the grit it had especially when we had to use it as bath soap, but one thing was clear, it got you clean and would just about take the hide off if you rubbed too hard or long. In addition, my grandma would use the same big pot to boil water to wash clothes in the lye soap she made from the hog lard. She would take her old rub board and set the ends in the pot of hot water; then she would rub the wet clothes with lye soap and push them up and down on the rub board until the clothes were clean. She would dunk them in the pot a time or two then twist most of the soapy water out before throwing the clothes in a tub of clean water to rinse all the lye soap out of the clothes.

One of the first things all us young boys were waiting for at the hog killing was the back straps or tenderloins to be taken out. We would take green hickory sticks which had pieces of hog tenderloin stuck on the end. We would hold the meat over the fire until it was roasted. The fresh meat would begin dripping moisture and would begin to turn brown. Then, the meat was taken off the stick and eaten. This was some of the best fresh meat I have ever eaten. After being stuffed with fresh tenderloin, all the boys would help with the hog preparation.

Back in the day, everyone had a smoke house that was used to cure the meat usually with hickory smoke. Grandpa's old smoke house had homemade wooden shingles that covered the roof of the building. Sometimes the old house looked like it was on fire because of the smoke coming out of the roof between all those wooden shingles. But after being cured, that was some mighty fine hams and also sausage.

Several of us boys would swap out in turning the meat grinder that was used for grinding up small pieces of the hog meat into sausage. Some of the sausage was placed in dry corn shucks that had the ear of corn removed; then after stuffing the shuck with sausage, the top of the shuck was tied together with a small wire or string. Once the sausage was packed in the dry corn shuck and tied, it was hung in the smoke house to be cured with the hams and the rest of the hog. Smoked sausage with my grandma's sage and pepper seasoning was the best you could eat.

In addition, the smoke house also had a salt box that was used to preserve the fresh hog meat. A lot of times, the sides of the hogs, also called middlings, were placed in the salt box and later cut up as bacon. Sometimes my grandma would wash the meat in hot water to remove the excess salt off the meat before cooking it for breakfast.

I remember that in the spring of the year, the meat had been in salt all winter, and I would ask Grandpa Dan Walker what was the all holes in the breakfast bacon. He would say, *"Son do not worry about those holes cause the meat is well cooked. After that meat stays a long time in that salt box, it will get skippers or zippers that will bore holes through the meat, but they will not spoil the meat."* The skippers were a type of meat maggot that bored holes through the meat even though it was covered with salt.

Of course, I could taste the meat getting a little stronger the older it got, but I knew better to complain about the taste because you did not disagree with Grandpa Walker. I learned to like the meat that looked like hoop cheese. Eventually when the meat got rancid, it would be discarded or fed to the dogs after grandma cooked the meat real good.

Nothing of the freshly killed hog was wasted not even the lungs. Grandma would soak all the blood out of the lungs and then boil them until they were very tender. Grandma fed me lights for a long time before I finally realized that they were the hog's lungs. I do not remember complaining about eating lights. In addition, my grandma would cook hog brains with fresh eggs and I thought that was one of the best breakfast meals.

Even the head, tongue, nose, and ears were not wasted. After the head was cooked and the meat removed from the bones, it was put in a pot and I would get to turn the meat grinder like making sausage, but the ears, tongue, nose, and all parts of the head and other parts including cartilage or gristle were ground to make souse meat; sometimes it was called head cheese. The cooked and ground souse meat was seasoned with sage, salt, and pepper then molded like butter. Then, grandma would usually place one of her old heavy metal flat irons on top of a plate covering the souse meat to squeeze out all the excess grease. After the grease was squeezed out of the souse meat, it was put in the refrigerator to cool; the souse meat was ready to eat. My grandpa and I loved souse meat with a little hot pepper sauce sprinkled over it and then placed on crackers.

Hog killings were a big family and neighborhood event that everyone was involved in during the preparation of the winter's meat supply. Most folks that assisted with the hog butchering were given a good portion of the meat to take home to feed their families. Some of our larger neighboring families that had many mouths to feed would kill and prepare as many as eight hogs over a three day period each fall. I remember the good times of fellowship and working together with the folks involved in the activity. The event was full of many wonderful memories of a true southern tradition that I as a young Celtic Indian boy participated in while growing up during hog killing times.

Murder and Wood Cutting

Survival growing up and staying many nights with my grandparents meant learning how to be self-sufficient and dependent on no one. My Wilburn Grandparents had purchased a forty acre tract of woodlands from Moody and Hattie Hogan of Speake Community. From those wooded acres, they cut the timber and cleared open plots of land to plant their crops. Shortly after the woods were cleared, it took back breaking work with a grub hoe, axes, and other tools to get the area ready to plant; they always called these new openings in the forest new ground.

I hated to try to cut roots with those big grubbing hoes, but I was always willing to help my Grandpa Arthur. Using a Georgia stock plow pulled by one old mule, they would try to till the land around big stumps and usually plant a patch of corn the first year of the planting season. After a few years, the rotten stumps could be pulled from the ground or burned until the land was ready for the row crop of cotton.

During the first year of planting corn, the land would produce a great harvest, but grandpa was always vigilant for attacks on his new corn crop by groundhogs, crows, blue jays, squirrels, and raccoons. Since the new ground was next to the forest, these creatures could destroy several rows of ripening corn. Grandpa and I spent many hours guarding the new ground corn patch with our 22 rifles, and sometimes grandpa would use his double barreled twelve gauge shotgun.

My grandparents cut fire wood and stove wood for many folks within a few miles of their place which they sold to help pay for their little piece of paradise. For a few dollars, my grandparents would cut firewood for other people to burn during the winter months and for their wood burning cook stoves.

I watched and helped many days as my grandparents cut stove wood with a cross cut saw and ax for their cook stove and wood to burn in the big heater. They never had power saws or chain saws and the wood cutting work was labor intensive. My job was never ending because I always stacked the brush in big piles which we would later burn. The piles of brush would be placed on the big stumps in order to burn them up.

Butch and Grandma Ila cutting stove wood

After their row crop fields were cleared of timber, they usually cut wood on the side of the mountain, and were more selective always leaving the better timber for shingles and boards. Grandpa loved to cut white oak for his fire wood; he would select an undesirable timber tree to use for firewood and stove wood.

To haul the cut firewood off the mountain, my grandparents depended on mule power. They would load the sled with firewood and the mule would pull the load to the house where it was stacked near the road in a cord or rick to be sold. It took many days of hard work to earn enough money to make the land payments from the wood cutting and faming small patches of cotton.

One day, Price Fuller and Emmitt McMillan rode their horses to my grandparents' house; Mr. Price Fuller sat on his horse and wrote my grandpa a twenty dollar check for a load of wood that he had got earlier. Little did Mr. Fuller know that this would be the last check that he would ever write for a load of firewood or anything else. Since my grandpa was not at home at the time, he gave the check to my grandma and told her, *"Give this to Arthur on what I owe him."*

The men told my grandma that they were riding through Sugar Camp Hollow and over the mountain to buy some wildcat whiskey. They were going to get the whiskey from a bootlegger by the name of Terrapin Lowery, who had his moonshine still in front of his house in a big sinkhole. My grandma told the men not to go because those folks had been drunk for over a week and been fighting.

Grandma had kept and took care of their kids during their parents' big drunk time to prevent them from being abused. Grandma told the men, *"Y'all better stay away from that place because all you will get is trouble because they have been drunk for a while."* The two men did not pay any attention to my grandma and told her that they would be all right that they were just going to get some of Terrapin's freshly made moonshine, and off they rode without a care in the world.

After what seemed to be a little over an hour, Mr. McMillan came galloping up to the house on his lathered up horse, and he wanted my grandma to help him because he had been shot. His arm was swollen real badly, his shirt sleeve was soaked in blood, and blood was dripping off his hand. He asked my grandma to get the scissors and cut his sleeve so he could have some relief. Grandma was reluctant and said, *"I do not want to go to court or get involved with anything to do with this shooting."* McMillan assured her that he just wanted some temporary relief because the shirt sleeve was very tight due to the extreme swelling. When grandma started to make the cut from his cuff up, the sleeve of his shirt just busted all the way to his shoulder.

Mr. McMillan told my grandma, *"Lutie has shot and killed Price and I made a dash for the woods as fast as my horse would go, but just prior to reaching the timber, I felt the bullet hit me in the back of the upper arm. Terrapin tried to kill me and would have had I not taken off on my horse; he shot at me several times!"* Later, Terrapin said, *"If I would have had my big rifle, I would have killed Emmitt McMillan."*

The story goes that Fuller did not like the cussing and started on the porch with an old scratcher spring. In self-defense and after being warned, Lutie grabbed a 22 rifle just inside the door and shot him in the head as he started up the steps to the porch. It was reported that Fuller had crawled to the back of the house before he died sometime during the night. It was eventually revealed that Fuller was shot in the head and did not die until several hours later; it was said that the lady who shot Fuller told her husband during the night, *"Go out there and kill that moaning son-of-a-bitch so I can get some sleep."*

In the meantime, McMillan had contacted the law, but they refused to go to the house until they got Mr. Shirley Smith to agree to go with them the next day. Mr. Smith was road commissioner and had known the family for years; he accompanied the law enforcement authorities to the house where they picked up the body of Mr. Fuller. Lutie Lowery was arrested and charged with murder.

While Lutie was in jail, my Grandma Ila kept her kids. The youngest girl was my age and she had two older brothers; eventually the kids were put in foster homes. After we got to be teenagers, I dated Terrapin and Lutie's daughter a couple of times, but she started seeing my best friend Jimmy Day and that ended our relationship. Much later in life, we became friends again; even though I seldom see her anymore, I still consider her a friend.

Prior to the children being placed in foster care, their dad came to my grandparents' house one night drunk and demanded to see his children. Since the kids were already in bed in the next room, my Grandpa Wilburn told him to leave and explained that the children were asleep. He was cussing and told my grandpa, *"General Mac Arthur I am going to see my kids and you are not going to stop me."* He always called my grandpa General Mac for the famous World War II General McArthur.

After being repeatedly warned, Terrapin Lowery entered my grandparents' house and started cussing my Grandpa Arthur. Without saying a word, my grandpa hit him so hard in the face that he knocked him through the door into the room where the kids were sleeping. The oldest son woke up and started yelling, *"Hit him again General Mac Aut, hit him again, hit him again."* Grandpa dragged Terrapine outside and told him to go home. After a few choice words from both men, Terrapin went back over the mountain to his house.

Now back to the wood cutting; I saw my grandparents make their own shingles, boards, and palings with a metal froe, wood mallet, and fork of a small tree. They would use steel and wooden wedges to split big logs into quarters, and then take off the heart wood to make shingles and palings. The wood shingles were about two feet long, four to eight inches wide, and about one half inch thick; the shingles would be used on the roofs of all their buildings.

The palings were boards made of white oak about five feet long and four inches wide. These boards would be sharpened on the end to a point before being used as a picket fence around the garden to enclose it from the chickens, dogs, and other animals. The sharp points on each picket also prevented the chickens from flying up to the top of the fence. For some reason, chickens would not light on a sharp point and they seldom flew over the fence into the garden. Such was the life of a Celtic Indian boy growing up and cutting wood with a cross cut saw and ax on the hills of North Alabama.

Cotton Picking

The coming of the hot dry late summer and early fall was not a time that I reflect on with a lot of enthusiasm and excitement, but rather a time to bow the back and crawl on your knees picking cotton. Not only would your knees and back get extremely sore from all that crawling and bending over, but the pointed burs of the cotton bolls would prick the ends of your fingers until they would just about bleed and sometimes they would bleed. We would start at the break of day and quit as the last rays of the sun were setting over the distant hills and hollows of the Warrior Mountains. At the end of the day, everyone would gather around the cotton wagon and wait for their pay in cash and coins for a hard day of work.

Each year during the peak of cotton picking time, school was let out so all the school kids could hit the white fields of cotton in the hottest time of the year. Of course, this was the only time of the year that I wanted to go to school, but instead, I had to strap on that cotton sack a try to get my poundage quota or face a whipping from my dad. Cotton picking became my motivation to go to college and get an education so that I would never have to pick another boll of cotton.

The highest rate of pay I remember getting was $3.00 per 100 pounds of cotton picked; therefore, when I was a youngster in elementary school, I was required by my dad to pick at least 150 pounds of cotton per day which would equate to $4.50 per day for forced child labor. My Grandma Ila Wilburn was a very kind sole and wanted me to pick my single row beside her as she picked two rows of cotton. She would put a big handful of cotton in my sack to encourage me to stay up with her. Grandma's cotton sack was nine feet long while I used a shorter six foot sack when I was elementary school age.

When we got into high cotton and my sack was about half full, I would lay down on my cotton sack and take an afternoon nap. The weather would be sweltering, but that nap felt so good in that real high cotton where no one could see me napping in the hot shade. I would even sweat during my nap, but I knew better than to nap too long because an accounting would be coming soon. My dad would give me a whipping if I failed to get my 150 pound quota for the day. My grandma would say, *"Come on son and get off your sack and get to picking because you know what your dad will do if you fail to pick enough cotton."*

I remember one year picking cotton for our neighbor Mr. Hansel Black, who was my dad's best friend. I was also friends with two of Mr. Black's boys-Phil Black and Larry Black. After a long day of cotton picking in the Kelly Patch just south of the Kelly Hole swimming area, Larry and I were walking toward his house when his mom passed us along an old field road in her car. I was tired and wanted a ride; therefore, I jumped on the trunk of the car as it passed along the field road.

Larry saw what I had done and tried to swing on the back door handle for a ride, but the car hit a small ditch crossing the field road and Larry fell under the back tire and was run over in the middle of the body. I vividly remember watching the tire run over his body as I was on the trunk of the car looking right at Larry when he fell under the car.

Even though we were just kids, we had to work the whole day just like the adults, but as kids, we made our share of mistakes. I felt extremely bad about the accident because I was encouraging Larry to ride with me on the car's trunk. This accident could have very easily ended Larry's life, but he managed to survive and we became lifelong friends.

After I got into high school, I graduated from a six foot sack to a nine foot sack which could hold about 100 pounds of cotton depending on how hard you packed the cotton in your sack. Once you filled your sack as full as you could get it, you hoisted the sack on your shoulder and carried it to the cotton wagon. I felt a great pride and relief to carry my full cotton sack to the wagon to be weighed and to get a drink of cold ice water that the farmers usually kept on the cotton wagon. Usually the farmer or one of his hands would weigh your sack of cotton, record your poundage, and empty your sack of cotton in the wagon. They would throw the empty sack back at you, so you could get back to picking a quickly as possible.

As I got older, my cotton picking ability improved and I was able to pick over 300 pounds of cotton per day and to pull over 600 pounds of cotton per day. Pulling cotton was a process of stripping the stalks including the cotton, bolls, limbs, and putting all that in your cotton sack. But I still could not pick more than my smaller aunt who could grab a whopping 400 pounds of cotton each day. Her hands were extremely fast and quick, and I never could pick the 400 pounds per day goal.

Picking cotton meant that you had to pull only the cotton from the bolls and keep the cotton free of leaves and debris. The reason for my increased motivation in cotton picking as I got into high school was the money I made and got to keep. Therefore, I would grab as much of that fluffy white stuff that I translated into dollars in my pocket.

I had saved over one hundred dollars from my cotton picking activities and was so proud of my accomplishments, but dad needed some cash for an emergency and offered to sell me his Browning automatic 12 gauge shotgun for the one hundred dollars I had in my savings. I was very happy with the gun deal with my dad; I now had bought my first twelve gauge shotgun with cotton picking money. The gun was of the highest quality being Belgium made with a gold trigger, ventilated rib, modified choke, and a cheek rest walnut stock; I still own that gun today which is a sweet reminder of the cotton picking times of a Celtic Indian boy in a field white with cotton.

Sawmill and Softball

I did a lot of things when I was growing up to avoid picking cotton which I thought was some of the hardest work that I have ever done. Finally when I was in high school, I got a part time at Elmore's dime store. The dime store was on the north side of the town square in Moulton straight across from the court house which was in the center of the town. Working for the dime store was good job, but it did not pay very much at all. Now I understand that everything was so cheap that they could not afford to pay much to their part time workers. The time I worked at the dime store was way better than picking cotton with sweat and dirt all over you by the end of the day; at least I could stay somewhat clean while I worked.

After working at the dime store for a while, Ms. Dean Cook helped me get another part time job which was a little higher paying at Piggly Wiggly grocery store in Moulton, Alabama. Mr. Clark Weatherwax, the owner and boss, gave me the job of sacking groceries with some other nice young men from Moulton. I worked with Mike Hill, John Cross, Phillip Boyles, Robert Harris, David Alexander, Golden Gene Terry, and Mr. Weatherwax's son, Roger Weatherwax. I finally helped get my high school friend James Steele a job at the store; we had fun and became great friends with our coworkers. John Cross and I were always up to mischief and had a lot of fun sacking and delivering groceries to the cars. I just thought I worked real hard, but I soon found out what hard work was all about when I got a full time summer job at the sawmill just before my first year of college.

My first job at the Grayson Sawmill in the Bankhead Forest was stacking lumber. I worked side by side with a real country red neck by the name of Thurman Jetton. Thurman was a man who liked the wild side of things and according to him grew up real rough. He had made moonshine for several of the men I knew who lived in the Moulton Valley. I was already familiar with those people because I was the designated driver for a bunch of drunks who visited every bootlegger in a three county region nearly every weekend.

Thurman Jetton was good to me and a very hard worker; he put up with a lot of verbal abuse while doing his job and never lost his cool while I worked with him on the lumber stacker. I knew that he loved to drink a little moonshine, but I never remember him coming to work drunk. He did have an eye for pretty women and let that be known; every time he saw one of the beautiful sawmill girls he would holler, *"Mossy jaw."* The girls seemed to pay no mind to his name calling and foolishness; they just went on about their business. Many years after my days at the sawmill had ended, I heard on the news where Thurman had beat a woman to death with an axe handle. You never know what people are capable of that you work side by side with for several weeks. The killing was the last that I ever heard of Thurman Jetton.

While Thurman and I worked together, he was real nice to me. Our job was placing strips of wood between each stack of fresh cut lumber so that it could be dried.

Two big, flat steel arms would lay down a large layer of lumber about 16 feet by 16 feet square and real quickly we had to place strips of wood on top before the next layer was placed on top of the last. The job was fast and furious; by the time you got the strips laid, another layer of lumber was on the way.

After about the first week on the job at the Grayson Sawmill, a lot of young and very pretty girls who lived in the sawmill houses and some who worked at the mill asked me and a friend of mine Bill Borden to be coaches for their softball team. Bill and I gladly accepted the challenge, but the problem was that neither one of us knew anything about girls softball.

Bill and I managed to get the sawmill to support the team and they even let us clean off part of the log yard for the field. Mr. John Clancy owner of the mill was willing to sponsor our girl's softball team. Mr. Clancy provided the space in the log yard for us to make a softball field; he had some of his heavy equipment to move logs and clean off the area for the field. Mr. Clancy paid Bobby Smith to take the road grader and level our Grayson Softball Field; Bobby operated the equipment at the saw mill and got our field in great shape.

All the team members including Bill and I picked up trash and raked the field clean; our softball field was on a flat ridge east of the mill which overlooked the beautiful forest valleys. The head of the valley just east of the softball field led to the Collier Creek Falls; an absolutely gorgeous waterfall that plunged into the deep canyon below. Below the falls were two stone columns that had supported the water wheel of a grist mill that had long ago belonged to Will Riddle. Occasionally, some of the girls and I would go to the falls to enjoy the sights and sounds of the forest.

One thing I remember about Grayson is the loud steam whistle similar to that of a train. Every morning at 8:00 am which was the start of work, the whistle would sound off; at noon each day at dinner time, the whistle would signal the time to go eat. Then, each afternoon at 4:00 pm which was the end of the work day, the huge whistle would blow and immediately every one quit work and started for home except Bill and me. We would head to the softball field to practice with our bunch of beautiful mountain girls.

Many years after I left the hard lumber work and had a family of my own, I would hear the whistle while hunting or hiking in the forest. After hearing that old lonesome whistle blow, it would bring back memories, both good and bad, of my days working and practicing softball with the lovely women of the forest sawmill.

The work on the lumber stacker was physical and tough; we were grabbing and laying 16 foot strips of wood between each layer of lumber. To make matters worse,

Cotton Townsend who was our immediate supervisor was not too friendly and would sometimes holler at Thurman and me to do our job faster. Thurman would talk under his breath how he did not like being hollered at, but I was getting fed up with the way I was treated. It was like working on a chain gang with an overseer that was just plain mean; I do not remember Cotton saying one kind word while I worked like a mule.

After working for a few weeks on the stacker, I had got disgusted being hollered at like a dog; one particular morning, neither Mr. Townsend nor I were in a good mood. He started hollering at me and Mr. Jetton to do our job faster; I hollered back telling him, *"You son-of-a-bitch, we are working as hard as we can."* Now at that particular moment, that was not the appropriate thing to call your boss; Townsend, who at one time was the Sheriff of Winston County, shut down the stacker and came running across that stack of lumber and said, *"Boy what did you say?"*

I thought for sure the fight was on, but I told Townsend that he heard what I said; he then rudely told me to follow him to the office which I did. Cotton Townsend was going to have me fired, but for some reason that did not happen and I still do not know why I kept my job. When we walked into the owner's office, Mr. John Clancy told Cotton Townsend to leave, I knew that I was going to be fired from my first full time job at the sawmill, but I was glad to leave that place. Mr. Clancy owned the Clancy Lumber Company that was at Grayson; he asked what had taken place and I explained to him that I did not like anyone hollering at me like a blank dog. I did not use blank, but rather not repeat what I told him; but I told him the truth.

I think that Mr. Clancy realized that it was hard to keep people working in some of the harsh sawmill conditions; I think he appreciated me taking a stand against a supervisor that I thought was overbearing. I know Mr. Clancy appreciated me helping with the team that he was sponsoring and all the extra hours I put in helping coach his girls that made up the Grayson Gophers softball team. He also remembered me eating at the same table each day at dinner, but we never talked much; he was the owner and boss of everyone at the saw mill and all the folks around showed him a great deal of respect because he had earned it.

Mr. Clancy had a hired a great cook Ms. Susie Bishop who would fix boiled cabbage, big speckled butter beans, fried potatoes, fresh squash, and delicious corn bread with huge pork chops or other meat each day at lunch. Paul and Susie Bishop also ran the boarding house at Grayson for Mr. Clancy. When the whistle blew for lunch, I always headed to the big dining hall were some of the workers would eat at the same table as Mr. Clancy. The good old country food was some of the best that I ever ate; the great meal only cost fifty cents and was worth every penny. Each day, I looked forward to that large glass of iced tea and all those freshly cooked vegetables. Mr. Clancy may not have paid his workers real high wages, but he subsidized the meals to keep the costs low enough for his hired hands; however, most of the laborers still brought their own lunch.

Mr. Clancy kind of smiled and said I have another job for you at this mill; of course, I was shocked that I was not fired immediately. I should have known that he was going to put me in the sawmill hell; the most dangerous and hardest work that I have ever done in my life was about to happen. I think Mr. Clancy wanted to see how tough I was; I think he was testing my grit to see if I could really handle the horrible and dangerous job of turning cants. Very few tough men would last over a week or two turning cants; the toughest job I know of anywhere.

Sawmilling was not the safest work or job that one could have; a lot of accidents happened, but I only know of one man that died as a result. The death was caused by a high stack of lumber falling and crushing the man to death. Another accident turned out to be a miracle; a 16 foot two by four board was slung so hard from one of the saws that it went through a man's chest. Mill workers quickly cut each end of the board off that was sticking through the man and rushed him to the hospital; doctors were able to save his life.

Several of the workers who ran knot saws had missing fingers from being cut off at work; Bill Borden refused to run a knot saw and Mr. Clancy also like Bill. Bill told him that he was going to school to be a dentist and that he must have all his fingers; he never ran a knot saw but I did. Bill would mow Mr. Clancy's yard in Decatur then take Mr. Clancy to Huntsville to get some whiskey. Bill would also mow the yard of the "Church of the Forest" that was built by Mr. Clancy. Each Christmas at the church, Mr. Clancy would give all the saw mill camp children wonderful gifts that he had personally paid for; in addition, he gave all employees a bonus.

I went to school with Dexter Garrison and his daddy Garvin Garrison had measured saw logs at the mill for years, but they put Dexter to work at the Grayson Sawmill turning cants. Every day that I saw Dexter, it looked like he had been in a fight with a wildcat; he was scratched up all over his arms. Dexter was as tough as they come, but had finally quit the job of turning cants. I was about to inherit his position since Mr. Clancy needed someone to work in the sawmill hell and I was about to be put to the test.

I did not have but one clue about turning cants; that clue came from my high school friend Dexter Garrison who told me about the rough job. When Dexter and I finished high school, we along with James Steele and Wayne Adair went on our graduation trip to Florida in my new Simca. The little car would not run more than 60 miles per hour and going uphill I was lucky to keep it above 50. We would have big 18 wheelers pass us while going uphill, but the little car would get over 40 miles per gallon on gas. The four of us could barely fit into the vehicle and we only had one bag apiece, but we were going to travel all over Florida which we did for about two weeks.

Now back to the cant turning job; I will never forget my adventure of turning cants which is half of a huge log that has been sawed down the middle into two halves. Each half of log had to be placed on its flat side before it goes through the bank of large band saws to be cut into boards. I was in a hole where a metal conveyor belt carried the half logs up an incline to a series of big band saws. As the half logs were going up the inclined conveyor, they had to be turned to the flat side with a cant hook or either you would have to wrap your arms around the log and roll them to their flat side.

One half of the log would come off the main saw that just split the logs down the middle in front of you. The other half of the log came off rollers behind you and would fall some four feet on to the steel platform. You had to be careful not to get in front of the log coming from behind you while you were turning the first cant. Some of the logs were so big that it took all your strength just to turn the log over. At the same time, you had to watch for the next log to fall on the steel rack.

I did not last as long at the cant turning job as my friend Dexter; shortly I went back to Mr. Clancy and told him that I was going to quit. I have no idea if he liked me or just needed some workers, but he said, *"I have a better job for you in the hard wood mill running a knot saw."* In other words Mr. Clancy evidently did not want me to quit working for his lumber mill; this was the first and last job that I could not get fired from nor could I quit. I knew that the new job I was going to would easily cut your fingers off, but I was willing to give it a try; I sure wanted away from the sawmill hell in the cant hole.

Mr. Clancy was a good man, but he also like the shine and was known to get drunk every once in a while. On one occasion, he got stopped by the Lawrence County law enforcement officers and was arrest for driving under the influence. The officers had no idea who he was and carried him to jail; upon arriving at jail in Moulton, they found over 100,000 dollars in his possession. Mr. Clancy was worth well over fifty million dollars; he built nice sawmill houses at Grayson for his workers. If a hired hand worked long enough at the mill, Mr. Clancy would give him one of the houses for a permanent home.

On another occasion, Mr. Clancy was picked up at his home in Decatur by Mr. Charlie Feltman who was his designated driver in a brand new Ford LTD; Clancy told Mr. Feltman to pull over that he had to take a leak. Charlie Feltman did not understand what Mr. Clancy wanted and did not pull over. Mr. Clancy got aggravated and just relieved himself in the back floor board of the new car. Charlie had to clean the car after he got Mr. Clancy to the saw mill; Charlie learned that if Mr. Clancy said something that he had better do it.

Mr. Clancy give me the new job of running a knot saw which was a little easier than turning cants, but not in the least less dangerous. You were standing right in front of a circular saw blade that stuck up from the metal table about four inches high and the saw was running wide open. As hardwood flooring came by on a conveyor belt, you had to grab the boards with bad knots or holes and cut those knots and holes out of the board. The good thing about working at the hardwood mill was my supervisor John Henry Bolan was just a nice boss; his wife Super Bolan also played softball on our team.

Since Mr. Clancy sponsored our girls' softball team, he provided the school bus and driver Mr. Charlie Feltman to carry us to all the away games. We played Addison, Nesmith, Sardis, Piney Grove, Double Springs, and a bunch of teams that I cannot remember. One thing I can remember is a fateful afternoon at Piney Grove, I was catching to warm up the pitcher while our catcher was getting her gear on, someone called my name. I looked over to see what they wanted, and about the time I looked around, a fast thrown softball caught me right between the eyes. The ball knocked me for a flip; I wound up with a sore nose and two black eyes.

Mr. Clancy also provided the new uniforms that our girls wore and also bought all our equipment including new softballs, gloves, bats, and anything else we needed. I cannot remember all the girls that played on our softball team that was called the Grayson Gophers. I do remember some of the players: Janet Wilson, Loree "Super" Blankenship (Bolan), Lowell "Cricket" Blankenship (Bumgart), Linda Bohannon, Myra "Cutie" Scott (Page), Annice Bushman, Sue Bushman, Linda Faye Blankenship (Clark), Sherry Luker, Janet England, and Betty Jean Ayers.

Finally, I was starting college at the University of North Alabama before Mr. John Clancy let me quit my job at the saw mill. Many years later the sawmill work would flash before my eyes; on February 6, 2008, a tornado destroyed my home that I had bought some four years earlier. The house was built by Mr. and Mrs. John Prueit in the late 1960's.

As friends of mine, Ray England and Frank White, were helping me take up the remaining red oak hardwood flooring from my storm damaged house, each of the boards were stamped on the bottom Clancy Lumber Company, Grayson, Alabama. In addition, the eastern hemlock rafters were stamped with Clancy Lumber Company.

I realized that Mr. John Preuit originally built the house at the same time I ran a knot saw in the hardwood flooring mill for Mr. John Clancy. The hardwood could very well be some of the boards that I cut the knots and holes out of when I worked at Grayson Sawmill; such was the life of a Celtic Indian boy who experience the hard life of sawmill workers of Appalachia.

Fishing Adventures

Night I Never Forgot

My grandpa and I would spend countless hours in the woods at night waiting for the coon and possum dogs to tree something. While waiting late into the night for the sound of the hounds to give that unmistakable baying, I would stretch out in the leaves and sometimes go to sleep while grandpa waited patiently for our dogs to tree. I never had a fear because I knew grandpa was watching guard as I curled up in the leaves.

Butch, Age 4, Wheeler Dam, July 1954

Occasionally, the silent stillness of the night would be broken with the sounds of a great horned owl that could be heard for miles. At other times, the eerie sounds of the screech owl would send shivers down my spine because my grandma told me that death tolls were occurring. I always wondered where someone was dying and I certainly did not want to be in that number way out in the woods; however, I never had a fear of being with Grandpa Arthur on the darkest nights.

Many times on weekends, my grandpa, uncles, daddy, and any folks that could pack into our old car would take off to the river for an all-night fishing trip. I love to be near the water at night fishing with my grandpa. Most of the times, my folks would also be drinking wildcat and having a big time, but being a small boy, I would just curl up on the bank besides my grandpa and sleep until he caught a fish. When I was a small boy, we did not have a boat and always fished from the bank. My favorite spot was below Wheeler Dam, but I also like Lock A and Spring Creek on the Tennessee River. Many times, I remember waking up on the river bank watching the sun rise.

Sometimes we would get to Wheeler Dam and the banks of the river would be lined with people; that did not bother my dad who was always a little intoxicated. We would have to stop at the bootleggers before making the fishing trip. Dad would have several beers and some wildcat before we got to the river. After arriving at Wheeler Dam, Brady would walk right among all of those fishermen lining the banks and take out his old casting reel. He would put big balls of bait and begin winding up like windmill blades whirling in a strong wind. People would scatter to get out of the way of two or three hooks he had weighted down with a big hunk of lead. Pretty soon, we had all the fishing room that was needed for everybody in our group to fish all night long.

One day a whole bunch of us arrived at Wheeler Dam for an all night fishing excursion; Brackin Hampton and Grandpa Arthur Wilburn had piled in the car with about eight people total. I had to sit in grandpa's lap because the car was so crowded. We had some 20 cane fishing poles tie to the top of the car. As we were coming down the road, a bunch of chickens were about to cross and daddy did not slow up. One of the chickens flew up and got stabbed by all those poles tied to the top of the car. Feathers went everywhere, but dad just laughed and kept on driving. The chicken stayed on the poles until we stopped at the Dam Store just prior to reaching our fishing spot at the dam.

Upon arriving at the dam, Brackin Hampton asked me to catch him some bluegill for bait; of course, I enjoyed catching bluegill around the rock banks. I caught a nice bluegill that Brackin put on a huge ocean fishing reel. Just after dark, Brackin and daddy left to get some more moonshine and that reel started grinding. I pick up the reel, but I did not know how to unlock the winding mechanism; therefore, I threw the reel down and started pulling in the heavy line by hand. Finally, I got the big fish to the bank; it was a largemouth bass that weighed over seven pounds.

One night, Grandpa Arthur wanted me to go with him, Brackin Hampton, and Jimmy Robbins to East Flint Creek just west of Hartselle, Alabama. Mr. Brackin Hampton was a coon hunting buddy of grandpa and I had been with them on several coon hunts; therefore, I had no hesitation going on an all-night fishing trip with grandpa and his friends. The four of us crammed into an old pickup truck with me setting in grandpa's lap. We put all our fishing poles, buckets of worms, flashlights and lanterns, and food in the bed of the truck.

After we got close to Hartselle, we turned south down an old dirt road about three fourths of a mile west of the bridge crossing East Flint Creek on Highway 36. The narrow road led south for about one mile prior to reaching the edge of the creek. We unloaded all the gear and set out our poles and waited for the catfish to begin biting. By about eight o'clock that night, we had several fish; Jimmy wanted my grandpa to go with him to get some whiskey. Grandpa wanted to know if I would mind staying with Mr. Hampton while he would be gone about an hour. Of course, I enjoyed watching our poles and catching those cats; therefore, I told grandpa that I would be fine as long as he would be back pretty soon.

At the time, I was only seven or eight years old and had no fear of being in the woods or on the creek bank at night; however, I was a little uneasy about grandpa riding with Jimmy who was about drunk already. Little did I know that it would be three days later before I would see my grandpa again. Mr. Brackin Hampton was also reluctant to give Jimmy the keys to his truck, but after Jimmy assured him that they would be back in a few minutes, Brackin agreed to let Jimmy drive his pickup truck to get the whiskey. After some six hours after Jimmy and Grandpa Arthur left, Mr. Hampton told me that they had left us and that we needed to start walking toward home which was some twenty miles away. I had already got cold and sleepy by two o'clock that next morning; therefore, I agreed to head toward home even though I knew it would take us a long time unless we could catch a ride.

Brackin Hampton and I hid all our fishing equipment in the woods and with a flash light, we started walking out to the main road. When we got off the little dirt road, I noticed an old clapboard house not far away with an old pickup truck parked in the front of the house. I told Mr. Hampton that I was going over to the house to see if anyone was home. He said that was some black folks who lived over there, and it was too early in the morning to wake someone up.

At the time, I was too cold, tired, and sleepy to worry about getting shot; and for some reason, I had no fear about knocking on the door. Mr. Hampton told me that he would wait by the road while I went up to the house. I walked up on the porch by myself and knocked on the door several times before I heard someone coming to the door. In a few minutes, the door open and a big black man said, *"Boy who are you?"* I said, *"Sir, I am Butch Walker!"* He looked at me and smiled and said, *"Do you know Brady Walker?"* I said, *"Yes sir, that is my daddy!"* He said, *"Lord how mercy, I grew up by your daddy and we used to box all the time in the cattle stall at your Granddaddy Dan Walker's barn."*

The black man went on to say that he was a Sharpley, and I think he said his name was Kenneth Sharpley; his family lived on the hill behind my grandpa Walker. I then told Mr. Sharpley, *"I have been left on the creek about six hours ago and I want to go home."* Mr. Sharpley told me, *"Come in the house and let me get my shoes and shirt on and I will take you home."* I then told Mr. Sharpley that another man was with me and could he ride with us. After about fifteen minutes, Mr. Hampton and I were riding toward home in Mr. Sharpley's truck. When we got to my house about daylight, I got my daddy up and he and Mr. Sharpley talked until long after daylight catching up on old times when they used to play and box with each other. I was never so glad to be back home.

Very shortly after arriving home, my dad and my uncles begin looking for Grandpa Wilburn. They found Jimmy Robbins, but he did not remember what happened to my grandpa. For the next two days, an intensive search with law enforcement authorities assisting was made for grandpa. My folks had looked everywhere with no luck or leads as to what might have happened to grandpa.

My grandpa was very introvert and did not like to be around a lot of people; therefore, after he got left around Hartselle, grandpa started walking across country toward home. He walked through the woods and stayed off the main roads until he got home. I was setting at the back door of grandpa's house on Sunday morning. I looked up the hill and saw grandpa walking toward the house. Finally, the long fishing trip ordeal was over and I was glad to see my Grandpa Arthur alive and well.

Mountain Rifle Fishing

Many times I think back to the old days of my boyhood when fishing in the Warrior Mountains was for food and not so much for fun. It was not that we did not enjoy catching fish on a hook and line, but many times, it was about getting the fish to eat any way we could. It was more about food and something to eat rather than the fun and excitement as it is today. If we could make a big fish basket out of chicken wire, use one of grandpa's old hoop nets, or fill a pool with green walnuts in the late summer to catch a fresh mess of fish for the dinner table, we did not see anything wrong with the catching method or technique that provided a meal for the table.

The same logic of providing food to eat applied to gigging or shooting suckers and red horse fish in their spring run with a rifle or bow. Red horse were a type of river fish that would run upstream along with the more common spotted suckers to the shallow waters of the West Fork of Flint Creek. The suckers sought out a shallow shoals and rapids with swift water and gravel bars to spawn and lay their eggs. Later the suckers would return downstream to the river with the next flood stage water after the weather got warmer in the early spring. The suckers and red horse were similar to the shows on spawning salmon, but they did not die after laying their eggs and are totally fresh water fish. Sometimes one shoal would have forty or fifty suckers and red horse competing in the shallow water to spawn.

I preferred shooting suckers with a bow that had a Zebco reel attached to the stabilizer bar. During the late summer when the creek bass would float near the surface, a well-placed arrow would provide fresh fish meal for the table. However, it was also fun trying to punch suckers and red horse with the gig attached to a long stiff fishing cane. The gig usually had three sharp barbed points that would stick into the fish; the fish could be brought to the bank to put on the stringer. Some of my uncles enjoyed snaring suckers and red horse with a fine wire attached to a long cane pole, but I liked the more active method of shooting or gigging the fish.

After a successful fishing trip, my Grandma Ila Wilburn had a pressure cooker that she would put on her wood burning stove to cook and can the bony suckers, red horse, carp, and buffalo fish that we had caught. Prior to being placed in the quart jars, the fish were scraped clean of scales, gutted, and their heads and fins cut off. Grandma Ila would stuff and pack the pieces of fish into the quart jars after they were cut into blocks. The reason the suckers, red horse, and other fish were placed into the pressure cooker instead of frying the filets was that the fish had so many bones that they were impossible to eat fried; therefore, the pressure cooker was used for fish that were full of bones in order to cook the bones until they were eatable.

Grandma Ila would add seasoning to the fish and completely fill the quart jars with water. The jars containing chunks of the fish would be placed in the pressure cooker; the fish would be cooked long enough that their bones would be brittle and soft. The bones could be eaten along with the flesh of the fish when they were made into patties. The canned fish would last for a long time; when we got ready for a mess of fish patties, Grandma Ila would open a jar and cook up a bunch for us to eat. These pressure cooked fish would be used to make of the best patties just like one would do with a can of salmon. I loved fresh cooked golden brown fish patties of those suckers, red horse, carp, buffalo, and other boney fish.

On warm summer nights, my dad, uncles, and I would head to shallow streams in the Warrior Mountains with tow sacks and 22 caliber rifles for our fish shoot. We all knew it was illegal to shoot fish with rifles, but when fish became hard to catch, it was worth the risk to have a mess of fresh fish. I reckon that we used tow sacks because they were available, cheap, and the sacks could be slung over the shoulder to haul out coons and possums in addition to a sack of fish. Most all the animal feed and cotton seed from the ginning process of many years ago was placed into tow sacks; therefore, nearly all the farmers had a bunch of uses for their tow sacks.

One creek in particular that we use to rifle fish was the upper end of Rock Creek just east of Upshaw off the Jasper Road or Highway 41. We would start at one bridge and wade the creek to the next bridge shooting fish as we went. The fish would be placed in the tow sack after they were shot in the head. We would use carbide lights and 22 short ammunition as we searched the clear water for fish that appeared to be asleep. Once the single shot rifle was placed under water and fired, it made very little sound that could be heard for just a short distance; this was very effective in keeping the game wardens from trying to catch us.

Most of the fish would be on or real close to the bottom of the stream. Usually, the fish would remain still until you could ease the rifle barrel into the water for the shot. Very carefully in order to prevent spooking the fish, we would stick the rifle barrel under the water within about four inches of the fish's head and pull the trigger. Most of the times, the concussion would kill the fish if the bullet happened to miss the fish's head. After the fish was shot, it would just roll over dead and you could pick it up and place in the tow sack which was dragged along in the water.

A long time hunting and hiking buddy of mine who is also a Celtic Indian of the Warrior Mountains is Charles Borden. He and his parents and grandparents did the same form of rifle fishing in the mountains. They too used a 22 caliber rifle that was placed into the water near the fish's head before the fish were shot. Charles and his family rifle fished on Brushy, Beech, Rush, and other creeks close to their home which was just south of Pine Torch Church in the William B. Bankhead National Forest. Charles said that they did not pressure cook the fish and most were too boney to eat.

Charles also said his favorite method to catch spawning suckers was with a stiff pole with a fine wire snare. Most of his snaring was done above the Pitman Bridge at the upper end of Brushy Lake on the shallow shoals in Owl Creek and Brushy Creek. A loop was made at the end of the wire with a white button placed above the loop to increase visibility. The snare was allowed to move downstream and eased over the fish's head passed the gills; then with a quick jerk, the snare would tighten around the fish's head just behind the gills. After the fish was snared, the suckers could be lifted to the bank just like with a fishing pole. In snaring suckers, one had to be very cautious and stealthy or you would spook the whole school of fish and they would run back into deeper water.

Shooting floating fish that were near the surface with a 22 caliber rifle or bow was another effective method of harvesting some food during the late summer. Once a fish was shot with the rifle, you had to get into the water to retrieve it, but with my bow and Zebco, I could reel the fish to the bank. I spent countless hours bow fishing the West Fork of Flint Creek; and during the right time of year, I would usually bring home a mess of fish.

Sometimes a big bass was shot with my bow along with other game fish which provided great table fare. Even though this was also illegal, the fish was used to feed the family and did not go to waste. In the days of my youth, life was good for a Celtic Indian boy growing up and learning to survive in the Warrior Mountains of North Alabama.

Fishing Hole

For many years, I followed my Grandpa Arthur Wilburn to the ancestral fishing hole that we called the Mastengill. Grandpa had fished the same hole with his dad and granddad in the same tradition that I was introduced to the fishing spot. Grandpa and I would walk to the Mastengill with poles in our hand and hopes for a fresh mess of fish. From the time I was born until my grandpa's death, he never had a vehicle of any kind; therefore, we walked every time we went to our favorite deep stretch of creek that was our fishing hole.

As a small boy, the only fishing equipment grandpa and I used were creek canes with lines that had floats or corks attached, lead that was beaten flat with a hammer and wrapped around the line for sinkers, and just plain old fishing hooks. Grandpa would cut our fishing poles along the creek and hang them by their small ends on high branches of the big white oak trees that grew in his yard; the poles would have a rock attached to the bottom to hold it straight until our fishing canes dried. Once the poles dried, grandpa would rig them for fishing.

Years ago, creek canes in our area grew as long as thirty feet in the rich alluvial woodlands along the creek bank, but in recent years, I have not been able to find native river canes anywhere in the Warrior Mountains that grow that big. It appears that most die after reaching only fifteen to twenty feet in length; their decline in growth may be due to air pollutants or other environmental factors.

After heavy spring rains, the creek would get dingy and grandpa and I would make the long walk to the Mastengill. Most of the time, we would catch a stringer of mud cats and bream that were delicious when they were cooked by my grandma. We would scale the fish, cut their fins and heads off and grandma would fry them on her wood stove. My favorite meal was the fresh creek fish along with cream potatoes, vinegar slaw, pinto beans, garden ripe tomatoes, and cornbread; of course, all the food except for the catfish and bream were from grandma's garden.

On special fishing occasions, Grandma Ila would pack the old cast iron frying pan, lard, meal, and all the essentials we would need to cook fresh fish on the creek bank. When we got to the Mastengill Hole, grandma would start preparing a place in the woods next to the creek bank where she would cook our meal so that we could have a picnic of fresh fried fish and other foods in the big sack. Those meals prepared by my grandma on that creek bank were some of the best food and wonderful memories I have growing up in the Warrior Mountains.

Two of my cousins also liked to fish as much as I did, but the only place we had while growing up was farm ponds and local creeks. Since one of my favorite places to fish was the Mastengill Hole on the West Fork of Flint Creek, I got my cousins to go with me to that ancestral fishing hole. The fishing spot was on the Alexander Plantation just west of the six acre patch and just south of the Walnut Ford at the mouth of Thompson and West Flint Creeks. The Walnut Ford was the crossing place of the old Poplar Log Cove Road that went just east of the Mastengill Hole.

Sandy, Butch, Danny

Most of the time, my cousins and I would walk from my home which was some two miles to the best fishing waters at the Mastengill; but one day after my granddad had passed away, my cousins Danny and Sandy Welborn decided that we could ride. Therefore, Danny Welborn drove his stepdad's old log truck from my Grandpa

Walker's on the Danville Road to my house which was some ten miles; then, from my house, we rode the old truck the two miles along an old log road to the place we wanted to fish. The problem was that the truck had no brakes and the only way to stop the truck was to gear it down until it got slow enough to cut off the switch to let it roll to a stop.

The only other problem with driving the old log truck was that neither of the three of us had a driver's license, but that did not stop us from trying to save a lot of walking time to our fishing hole. After they got to my house, we loaded my Zebco 33 fishing reel and rod into the cab with their rods since the truck had no bed.

Two steel posts on each side of the truck's steel frame held the logs in place, but provided no place to store our fishing gear; therefore, we barely had enough room for Danny to shift the gear stick in the middle of the floor board. Every time he had to shift, Sandy had to slide into my lap, and after grinding the gears trying to shove the shifter into the correct gear, it sounded like the transmission was going to fall out on the ground.

Finally, we made it to our fishing spot where we tried to catch a stringer of largemouth bass. In the past, we had caught a lot of bass fishing with creek chubs or minnows we called steel backs using cane poles, but most of the time, the bass would get off when we tried to swing them up on the high banks. We would catch the creek chubs in a minnow basket made with scrap screen wire or we would use a minnow seine to catch our live bait. But this particular day, we were armed with our Zebco 33's and some cheap artificial bait; we knew that we were going to catch a bunch of creek bass. Despite our plans to catch a lot of fish, we came up empty handed because the bass were not biting our lures and we did not have a bucket of creek chubs.

On one particular occasion, my cousins and I went to the Mastengill fishing hole on the West Fork of Flint Creek with one of Sandy's school friends whose name was Paul Hogan. We got to a large drift that had caught on a log laying across the creek. At the drift, leaves and debris had built up to about three inches thick and small green grass and vegetation was growing on top of the drift making it look like solid ground. Paul Hogan thought that the drift was solid ground.

Since Paul wanted to cross the creek to the other side, he jumped off a high bank on to the floating drift. After he hit, all we saw was a big splash with his cap floating along with the rest of the trash. Paul went completely out of sight and finally came up covered with all that mess covering his body. At first, we thought that Paul was gone for sure, but he finally popped back up through all those limbs, twigs, leaves, and trash. Seeing this sight, we all rolled on the bank with laughter, and Paul with soaking wet clothes and covered with trash walked out on the far bank. He looked at us and said, *"I had no idea that was water which was over my head."*

Now back to the old log truck ride; after fishing several hours, we finally started back to my house and climbed into the old log truck with all our rods stuck in beside us in the cab. As we got to a high hill on the log road, my cousin Sandy and I decided to jump out and leave the downhill ride with no brakes to Danny. As we were exiting the truck cab, some of the rod tips stuck out the window and the line wrapped around the back tandem tires. The line jerked the rods out of the cab and wrapped them around and between the tires.

Of course, the rods and reels were crushed as the old truck without brakes went wide open down the hill before it finally came to a stop. Sandy and I laughed as we saw Danny bouncing up and down as he went down the steep rocky slope; Danny did not think the ride was very funny. This was the first and last time we used that old truck to go on a fishing trip, but the memories of our adventures and fishing hole will live with us for the rest of our lives.

Buried Waterfall

When I was about eight years old, my dad and I went fishing with my Uncle William Roy Walker to one of the most beautiful yet mysterious places I remember visiting as a small country boy. In the late afternoon as we were making our way down the hill, you could hear the roar long before you could see what was making all that noise.

I remember the eerie sounds of wind and water were emerging from a deep canyon as the noises mixed with the thunderous roar of water crashing into a deep clear pool some 50 feet below. Just upstream was another sound of a waterfall with the same size and magnitude of those we were approaching. The sights and sounds of that afternoon are still a vivid memory of a fishing trip which lasted well into the night.

After dad parked his old Chevrolet car on the side of the road on top of the hill, we walked a long way down a trail to the place called Clear Creek Falls. The double waterfalls were about 250 yards apart with each waterfall dropping some 45 feet from sandstone ledges. These waterfalls were located in Section 9 of Township 12 South and Range 7 West on Clear Creek about a mile from its junction with Sipsey River.

We finally made our way to a large flat rock beside the creek as it plunged over the ledge some 45 feet above the pool of water we were going to fish. After nightfall, the sky was totally black and made the place seem even more mysterious to a young boy. I remember throwing my line with a small lead sinker and hook full of worms into oblivion not knowing when or where it hit except the line stopped coming off my little Zebco 33 reel. After dark you could not see nor hear the bait strike the water because of the roar of the two largest waterfalls in the Warrior Mountains.

Lower Clear Creek Falls

Clear Creek Falls were known by some folks as the "Falls of Black Warrior" and were a major landmark to the Indians and early settlers of the area. The falls became historically important during the Civil War as a campsite for the Union Army.

According to the *Annals of Northwest Alabama* by Carl Elliott (1972), General James H. Wilson formed the world's largest cavalry of 13,480 mounted Union soldiers at Gravely Springs in Lauderdale County, Alabama. The Union troops were armed with Spencer repeating rifles, and they were riding some of the best horses in the country. After being split in Lauderdale County into three units, the brigades of Wilson's army united and camped near Clear Creek Falls on March 25, 1865. One brigade of the Yankees of Northern Aggression traveled by way of Kinlock and Hubbard's Mill in

Lawrence County, Alabama on March 24, 1865, before uniting with the rest of Wilson's command at Clear Creek Falls on the following day.

The 27 year old boy general was Major General James Harrison Wilson; his Union army went from Clear Creek Falls to capture Selma, Alabama, on April 2, 1865, and four other fortified cities in Alabama including Birmingham and Montgomery. On Easter Day on April 16, 1865, Wilson's army captured Columbus, Georgia, which was considered the last major battle of the Civil War. During May 1865, Wilson's army captured Confederate President Jefferson Davis as he was fleeing through Georgia.

As a young boy on an exciting fishing trip, I was totally unconcerned with the past history of the falls; however, after reaching the edge of a large flat rock cliff next to the creek which was plunging some 50 feet, we set down our lantern, bait, and fishing equipment. We selected a place next to the creek on a flat sandstone rock at the edge of the bluff. I was in total amazement that we were going to fish off that cliff some 50 feet above the pool below. At first, a feeling of fear overwhelmed me as I thought about a fish pulling me off the high perch into the swirling pool of water a long way below where I was sitting.

Major General James Harrison Wilson

As soon as we had cast our bait into the pool of water many feet below, we began catching bream on the worms. We fished late into the night by the light of the old lantern and only caught a few small catfish. I will never forget the trouble of trying to turn the little reel handles to get a fish to the top of the falls. On almost each occasion, the fish would get loose before we could get them to our precarious perch high above our fishing hole. We fished until about midnight before taking our catch up the hill to the old car.

Today, the old fishing hole along with all its glory and history is gone; so are the spectacular falls of the Warrior Mountains. A few years after the memorable fishing trip about 1957, Lewis Smith Lake Dam flooded the great falls in the early 1960's. Now only a depth finder on a boat can locate the falls of Clear Creek on Smith Lake. As you cross over the top of the falls in a boat, the depth finder will instantly drop or rise about 45 feet. The great falls of the Warrior Mountains now lie deep under the backwaters of Smith Lake with all their history and beauty buried forever in a watery tomb.

Upper and Lower Clear Creek Falls

Trapping in Hill Country

Trap Line

On a cold December morning before daylight, my grandpa Authur Wilburn left his old log house with his Uncle Hiram Johnson to check trap lines on Indian Creek. Grandpa and I had made a deal to work our trap lines during my Christmas vacation and split the money. I had been staying each night at my grandpa's house, but mother made me stay home that night because grandpa's uncle was spending the night.

I was a small fifth grade boy attending Speake School, but had arranged with my grandpa to run the trap line during the two weeks we were out for Christmas. We had set over 100 traps that stretched a circuit of nearly 20 miles through the Warrior Mountains. The complete route was so long that the trip would require us to start prior to daybreak and continue many times after dark. My Grandpa Arthur never owned a vehicle; therefore, we walked all the places we trapped, hunted, and fished.

My grandpa's home was on the west side of Mull Johnson Mountain about five hundred yards downhill from the Hattie Hogan Spring. The east edge of their land was bordered by a 40-acre block of U.S. Forest Service Property. The south and west side of their land was bordered by the vast Alexander Plantation, to the north was Cedar Mountain, to the west was Brushy Mountain, and to the southwest was Sugar Camp Hollow. I was supposed to be at grandpa's house before daylight, but my parents overslept. By the time I got to my grandparents' house, Grandpa Wilburn and Uncle Hiram had been gone about one hour. I told my grandma that I could catch up with the men. Reluctantly, she allowed me to strike out by myself.

About 7:30 that morning, I caught up with Grandpa Arthur and Uncle Hiram just east of the Mastengill Hole on the West Fork of Flint Creek. By the time I finally caught up with the trappers, I had gone about two miles on a heavily overcast and cold day. At that time, they were walking the Poplar Log Cove Trail that crossed the Flint Creek at the mouth of Thompson Creek on the Old Alexander Plantation which was always called the Walnut Ford. The ford was known as Walnut Ford because the bottomland along Thompson Creek was covered with gigantic black walnut trees.

At the Walnut Ford was a large field known as the Cyclone New Ground. The field lay to the southwest of the ford and was cleared by a cyclone or tornado. When the cyclone came through, it blew the top off Jake Alexander's old plantation house. The house had been built by his father Thomas Jefferson Alexander and there was actually four plantation houses built on the same floor plan. According to my Uncle Curtis, a hired hand, Ed Welborn, was upstairs in bed with the typhoid fever; the storm left Mr. Welborn in bed, but removed the roof.

From Walnut Ford at the mouth of Thompson Creek, the Flint Creek Trail proceeded toward High House Hill passing between the Nichols Cemetery and the Gray Cemetery. The trail crossed Gillespie Branch and up High House Hill, and passed southwest along the ridge crossing the High Town Path and on toward Brushy Creek. The Poplar Log Cove Road preceded northwest from the mouth of Thompson Creek toward Moulton with the southeast portion we were walking going toward Poplar Log Cove Spring at the headwaters of West Flint Creek.

The old Poplar Log Cove Spring became the home site of Mr. Tom Poole and the beautiful valley was known by many people as Tom Poole Hollow. The road went right by the edge of Mr. Tom Poole's yard. The spring was just a few yards behind Mr. Poole's house and the branch ran beside his home site. In Mr. Poole's day, all travelers would stop at his house to get water before heading to Basham Gap and Cave.

From Mr. Poole's, an old road continued southeasterly toward Piney Grove and was called the Black Warriors' Path. When I was a young boy following my grandpa on the trap line, these old roads I speak of were only trails that were worn deep into the hills and hollows they traversed. At the time of my trap line adventures, the old roads were abandoned, over grown, and not used by any motor vehicles, but they provided easy walking through the forest.

The morning was extremely cold and I did not take enough time to dress as warmly as I should. I remember the cold just seeping through my clothes every time we stopped to check or re-set our traps. The only traps we checked while heading to our final destination at the upper end of Indian Creek were those which would be out of the way on our return home. The complete round trip was some twenty miles which ended approximately four hours after first darkness.

I had caught grandpa and Uncle Hiram just past the mouth of McVay Hollow. As we proceeded along the Old Poplar Log Cove Trail, I listened to the two men talk about the people who lived along the old road when they were young boys. Even though the trail was no longer an old horse and wagon road, my Grandpa Arthur always tried to point out where everyone had a cabin.

On the north side of the Pearson Field was a large log cabin near the mouth of Lindsey Hollow. At the upper end of the Six Acre Patch, which was the last southeastern most field on the Alexander Place, was large log house with three chimneys and a hand dug rock-walled well forty feet from the house. Between the house and well was a dug out rectangular hole that may have been a root cellar.

In the mouth of McVay Hollow on the north side of the branch, a large log house with an old rock chimney was rotting down. It was probably the home of a member of the McVay family. As I got to the old McVay Place, I was extremely happy to see my Grandpa Wilburn and Uncle Hiram Johnson near the middle of the Six Acre Patch. I had already made up my mind to go back home if I had not caught up with them before the last field on the Alexander Place.

We proceeded south and east out of the Six Acre Patch, through the woods past the three old chimneys to the Matt Pearson Old Field. We continued past the mouth of Lindsey Hollow, across Blizzard Branch, crossed the Blowing Spring Road, and up the hill just south of the Old Friendship Cemetery; we passed the old cave just south of the road on the hill and back into the West Flint Creek bottom toward Indian Creek.

At the mouth of Indian Creek, we sat down on the side of the old trail and ate our lunch. As always, Grandpa Arthur offered me some of his food. We never carried water because we knew the location of every spring and we would sometimes drink from the little feeder streams. After finishing lunch, we went up Indian Creek to check the most distant traps.

Butch, Grandpa Arthur, and Mike with our trapline catch in February 1964 just a month before grandpa died

On the east side of Indian Creek not far from its junction with Flint, the old Indian Creek Trail led south toward Hickory Grove. The trail serpentined its way down the hill from the east and turned south along the creek's eastern bank, then traversed up the valley to the High Town Path at the creek's headwaters.

On Indian Creek, we had three raccoons within a short distance. I placed the coons in a tow sack which was swung across my back. The sack of animals helped keep me warm on the long trek back toward home. All three helped bear the burden of animals. We would not clean the animals in the woods because we kept the meat to eat and to sell the surplus.

When we got back to the Pearson Field about 4:00 p.m. that afternoon, snow began falling so thick you could hardly see over twenty yards. By the time we got back to the Walnut Ford and hit the Flint Creek Trail which led toward the Alexander Bridge and Cedar Mountain, the snow was three to four inches deep. I well remember looking into the sky, watching those big flakes of snow falling like a swarm of bees. By the time we reached the old wooden bridge, the snow was five to six inches deep and was well over my shoe tops. My feet felt like chunks of ice.

Uncle Hiram said he was walking home. He lived about two miles west from the bridge, past the old Alexander plantation home, and past the entrance of the Welborn-Alexander Cemetery. Grandpa and I wished Uncle Hiram well and thanked him for helping carry our day's catch. I remember well that grandpa looked at me and said, *"Butch we have about a dozen traps left on the Old Suck Branch and into Beech Bottoms. Let's*

Snow in February 1958

check those tonight because they will be snowed in for the next few days." I agreed with grandpa even though I felt like I was freezing to death.

We got to the Old Suck Branch and found a large boar mink in our first trap. We continued checking all the traps before crossing the south end of Brushy Mountain toward home. I was tickled to death to get to grandpa's home by about 8:30 p.m. that night. It was a great feeling to stand next to the old wood stove and thaw out from a day that was extremely cold. Shortly after warming by the fire, I started skinning the day's catch. Grandpa never cleaned the animals; that job was left to me and my grandmother. Sometime around midnight, we had all the hides stretched and all coons and possums soaking in pans of water in the refrigerator. The foot of snow stayed on the ground for about a week.

The above true story was blazed into my mind as an unforgettable memory of the largest snowfall I had experienced in my lifetime of walking the Indian trails of the Warrior Mountains. It represents only one day that I walked portions of the Flint Creek Trail and Poplar Log Cove Trail. Since that day in the late 1950s, I have walked these old Indian trails many times, which were also walked by my Indian ancestors for hundreds of years; I feel the spirits of my ancestors when I walk the trails that they walked.

Bobcat Hole

On the southwestern end of Mull Johnson Mountain is a unique hole in a limestone outcropping about half way between the top and bottom of the hillside. The hole is unique in that water can always be heard crashing against the rocks way down deep in the mountain. When I was a small Celtic Indian boy, my grandpa showed me the hole and told me that it was used by many different kinds of furbearing animals. Grandpa Arthur always told me that the hole was at one time very dangerous because the near vertical shaft at the entrance was wide open. Grandpa and his dad, who was my great grandfather Sandy Welborn, placed large rocks over the hole to prevent people and dogs falling into the cave opening.

My great granddaddy had also trapped at that hole when he was growing up, and it was on a cold wet day on a trap line with his son Arthur that my great granddad, Sandy Welborn, contracted pneumonia and died within a few days. At that time, penicillin was not available, and even though he was a tough Celtic Indian man, he lost his fight against the disease. He died within a mile west of the bobcat hole in a large clapboard house that stood on the hill just east of the Alexander Bridge that crossed the West Fork of Flint Creek.

After many years had passed since the death of my great grandfather Sandy Pascal Welborn, I was trapping the bobcat hole. That hole was not completely blocked, and raccoons and bobcats still used a small opening into the underground waterfall on the mountainside. Therefore, the entrance of the hole became an important place that I would trap in the long tradition of my ancestors.

The reason I called the opening the bobcat hole is because my cousin and I caught four bobcats in one trapping season at the entrance to the cave. The set was made at the opening of the hole and had a drag brush attached to the trap. A drag brush was used to prevent a dead pull that would allow larger animals to sometimes get their paw out of the trap. The brush could be dragged away from the set, but would leave a trail in the leaves until it finally hung up on briars or small bushes.

Sandy Pascal Welborn

One day, I was checking the trap at the hole and was not paying close attention as I was approaching the area. I had no idea that a big male bobcat was in my trap and had pulled the drag brush along the trail that I was walking. The bobcat obviously had heard me coming along the trail and waited in ambush. It was a good thing that the drag brush had hung solidly because when the bobcat jumped toward me, I was caught completely off guard, scared to death, and froze momentarily in my tracks. It did not take me but a second to put a 22 bullet between the bobcat's eyes. From then on, I approached that particular trap with extreme caution.

A Celtic Indian friend of mine Michael Offutt related a similar story that I must share: *"A local beagle club was having problems with predators getting in and killing out the rabbits they had stocked for their dogs to run, and had called Lamar Marshall and me in to trap them. We made a bobcat set next to the private dirt road that led to the club, and had secured it to a discarded wooden shipping pallet. The next morning, the pallet and all was gone. Our friend, Lamar, thinking a large hound must have gotten in it and dragged it off, went searching the brush for it. He immediately came panting out of a briar thicket, announcing that we had caught "a big tom" and he was in the briar patch."*

"I wanted to get some live pictures of it before we had to dispatch the bobcat, so I began easing into the brush with my camera looking for its location. All of a sudden, I felt a push from behind. I stumbled forward trying to keep to my feet, wanting to avoid falling in with the cat. As I reeled away, (I'm sure I called our friend Lamar everything but a child of God at that point), he was laughing hysterically. I was not amused. Once I regained my composure, while keeping an eye on my companion, I was able to get some decent pictures. After a single round to the cat's head from his .22 rifle, it lay lifeless."

"I carried the rifle and my camera back to the truck while our buddy retrieved the "dead" bobcat. I was sitting on the tailgate, putting things away when I heard him yell. There standing in the middle of the road, holding at least 35 pounds of cat by the hind legs; he shouted, "He ain't dead, come shoot him again"! Sure enough, the big old tom was beginning to squirm in his grip. I calmly asked, "Do you promise to never push me at another bobcat, and will you say you're sorry"? He yelled back, "I'm not kidding, shoot 'em again!" And he wasn't kidding, that cat was getting lively. I asked again, "Are you gonna promise never to do it again, and are you gonna say you're sorry?" At the top of his voice, he said, "I can't keep holding him, and I can't let him go. Come shoot this thing!" I replied, "You gotta promise and say you're sorry!" "Alright, alright, I promise and I'm sorry. Now shoot it," he answered. Smiling broadly, I took my .22 pistol from my pocket and walked up a put a couple of more shots into the big cat's head, which ended the struggle."

Now back to my story about the bobcat hole; in addition to bobcats, I caught raccoons at the entrance to the underground waterfall. On one occasion, I broke the butt plate of my 410 shotgun on a coon that got away. The incident occurred one afternoon after school when I was checking my trap that had a large boar coon that was well alive. In order to prevent putting a big hole in the pelt with my shotgun, I decided to take a big stick and knock the coon in the head which I did.

The problem was that I knocked the coon out of the trap; my stick broke into, and I had only dazed the animal. He started toward the hole; therefore, I hit at him with the butt of my shotgun. Instead of hitting the coon, the stock plate hit a rock. I was not about to grab that mad coon and he got into the hole and escaped. At that point besides being very angry about losing my coon, my favorite squirrel gun had a broken butt plate.

My friend Michael Offutt also related a similar coon story worthy to share: *"I was helping our mutual friend Lamar Marshall run his trap line along the waterways of Blount County. He had been laid off and was trapping that season to provide for his family. We were targeting mink and raccoon, and an occasional fox if we found their sign. The clouds were approaching as we launched the canoe into a stretch of the Locust Fork of the Warrior River. A big rain was coming and we had to pull all the traps before the river rose and washed them away. A young coon was caught in one right on the edge of the water. We slid our craft up to the bank, and our friend, got out with his "trapping stick". It was a long hardwood staff that he had found one day on the river that had been de-barked by beavers and had seasoned out on the rocks lining the banks. He had fashioned a steel hook on one end for retrieving traps that were underwater. After administering a couple of hard whacks to the raccoon's head, it rolled over kicking and then lay motionless. He released its leg from the trap and pulled the stake."*

"Before he threw the set and the animal into the canoe, I told him, "You'd better make sure that coon is dead!" Confidently, he replied, "Oh, it is dead alright," as it landed between the seats of our boat. A little while later, on downstream, we were picking our way through a rock garden, a shallow shoal with protruding rocks. I was in the front of the canoe, helping guide the laden craft between them when the clamor and sudden violent rocking of our boat happened. It sounded like all hell had broken loose and I firmly anchored the end my paddle into the rock bed trying to steady us and prevent us from being capsized."

"I had never heard such violent sounding growling and snarling, and it was coming directly from behind me. I wheeled my head around to see a sight I shall never forget. Our friend was standing on the very tip end of the stern, wildly fighting back the resurrected raccoon with his paddle. After knocking the beast into unconsciousness again, we resorted to drowning it for good measure. The rest of the trip went well except for the rains caught us and I got hypothermia so bad that I could barely walk up to the bridge where we took out. It took a while with the truck's heater running full blast before I was able to recover; oh, the memories!"

Once again back to my bobcat hole story about the coon and my 410 shotgun. The butt plate of my gun was broken and I was totally disgusted that the coon had got away. I was aggravated at breaking a piece of my gun and could not afford to buy a new one; therefore, I took epoxy glue and repaired the broken piece. The glue hardened and filled in the broken butt plate, and it is still holding today.

Anytime I see the gun, I get to share my story of the coon that got away and the patched butt plate provides a great conversation piece of the little shotgun. To some people, the story may sound frivolous, but at that time, raccoon hides were bringing about fourteen dollars each and the carcass would sell for another three to five dollars. Back in the early 1960's, that was big money to a fourteen year old Celtic Indian boy roaming through the Warrior Mountains trying to make a little hunting and trapping cash.

A few years ago when I gave my old 410 shotgun to my five year old grandson Brady Sutton (White Raven), I told him the story about how I had broken the butt plate trying to kill the coon. It is my hope that White Raven will remember the story that goes along with his passed down shotgun, and that he to can pass the gun to his grandson.

In addition, I need to take White Raven to the bobcat hole and show him the opening and let him listen to the water falling way beneath the ground. I need to tell him that his ancestors long ago listened to that same sound of the crashing waters. It is good to keep old traditions alive and the only way we can do that is pass it down to the future generations! Since my grandchildren including White Raven and Little Turtle will be the next modern Celtic Indian kids of the Warrior Mountains, I must pass along all I know so that they too can share my love of the land of our ancestors. My Granddaughter Ashtyn Allred has developed a deep love for all of God's creatures; I am sure she will share my love of the ways of the wild!

Mink for Christmas

As I was growing up near the foot of the Warrior Mountains, my parents were not making a bunch of money working in local shirt factories for minimum wage or slightly a little higher. Therefore, we survived with the bare essentials in order for my parents to pay bills and buy a few groceries. One particular Christmas was extremely difficult for my family and there was not enough money for presents for my siblings and me. Times were tough financially for my folks living in a little frame house in Hickory Flats Hollow near the base of Mull Johnson Mountain.

Since my dad was aware of the trapping skills that I had learned from my grandpa, he asked me to help him catch some furbearing animals that he could sell for a few dollars that would be used for Christmas. Dad told me that he and mom would not have money for Christmas unless our trapping was successful. If we caught any furbearing animals, dad planned to sell the hides and use the money so he and my mom could buy us kids some presents for Christmas; otherwise, he said, *"There will be no Christmas at our house."*

I had bought my own steel traps with the money I had earned from picking cotton and from the selling of hides from coon and possum hunting adventures, in addition to my trapping activities; therefore, I had accumulated several steel traps of various sizes from zero to number two double springs. The various sizes of traps were used for different types of animals that I was trying to catch. The bigger the animal that I tried to catch usually required a larger trap in order to hold the animal securely. Sometimes a large animal could pull out of a small trap.

Anyway, my dad sought my assistance for acquiring Christmas money; for that reason, this was the only time I remember that he and I worked together to catch some furbearing animals. My dad did not have a trapping license; he could not afford to buy a license for a short period prior to Christmas to trap for a little extra cash.

However, dad would take the chance that he would not be caught trapping without a license; at that time, I was too young to be required to have a trapping license. Therefore, dad and I loaded the gear we needed in the trunk of our old family car so we could travel outside the area that grandpa and I were already trapping. Some of the more distant places near the headwaters of the West Fork of Flint Creek were out of the area for my grandpa and me to run a trap line because it was too far to walk.

After loading up some of my traps in our old car, we headed into the Warrior Mountains where I thought we might catch some furbearing animals for some quick cash. Dad wanted to try catching mink or raccoons because he knew they would bring the best price, and he did not have long to get some money for Christmas. Since grandpa and I could only work our trap line as far as Indian Creek, Dad and I headed out to the Chenault Bridge on the upper end of the West Fork of Flint Creek. This area was some two miles east of the closest trap that grandpa and I had on our trap line.

The Chenault Bridge was named after the Isaac Chenault family that had lived on the top of the hill to the south of the bridge prior to the creation of the William B. Bankhead National Forest. The creek bottom dad and I decided to trap was on the United States Forest Service property at the lower end of Poplar Log Cove and east of the bridge. The upper end of the cove was cleared with large fields and was about one and a half miles to the east of where we planned to trap for a few days. The Poplar Log Cove had been settled by members of the Hunter, Doss, Hampton, and Poole families in the 1800's.

We went up the creek a little piece from Chenault Bridge toward the junction of Wiggins Creek and the West Fork of Flint Creek. Here we found some good sign of mink activity; therefore, we made several sets trying to catch some of the more expensive mink that at the time was bringing some twenty dollars for each big boar mink. Dad and I knew that we did not have but a few days to make the money needed to have some kind of Christmas and I was hoping we would not be disappointed. My grandpa had taught me well on how to find the right spot and how to make an effective trap set so as to catch the wiliest animals.

Grandpa had showed me many times where the mink had a habit of using undercut banks next to deep areas in the stream looking for crawfish, fish, and other things to eat. Armed with this knowledge, dad and I placed our traps at the bottom of the steep sides of the washed out banks; these areas created a perfect location and runway to catch the mink between the edge of the high overhanging bank and the deep water.

Patiently, I took my knife and cut out a small depression in the mud bottom of the runway the size of the trap; then I placed the trap so that the jaws were even with the rest of the ground. Very gently I placed a single layer of wet leaves over the trap to make runway level, and reached into the creek for a handful of mud which I squeezed over the leaves. As the muddy drops covered the leaves, you could not detect that the trap was ready to catch a mink because it was perfectly camouflaged and looked like it was part of the original clay bank. Sure enough the method worked to perfection and the next day, dad and I recovered two big boar mink that had got caught in our traps.

We brought the mink to the house where I skinned them and placed their hides on my drying boards. The animal's fur was always against the wooden board and his pelt was on the outside so it would dry completely. The mink drying boards were made from thin white oak boards that my grandpa made with his froe, wooden dogwood fork, and wooden hammer.

Grandpa Arthur would take a bolt of white oak some four feet long and split off several boards; then he shaped the thin boards with his pocket knife to a rounded point for the mink's head. The boards were some four feet long and three inches to five inches wide depending on the size of the animal. Other drying boards were developed for the different sizes and shapes of the furbearing animals that we caught.

After we stretched the mink hides, my dad and I drove to Mt. Hope to see my fur buyer Mr. Earl Martin. Even though the mink hides were not dry, Mr. Martin gave my dad twenty dollars for each of the big boar mink. The sale of these two mink hides was shortly before Christmas day; my mother and daddy made a trip to town to buy Christmas presents with the forty dollars that was collected from the sale of the mink furs.

After this Christmas and before my dad died, I heard him say many times that we would not have had Christmas that year if it was not for the luck of catching those two boar mink. After that short Christmas trapping episode, I do not remember my dad ever trapping with me again. Such was the times when I was a young Celtic Indian boy who trapped with his dad on the creek bottoms of the West Fork of Flint Creek in the mountains of North Alabama.

Hunting in Appalachia

Bow for an Indian Boy

One day when I was about eight years old, my great grandpa, George Curtis, told me to help him with a special gift that he was going to make for me. I was extremely excited and could not wait until the next day when we would start the project.

My great grandpa, George Baxter Curtis, was a great woodworker and made walking sticks, ax handles, hoe handles, hammer handles, and all kinds of hickory wood handles that he sold for a little extra money. My great grandpa's love in his last years was his woodworking activities. He made and sold hundreds of his walking sticks and handles for all kinds of tools out of the finest hickory. Mr. Charlie Stewart of Hartselle would buy bundles of these walking sticks and handles to sell in his store.

My great grandpa George Baxter Curtis, 1/8 Cherokee, made me a bow before he died

I would stand and watch grandpa with his old pocket knife smooth the wood handles until they were perfect. He was also an old timey blacksmith. For hours, I would turn the handle of the blower to heat the metal until red hot. When the metal got just right for him, grandpa would take tongs and weld the metal by beating it with his hammer on the anvil.

As a reward for me helping him, grandpa told me he was

going to make me a traditional Cherokee bow. The next morning I was in a hurry walking and running down the dusty road to grandpa's house next door. I could hardly wait as grandpa gathered the tools that we would need to cut down a perfect white oak tree.

Finally, we were on our way to the woods loaded down with the tools. As we walked up the mountainside a long way, grandpa would inspect each white oak we passed. After looking at several white oaks, he finally selected one that met all his qualifications. He looked up and down the tree, walked around the tree, looked at me, and said, *"This is the perfect tree to make you a bow."*

My great grandpa George Curtis' woodworking and blacksmith shop notice homemade mule drawn hay rake in front

We sawed with the old cross cut until my arms were beginning to ache, but I was not about to quit until the tree was down. At last the big tree fell and I felt a great relief; however, grandpa marked off about eight feet and we begin to saw the trunk again. After the log section was cut, my great grandpa took metal wedges, a sledge hammer, and began to split the tree into two halves.

After the metal wedges started splitting the tree, large wooden wedges were used to finish the job. The two halves were then split again into quarters. Grandpa took each quarter and removed the red heart wood with the wedges. After he removed the heartwood, grandpa split each sapwood quarter section and created a total of eight pieces he called bolts. After removing the bark, he then placed two of the best bolts on his shoulders and I gathered as much of the tools as I could take; we started the walk back home.

George Curtis and Brady Walker

When the bow was finished, grandpa took several pieces of the oak and began making arrows. He carefully shaped the arrows and finally placed split turkey feathers for fletching which were attached with waxed string. Grandpa also took the waxed string to make the bow string. The bow string was made of many strands of the waxed string which he twisted together leaving a loop on each end. After the bow dried, grandpa again twisted the string until it was the correct length for the bow. Grandpa always kept a big block of beeswax for waterproofing which he rubbed up and down the string.

Finally when the bow and arrows were dried and ready, grandpa instructed me on being careful while I handled the bow because it was a dangerous weapon. The bow was nearly five feet long, very strong, and was an excellent piece of my grandpa's craftsmanship.

My first memorable hunting trip with the homemade white oak bow was to the Mastengill Hole on the West Fork of Flint Creek. The Mastengill Hole was named because a man of the same name had drowned in the creek at that location. My hunt was in late August and the creek had dried up into potholes full of fish. I shot the fish with my bow as they would come to the surface. After killing some 20 fish, I headed to my Grandma Ila Wilburn's house because she always cooked the best fish dinner I ever ate. My favorite meal she cooked was fresh fish, pinto beans, cream potatoes, vinegar slaw, with hot corn bread sticks.

My great Grandpa Curtis gave me a labor of his love that will never be forgotten; he gave me a traditional weapon that our ancestors used for thousands of years. Someone finally took my homemade white oak bow; I cried at the loss of such an important piece of my personal history, when I was a young Indian boy roaming the woodlands hunting with my bow.

For the rest of my life, the bow will be my choice for hunting. Presently, I have taken over 110 whitetail deer; I have never killed one with a gun and have no intentions to ever do so. I thank God for people like my great grandpa who filled my childhood days with such precious memories. You should also leave a lasting memory with a child, but make sure the memories are worth sharing for generations to come.

Grandpa's Love

As a little boy growing up at the edge of the Bankhead Forest of the Warrior Mountains, I was carried to the woods by my Grandpa Arthur Wilburn when I was too small to make a long trek with my short legs. My first memory was setting on a log beside my grandpa watching a gray squirrel cutting a hickory nut high up in a very large tree. I remember him trying to get me to be still and quite so he could kill the squirrel for us to eat. After waiting for what seemed to be an eternity, grandpa finally killed the squirrel with a 22 caliber rifle.

I learned at a very young age to love to eat squirrel tongues, cheek muscles, and finally the brains. The head was my favorite piece of squirrel to eat, and as a young Celtic Indian boy, I was raised on squirrels and other wild meat. It was in this old timey tradition that I loved to be in the woods hunting and learning as much as I could about the forest; I lived the old ways and the ways of the wild.

When I was about five years old, me and my dad traded "Ole Blue" for my own 22 rifle. Ole Blue was my big blue tick hound that would knock me down when he was excited about getting some petting. The dog was much bigger than I was and sometimes difficult for me to control. I really hated to trade my old hound dog, but dad had told me that a black man in Oakville had a rifle he would trade for a good squirrel or coon dog.

I loved my dog, but I really wanted a 22 rifle of my own so I could go squirrel hunting with my grandpa. I agreed to the trade; therefore, my dad and I loaded up Ole Blue and headed to Oakville. The man promised me that he would take care of Ole Blue and that I could come visit him anytime I wanted. Finally, I had my own bolt action single shot 22 squirrel rifle and could not wait to show it to grandpa.

Squirrels were the favorite game of Grandpa Arthur and Butch

My first hunts with grandpa were not very long, but their memories have lasted a lifetime. He was very patient with me and made me understand the importance of being still and quite while hunting squirrels. Grandpa had a double-barreled 12 gauge shotgun that I could barely pick up, but he always let me have the first shot or two with my rifle. If the squirrel started running away, grandpa seemed to always be a sure shot with the big gun.

My old 22 rifle was difficult for me to hunt with because I did not have the strength to pull the plunger back. The rifle had to be cocked by pulling the plunger back with your thumb and index finger. Initially, it was probably a good idea and benefit to me and others that I could not cock the rifle which made it much safer for me to carry the gun through the woods. When we would get ready to shoot at a squirrel, grandpa would cock the rifle for me. For the first year he carried me squirrel hunting, grandpa was always there to cock my rifle and always give me the opportunity to shoot the squirrels.

The Christmas when I was six years old, my grandpa ordered a brand new Remington single shot bolt action 22 rifle. The new rifle cocked automatically when the bolt was pushed forward, but would not shoot until you flipped the safety button off. The safety on the new 22 rifle was easy for me to push on and off, and grandpa allowed me to practice my shooting accuracy with the new rifle.

Shortly after he purchased the new gun, we went squirrel hunting with both of us carrying our 22's. After our squirrel dogs treed, we saw the squirrel hugging a limb high in the tree. Instead of cocking my rifle, grandpa handed me his new 22 rifle and took my old rifle. He whispered, *"Just push the safety off and kill that squirrel."* For the rest of the day, grandpa let me hunt with his new rifle.

When we got back home, grandpa asked me if I liked his new rifle. I told him I loved the gun because I did not have to have his help to shoot it. He then asked me, *"Butch would like to trade your old rifle even for my new 22 Remington rifle? I like your old rifle and you like my new one so well that we might as well trade rifles without any boot."* Grandpa said he could shoot my rifle better; therefore, I agreed to trade. Of course, I was tickled to death and was glowing with pride over my new rifle that I could shoot by myself.

Butch and Grandpa Arthur were hunting and trapping partners

At the time, I did not understand why he really wanted to trade, but grandpa was my best friend in the world. Now, many years later, I realize the love my grandpa had for me. I believe to this day that my grandpa intended for me to have the new rifle when he ordered it.

On March 15, 1964, my Grandpa Arthur drowned near the Houston area of Smith Lake, and I lost the best friend in the world; the best friend that I have ever had in my life. Today, I still cherish the 22 rifle he traded me when I was a little boy, not only because of its memories, but because it was truly a gift of love that I will never forget. Before it is too late, you need to make a precious memory for a child that will last a lifetime, but be sure those memories are worth being shared and remembered!

Conclusion

Finishing a Dream at Oakville

Many years ago, my dad, uncles, grandpa, and I would go fishing at Oakville Pond to catch crappie for the dinner table. Oakville was the closest place to where we lived that we could catch a mess of crappie. The pond was located on the property of Mr. John Wiley and Mr. P. B. Lowery; all my folks liked to fish for crappie in the lake.

We would sometimes go to Oakville Pond through John Wiley's hog pasture. I hated to fish from the bank of the Wiley property when I was a small boy because of the huge hogs that roamed the pasture around the lake; those hogs were big enough to eat me for lunch. Also to get to the water, we would go by P. B. Lowery's home and drive around a field to fish near the dam. Sometimes we would go by Mr. John McCay's house along an old field road that actually crossed the west corner of the big ceremonial Indian mound; most times we would stop and walk to the top of the mound and view the surrounding flatlands and lake.

Initially, Oakville Pond was formed because hogs filled the sink and stopped the water from flowing underground to the creek. In the original surveys around 1817, a huge spring at the upper end of a long depression flowed with an abundance of water that poured into a huge crevasse and disappeared underground. The fourth judge of Lawrence County, Alabama, Charles Gibson built a hog pen around the sink and the hogs eventually stopped the water from flowing underground to the Big Oak Spring directly west of the crevasse on the edge of West Flint Creek. The area flooded and a disease called the "Bloody Flux" led to the death of many residents; the Town of Oakville was abandoned around 1850.

Mr. P. B. Lowery had dug out a large portion of his part of Oakville Pond by a big drag line. Howell Smith ran the dragline machine; he would cast the big bucket by swinging the boom and releasing the cables at the correct time. Howell Smith was so good with the dragline that he could cast the steel bucket as good as I could cast my little Zebco 33 spinning reel. He dug out the Lowery portion of the pond to the big Oakville Spring that was at the upper end of the long depression; the spring in the early days had been the center of the square of the Town of Oakville that was incorporated in 1833.

Eventually, John Wiley and P. B. Lowery decided to reduce and control the amount of water that was backed up into the pond by dredging and blasting out a canal from the pond to the West Fork of Flint Creek. The two men secured the help of the

Corps of Engineers who devised a plan to blow the ditch with dynamite; holes were drilled from the pond to the creek and the holes were filled with explosives. In two separate blasts the ditch was formed between Oakville Pond and West Flint Creek; school children from Speake School were allowed to come to the big Indian mound at Oakville to watch the explosions.

According to the people who attended the blast, there were two separate explosions; the first blew the channel from the pond to about half way to the creek and the second blast completed the ditch to the creek. This was justified by the Corps of Engineers by reducing the mosquito breeding populations that caused yellow fever and malaria; along the Tennessee River Valley, the Corps drained a lot of wet lands to protect the people from mosquito borne diseases. However, the ditch did not completely drain the lake which had a great population of crappie, bass, bluegill, and other species of fish; fish from the Tennessee River could swim into the pond during times of flooding.

Since Oakville Pond had a lot of button willow bushes that grew out into the water several feet from the bank, my dad Brady Walker and I would use an old flat bottomed wooden boat that a black friend of his kept in the pond. The only problem with the boat was that it leaked and I spent most of my time dipping out the water that would always get my feet wet. I remember one particular crappie fishing trip in March that was extremely cold; my dad and I caught a bunch of crappie by placing minnows around the bushes with long canes. Even though we were catching crappie, I was freezing to death and my feet were wet on top of being cold.

As we fished the pond when I was a little boy, I remember looking at the big ceremonial Indian mound and the burial mound while we fished for crappie, bass, catfish, and bream; both mounds were in sight of the pond and my dad told me that my Indian ancestors may have helped build the structures. We had two relatives buried on top of the Copena burial mound at Oakville. Elizabeth Walker was buried on top of the mound; she was the wife of Dr. Tandy Walker, Jr., who is buried in the old McDonald Cemetery in Moulton.

Tandy Walker Sr., who secured the release of Martha Crawley from the Creeks in 1812, was the brother of my fourth great grandpa William Walker; Tandy and William were Indian traders and are buried side by side at Old Nectar. In the late 1700's, the Chickamauga Indian village at Oakville was a trading center at the cross roads of the Black Warriors' Path and the Coosa or Muscle Shoals Path. In addition, a distant Aunt Sarah Walker who married William Hodges was also buried on top of the mound; she was the daughter of William Walker.

As a small boy, I walked the surrounding fields in the creek bottoms along the West Fork of Flint Creek looking for arrowheads; I also roamed over the top of the mounds and I visualize these Indian mounds being protected. The little mound was also in a pasture which enclosed hogs which had rooted up tombstones and made a mess of the burial place; a 100 feet long pig parlor was built against the base of the burial mound, and years later was the first thing that I got to help tear down after the purchase of the property. The big mound which contained a little over an acre of flat ground on top was being farmed with corn and the last crop I remember being on the big mound was watermelons. Mr. Red Wiley gave my dad and me five or six of those big round green watermelons; they were some of the best watermelons I ever ate.

Then fast forward some thirty years, I became director of the Lawrence County Schools' Indian Education Program. I spent the first several years with the Indian program trying to find a permanent location for our Indian program office and museum which was temporarily housed in the old auto body shop of the county's vocational building in Moulton. One day a series of events began to happen; in the spring of 1990, Jane Weeks, Director of Alabama Indian Affairs Commission, called and asked if I would like our program to participate in an Indian Youth Leadership Project; of course, I jumped on the idea.

In addition, Dr. Don Hinds was assistant director of the Alabama Department of Economic and Community Affairs (ADECA); he was directing the funding for the Appalachian Regional Commission (ARC) Indian Youth Leadership Project and loved hiking. He asked if I would take him and his wife into the Sipsey Wilderness; several people including the families of Larry Black, Larry LouAllen of the Lawrence County Commission, Charles Borden, Lamar Marshall, along with Dr. Hinds and his wife got together for a camping weekend in the wilderness area with me and my family.

Dr. Don Hinds and our group spent the weekend hiking, horseback riding, and enjoying the wilderness area of the forest; after this adventure, a lasting relationship between Dr. Hinds and I was formed. Dr. Hinds kept up with all the activities going on at Oakville and was an integral person in seeing the facility completed; for years after the project was finished, Dr. Don Hinds would stop by the facility and spend hours with me.

The Indian youth leadership project was funded by the Appalachian Regional Commission that was basically controlled by United States Congressman Tom Bevill; Congressman Bevill wanted to do some economic development in Lawrence County and provided some $62,000 dollars to purchase some 26 acres of property containing the two Indian mounds from Mr. Travis Clark and Ms. Joyce Lowery Hames. The Indian youth project included the following Lawrence County Indian students: Stacy Lemley and Tracy Parker who were the youth supervisors; Jessica Bowling, DeWayne Peebles, Joey

LouAllen, Michelle Waldrep, April Sivley, Lori Black, Mark Evans, Chad Harville, April Braidfoot, Michael Gibson, Christy Loosier, and Christina _____ were members of the team.

One day from Washington, D.C., Dr. Hinds called me and asked if he got us the money would we build a building to house our Indian program and museum; without hesitation I jumped at the offer. Some $150,000 dollars came through ARC and was used to complete the outside portion of the office and museum building; getting the other $150,000 from the Lawrence County Board of Education required me to put my job and career on the line. When I was appearing before the board on the first occasion during Mr. Patrick Graham's administration, I asked the board to fund completion of the building interior but was totally ignored and the board went on to other business.

I kept attending board meetings asking for funds from the board to complete the inside of the Indian building at Oakville; finally at one board meeting, Mr. Wendell Logan asked that the rules be suspended and to discuss the possibility of completing the museum and office building for the Indian program. After a series of procedural moves, a motion was made and approved by the board; after two long years of the shell-in setting vacant and five years from the beginning of the project, the board approved the completion of the Oakville office and museum for the Indian program. After the building was completed in 1995, Congressman Tom Bevill was the very bright spot during the attendance to the building dedication; the congressman was very instrumental in providing funding for the purchase of the mounds and beginning of the Oakville Indian Mounds Education Center. In the front of the Oakville Indian Mounds Council House Building, Congressman Bevill and I had our picture taken together while shaking hands; we had finally accomplished a dream that I had as a young Celtic Indian boy many years before.

After the handshake with Congressman Bevill, I was not finished with the project and for some 14 more years I poured my heart and soul into the project. By the time I retired in 2009, we had purchased a total of some 120 acres of property, paved the roads, built a 60 by 32 feet work center, constructed an amphitheater, finished two outside restroom facilities, made a walking bridge across the lake, and established a festival area with a dance arena. Now at last, the mixed blood Indian people and children of our county had a facility that was the pride of their ancestral lineage, heritage, and culture.

Good or Bad; did I choose?

Did I choose to be good or bad? Did I have a choice? Was my behavior in my genes? Did mother and daddy cause me to act the way I do? Did my surrounding dictate who I am? I am not sure about these simple questions! I will closely examine of my mother and father; I will also reflect on my grandparents. Did they influence what I did in life or did I really have a choice?

My mother Novel Wilburn Walker had a saying that I heard all my life, *"Son every tub has to set on its own bottom."* She taught me from the time I was a small boy that I had to be responsible for my actions; not the actions of others but only mine. She always told me that I had a choice; at every fork in the road, I must choose the direction that I would go. I could choose to do the right thing or I could make an unwise choice that might cost me in the end, but I did not make one decision solely independent from the influence of my parents. The only exception was decisions that would bring shame to my mother would never be considered.

Mother, like her mother, was not in a habit of gossiping and did not talk about people. My mother had another saying that I have used a great deal in my life, *"If you see a pile of shit and stir it up, you are going to get some on yourself and everyone around you."* My mother did not like gossip and neither do I; gossip can hurt everyone that participates even more than it hurts those that the gossip is about. In other words, she did not spread rumors and did not allow me in her presence to talk ugly about anyone.

Her mother and my Grandma Ila also had a saying, *"If you cannot say something good about someone, do not say anything at all."* I know that these sayings kept my foot out of my mouth on many occasions; the teachings of my mother and grandmother prevented me from talking about others and spreading gossip and hurt. As in the paraphrased biblical text Jesus Christ says, *"If you have done it to the least of these, you have done it unto me."*

I have a lot of things that my mother passed on to me but slow to anger was not one of those; I am explosive as gunpowder, but as quick to forgive as the smoke from the shot goes away. Thankfully, I do not hold grudges, but spiritually my convictions maybe more on the shifting sands than on the solid rock on which my mother and my grandmother stood. Because of the love for my mother and grandmother, I was careful not to do things that would bring disgrace upon them, to make them feel hurt or pain for what I had done, but at times, I failed.

My mother was an example to me; as a church going lady, she lived at home the way she acted in church, a morally strong woman. Mother was very introvert like her father Arthur Wilburn; neither mother nor her father liked to be in crowds of people. Even though she was usually quiet, when she said something, she meant it. I seldom saw anger in my mother and she was slow to get mad and never had the tendency to get even;

maybe disgust about the way my dad acted on occasions, but somewhat subdued in her emotions.

I am possibly more introvert than either my mother or grandfather because I hate big crowds and I am very uncomfortable around a lot of people. One time during a workshop activity with some 40 people, the presenters did a Briggs and Myers personality profile; I was the most introvert in the group and my best friend was the most extrovert of the group. The workshop staff lined everyone up by their scores from most outgoing to the most inhibited; my friend was in the front of the line and I was the last person at the end of the line.

My mother was a very compassionate and loving woman; I too am passionate about things I do and I love my girls and my grandchildren with all my heart. In other words, I usually put my heart and soul into something that I believe in with all my being. I give things that I do my best effort because I was taught that if it was worth doing, it should be done right the first time.

My dad Brady Walker was very outgoing and never met a stranger; if he did within a few minutes, dad was a stranger no more. He did things in life that had the opposite influence in my behavior; he drank beer and whiskey, smoked cigarettes, and give me several severe whippings. But to my daughters Amber Walker Allred, Brandy Walker Sutton, and Celeste Walker Weller, Brady was kind and did everything in his power to make them feel the love he had for my girls and his granddaughters.

His actions had a reverse effect on me; I never drank whiskey or beer, I dislike being around people that smoke, and I did not spank my girls beyond reason. I chose and made the decision not to be like my dad with the drinking, smoking, and whippings; I had enough of that behavior growing up and sure wanted to get away from it when I was young and have no desire to ever do those things.

However, I must admit there are a few things my dad passed along; he had a quick temper, did his share of cussing, and did not mind letting others know what he was thinking. I wish I could have chosen not to have a quick temper and maybe I could, but it still happens to this day; the good thing about my temper is, it is a flash in the pan. I can be fired up in a moment and in the next moment be mild and mellow. I can apologize or ask forgiveness in a heartbeat after being mad enough to kill someone. I might have chose to cuss a little or lot depending on the situation and most of the time, it does not take me long to let people know how I feel either good or bad!

My dad also liked to play bad pranks on relatives, friends, and some people he did not consider either; on the other hand, I do not like pranks or things that embarrass people. Of all the things my dad did, he did not believe in lying for any reason; my dad always said, *"You can go to hell for lying as quick as anything you do."* That did not mean he tried to live a life without sin, but he did not like anyone lying to him especially me; therefore, I do not lie and do not like to be around people that stretch the truth until you cannot recognize fact or fiction.

Brandy, Amber, Brady, and Celeste

I had the choice to do bad or good, but I did some things because of the genes that I received from my parents and grandparents. All factors did have an impact on my personality through the characteristics they passed to me; however, some things I wish that I did not do such as temper flares that seem awfully difficult to control. I see my mother and my daddy in most parts of my life, but I know that I am a combination of both and not completely like either one. I know that I am their son; I see both mom and dad in whom I have become.

My environment also had an impact; growing up in an isolated area could have been a factor in my loner attitude. I do not walk to the beat of the drum; I do not want to lead and I am sure not going to follow! Some leaders do not have enough gray matter in their head space to lead especially those with an ego bigger than their common sense;

there is no way that I will follow a person who thinks he is better than I am or better than he really is.

      I am country hillbilly and proud to be a Celtic Indian redneck from the hills and hollows of the Warrior Mountains; I do not like preppy and designer clothes people who class themselves out of my world. I like the wild meat, beans, taters, turnip greens, and cornbread people who like the simple things of life; give me my tennis shoes, hunting boots, t-shirts, and blue jeans and leave me alone in the woods or on the water. Let me choose to be good or bad and give me the choice; do not force me to your ways but accept me for who I am!

Index

Adair, Wayne, 164
Alabama Volunteers, 11
Aldridge Grove Cemetery, 106
Aldridge, Earl, 140, 142
Alexander Bridge, 135, 185, 186
Alexander Hole, 136
Alexander Motorway, 111
Alexander Place, 18, 109, 182, 183
Alexander Plantation, 18, 19, 20, 36, 56, 74, 108, 109, 136, 175, 181
Alexander, David, 161
Alexander, Don, 109
Alexander, Jake, 18, 109, 181
Alexander, Quillar, 18
Alexander, Thomas Jefferson, 18, 109, 181
Allred, Amber Walker, 205
Allred, Ashtyn, 190
Armor, Lora Dale, 24
Armstrong Spring, 53
Atmore Prison, 105
Ayers, Betty Jean, 166
Barrett, Ervin, 83
Basham Gap, 182
Beason, Harold, 24
Beech Bottoms, 74, 108, 126, 185
Bell, Conrad, 141
Beta Club, 102
Bevill, Tom, 202, 203
Bishop, Susie, 163
Black Dutch, 4
Black Irish, 4
Black Warrior Forest, 11, 61, 108, 109, 128
Black Warriors' Path, 182, 201
Black, Hansel, 35, 37, 82, 159
Black, Larry, 159, 202
Black, Lori, 203
Black, Nell Robbins, 36
Black, Phil, 159
Blankenship, "Cricket", 166
Blankenship, Linda Faye, 166
Blizzard Branch, 183
Bloody Flux, 200

Blue John, 125, 126, 127
Bohannon, Linda, 166
Bolan, John Henry, 166
Bolan, Lucy, 20
Bolan, Super, 166
Borden Cove, 55, 56
Borden Creek, 53, 55, 56
Borden, Bill, 162, 164
Borden, Charles, 50, 173, 202
Borden, Christopher, 55
Borden, David, 55
Bowling, Jessica, 202
Boyles, Phillip, 161
Braidfoot, April, 203
Brushy Creek, 173, 182
Brushy Lake, 173
Brushy Mountain, 74, 108, 126, 181, 186
Bryant, Phillip, 141
Bryant, Ted, 141
Buffalo Trail, 56
Bushman, Annice, 166
Bushman, Sue, 166
C. C. Smith, 50, 124
Camp Davies, 10
Capsey Creek, 88
Carnation Milk, 92
Carter, Jerry, 141
Cave Springs Cemetery, 12
Cedar Mountain, 74, 81, 126, 181, 185
Cedar Run, 7, 11, 70
Cheatham Road, 53, 54, 55, 56
Cheatham, Bobbie Nell, 20
Chenault Bridge, 191
Chestnut Ridge, 74
Church of the Forest, 164
Civil War, 9, 10, 18, 63, 70, 178, 179
Clancy Lumber Company, 163, 166
Clancy, John, 162, 163, 166, 167
Clark, Travis, 202
Clear Creek, 177, 178, 179, 180
Clear Creek Falls, 177, 178, 179
Collier Creek Falls, 162

Confederacy, 10
Confederate, 7, 11, 70, 179
Cook, Dean, 161
Coon Dog Cemetery, 147
Crawley, Martha, 201
Cross, John, 161
Curtis, Alvin, 82
Curtis, Bessie, 54, 68
Curtis, George, 1, 53, 66, 194
Curtis, Ila, 7
Curtis, Kate, 67
Curtis, Minnie, 7, 54
Curtis, Steven Jonathan, 54
Dam Store, 169
Danville High School, 101, 102, 133
Danville School, 90
Day, Jimmy, 158
Delashaw, Howard, 139
Devil's Well, 55
Doctor Clear, 68
Dodd, Bruce, 145
Drag Strip Road, 109
Draper Prison, 104
dynamite, 23, 33, 114, 201
East Flint Creek, 76, 169, 170
Elam Creek, 110, 140
Elam, Waymon, 15
England, Janet, 166
England, Ray, 166
Evans, Mark, 203
Fairview Methodist Church, 54
Feltman, Charlie, 165, 166
Fish, Experience, 10
Fitzgerald, Sally, 109
Flint Creek, 72, 74, 76, 84, 108, 109, 134, 135, 171, 174, 175, 176, 181, 182, 185, 186, 191, 196, 200, 202
Forest Service, 34, 55, 56, 181, 191
Fort Jackson, 102
Freeman, Marie, 25
Fretwell, Neal, 39
Fuller, Price, 156
Garrison, Dexter, 164
Garrison, Garvin, 164
Gibson, Charles, 200

Gibson, Michael, 203
Gillespie Branch, 182
Glover, Kathleen, 22
Glover, Richard Hansel, 22
Graham, Patrick, 203
Gravely Springs, 178
Grayson Gophers, 163, 166
Grayson Sawmill, 161, 162, 164, 167
Griffin, Lonzo, 138
Hall, Foy, 140
Hall, Hoy, 140
Hall, Tom, 18, 140
Hambrick, Annie Mae, 34
Hames, Joyce Lowery, 202
Hampton, Brackin, 169, 170
Hampton, George, 86
Hardin, Wes, 76, 78, 114
Harris, Robert, 161
Harrison, Hattie, 25
Hartselle Clinic, 93
Harville, Chad, 203
Hattie Hogan Spring, 30, 56, 181
Hayes, Donna Jean, 102
Hickory Flats Hollow, 34, 190
Hickory Grove, 86, 185
High House Hill, 182
High Town Path, 56, 182, 185
Hightower, Rethal, 141
Hill, Floyd, 140
Hill, Hoyt, 140
Hill, Mike, 161
Hill, Newt, 31
Hinds, Don, 202
Hodges, William, 201
Hogan, Hattie, 30, 56, 155, 181
Hogan, Larry, 25
Hogan, Moody, 56
Hogan, Paul, 176
Hubbard's Mill, 178
Indian Creek, 108, 110, 181, 182, 183, 185, 191
Indian Tomb Hollow, 11, 74, 110
Irwin, Price, 43, 70
Jackson, Stonewall, 11, 70
Jacobs, Doshia, 24

Jacobs, Joe, 18, 108
Jacobs, Tass, 139
Jacobs, Willie, 139
James, Euel, 49, 50
Jarrett, Raford, 141
Jarrett, Reford, 141
Jasper Road, 10, 12, 13, 88, 91, 173
Jetton, Thurman, 161
Johnson, Ava, 25
Johnson, Barbara, 24
Johnson, Biddie, 126
Johnson, Don, 124
Johnson, Dora, 7
Johnson, Elizabeth Angeline "Betty" Hill, 63
Johnson, Hiram, 40, 181, 183
Johnson, Isaac, 95
Johnson, Mull, 26, 56, 74, 77, 128, 181, 186, 190
Johnson, Omie, 126
Johnson, Robert, 7
Johnson, Shirley, 20
Keeling, Charles, 41, 64, 103, 107
Keeling, Larry Joe, 103, 106
Keenum, Roger, 24
Kelly Hole, 134, 135, 159
Kentucky Bell, 25
Kerby, Leo, 50
King's Mountain, 10
Kingfisher, 9
Kinlock, 178
Korean War, 36
Lackey, Columbus, 86
Larrymore Mountain, 26, 128
Lebanon Methodist Church, 35, 51
Legg, Hoover, 140
Legg, Joel, 10
Lemley, Stacy, 202
Ligon, Snooks, 83
Lindsey Hollow, 182, 183
Little Turtle, 66, 190
Lock A, 169
Logan, Wendell, 203
Lolly Grocker, 65
Long, Kenneth, 140

Long, Wade, 140
Looney's Tavern, 10
Loosier, Christy, 203
LouAllen, Joey, 203
LouAllen, Larry, 202
Lowery, Bryant, 138, 139
Lowery, Lutie, 157
Lowery, P. B., 200
Lowery, P. B. (Bryant), 137
Lowery, Terrapin, 156, 158
Loyalty Oaths, 10
Luker, Glen, 141
Luker, Sherry, 166
Lye Soap, 30, 153
Marshall, Lamar, 188, 189, 202
Martin, Earl, 121, 123, 192
Mastengill, 84, 108, 113, 174, 175, 176, 181, 196
Mastengill Hole, 84, 108, 113, 175, 181, 196
McCay, Aubrey, 140
McCay, Don, 140
McCay, John, 138, 200
McLemore Cemetery, 54
McMillan, Ben, 137
McMillan, Emmitt, 156, 157
McVay Hollow, 74, 108, 182, 183
Melson, Luther, 20
Monroe Crossroads, 10
Montgomery Creek, 53, 54, 55, 56, 61
Morgan, Yolanda, 102
Moses, Delaine, 52
Mountain Springs, 56
Mt. Hope High School, 24, 50
Mt. Hope School, 50
Mull Johnson Mountain, 26, 56, 74, 77, 128, 181, 186, 190
Muscle Shoals Path, 201
Nance, Charlie, 121
Nelson, Elizabeth, 11
Oakville Indian Mounds, 3, 203
Oakville Pond, 72, 140, 200, 201
Offutt, Michael, 57, 99, 188, 189
Oil Well, 53, 55
Oil Well Road, 53
Old Blue, 197

Old Bulah, 11
Old Houston, 10
Old Nectar, 201
Oliver, A. J., 31
Oliver, Glenn, 31
Orr, Denny, 138
Outhouse, 30, 45, 96, 97, 98, 120
Owens, Claudia Ann, 61
Owl Creek, 173
Parker, James (Jim), 55
Parker, Mary Ellen, 55
Parker, Tracy, 202
Pearson Field, 182, 185
Pee Wee, 113, 122, 123, 124
Peebles, DeWayne, 202
Piggly Wiggly, 65, 161
Pin Hook, 52, 137, 140, 141, 142
Pine Torch Church, 173
Piney Grove, 140, 141, 166, 182
Pinhook, 90
Pitman Bridge, 173
Pointer, Aaron, 139
Pointer, Charlie, 138, 139, 140
Pointer, Dee, 139
Pointer, Louie, 139
Poole, Tom, 182
Poplar Log Cove, 18, 109, 175, 181, 182, 186, 191
Possum, 73, 118, 119, 120, 121, 122, 125, 126, 127, 143, 168, 191
Prater, Sylvia, 22
Praytor, Truman, 72, 131
Preuit, Clebe, 138, 139
Preuit, John, 139, 167
Proctor, Donald, 149
Proctor, Johnny, 149
Proctor, W. D., 7
Proctor, Williemuryl Welborn, 149
Rat Poison Gap, 53, 55, 56
Red River, 8
Reeves, Boyce, 24
Revolutionary War, 10
Riddle, Will, 162
Ridge Road, 53, 56
Robbins, Jimmy, 169, 171

Rock Creek, 173
Rush Creek, 86
Sanderson, Grady, 141
Sapp, Brenda, 102
Scott, "Cutie", 166
Sears and Roebuck, 45, 98
Segars, Martha, 4, 7
Segars, Pascal Sandy, 4, 7, 11, 70
Segars, Sarah Mandy, 7, 11
Sharpley, Kenneth, 171
Shelp, 122, 123
Shelton, Jackie, 24
Sherrill, Linda, 20
Shirt Factory, 34, 46, 49, 59, 105
Sipsey River, 177
Sivley, April, 203
Slate, Ralph, 102
Slaten, Frankie, 20
Slaughter's Mountain, 70
Smith Lake, 38, 50, 71, 72, 180, 199
Smith, Bobby, 162
Smith, Burly, 25
Smith, Howell, 200
Smith, Jess, 68
Smith, Raymond, 140
Smith, Shirley, 157
Social Security, 60
Sparks, Mary Elean, 53, 54
Speake High School, 22, 24, 34, 47, 50, 51, 101, 102, 133
Speake School, 20, 21, 22, 49, 181, 201
Speake, Charlie, 35, 38
Speake, Jimmy, 137, 140
Spring Creek, 169
Steele, James, 22, 161, 164
Stewart, Charlie, 194
Stover, Floyd Lee, 138
Stover, Johnny, 138
Sugar Camp Hollow, 63, 71, 74, 108, 156, 181
Sutton, Brady, 190
Sutton, Brandy Walker, 205
Swan Creek, 113
Tar Springs Hollow, 88
Tarzan, 46, 129

Taylor, Babe Ruth, 138, 140
Taylor, Buddy, 137, 138
Taylor, Hosey Lee, 138
Taylor, James Andrew, 138
Taylor, Rayford, 138, 140
Taylor, Wayne, 138
Taylor, Wyman, 138
Tennessee River, 34, 110, 112, 169, 201
Terry, Golden Gene, 161
Thomas Jefferson Hotel, 102
Thompson Creek, 108, 110, 181, 182
Thrasher, Ocie, 38
Tonnical Branch, 111
Townsend, Cotton, 163
Tripoli, Libya, 63
Truck Wagon, 130, 131
Truddle, 114
Union Army, 10, 178
University of North Alabama, 2, 102, 166
Upshaw, 173
Vaughn, Mary Ann, 11
Vernon, Larry, 23
Waldrep, Michelle, 203
Walker, Brady, 1, 13, 20, 38, 90, 94, 111, 170, 201, 205
Walker, Butch, 2, 170
Walker, Dan, 13, 15, 39, 94, 95, 154, 170
Walker, Diane, 26, 38
Walker, Elizabeth, 201
Walker, Hulda Christine, 11
Walker, James W., 8
Walker, Jonathan, 10
Walker, June, 26
Walker, Kenneth, 14
Walker, Lucille, 63, 88, 94, 95, 98
Walker, Sarah, 201
Walker, Sidney, 63
Walker, Tandy, 201
Walker, Thurman, 15, 89
Walker, Vady, 30, 94
Walker, Vady Legg, 88
Walker, Vicey Stevens, 101
Walker, Violine, 7, 101, 103
Walker, William, 10, 63, 201
Walker, William B., 8, 10

Walker, William Roy, 15, 63, 89, 177
Walker-Big Spring Cemetery, 11
Wallace, George, 22
Walnut Ford, 175, 181, 182, 185
Warrior River, 7, 8, 189
Wayne, John, 98
Weatherwax, Clark, 161
Weatherwax, Roger, 161
Weeks, Jane, 202
Welborn Cemetery, 11, 52, 73, 90
Welborn, Augustive (Gus) T., 11
Welborn, Carl, 35, 36
Welborn, Celia, 7
Welborn, Danny, 80, 133, 175
Welborn, Don, 97
Welborn, Ed, 182
Welborn, Gideon, 11
Welborn, Grover, 38
Welborn, Gus, 7
Welborn, Lockey B., 4, 7, 11
Welborn, Mamie, 76, 77
Welborn, Martha Elzey, 11
Welborn, Mary Elizabeth, 4, 7, 11
Welborn, Pascal Sandy, 7, 70
Welborn, Rayford, 39, 73
Welborn, Ronnie, 103
Welborn, Sandy, 42, 101, 133, 175, 186
Welborn, Willard, 7, 65, 101, 103, 106, 111
Weller, Celeste Walker, 205
Weller, Myla Marie, 66
West Flint Creek, 36, 72, 108, 109, 110, 112, 113, 114, 115, 182, 183, 200, 201
Western Auto, 72, 131
Wheeler Dam, 169
White Raven, 9, 190
White, Frank, 80, 166
White, Manco, 20, 86
Whitson, Doc, 149
Wiggins Creek, 110, 191
Wilburn, Arthur, 1, 40, 48, 70, 94, 108, 140, 142, 147, 169, 174, 197, 204
Wilburn, Cadle, 20, 35, 41, 63, 136, 137, 140
Wilburn, Curtis, 20, 54, 63, 81, 109
Wilburn, Ila, 1, 18, 61, 110, 159, 172, 196

Wilburn, Mary Lou Hood, 38
Wilburn, Mike, 26, 109
Wilburn, Novel, 13, 20, 51, 74, 204
Wild and Scenic Rivers, 56
Wiley, John, 138, 200
Wiley, Lynn, 140, 149
Wiley, Red, 202
Wilson, Janet, 166
Wren Mountain, 83
Yeager, Dallas, 109
York, Carl, 141
York, Cranford, 141
York, Donnver, 141
Zip City, 145

Rickey Butch Walker is a lifelong native son of the Warrior Mountains. He descends from Cherokee, Creek, and Celtic (Scots-Irish) people who migrated into the hills and coves of the mountainous region of north Alabama some 250 years ago. He, as was his father, is a member of the Echota Cherokee Tribe of Alabama. His Indian name is Fish Bird in honor of his fifth, fourth, and third great grandmothers-Catherine Kingfisher, Experience Fish, and Elizabeth Bird.

The kingfisher and fish bird (Osprey) love to fish and so does Butch. In addition, the osprey is of contrasting colors of black and white which identify Butch's character. Things that rule his life are true or false, yes or no, and black or white with virtually no gray areas; therefore, he lives his life somewhat as an open book. Also, according to Indian legend, the birds of prey soar high in the sky and carry the prayers of the earthly creatures to the great spirit. Fish Bird (Butch) has his entire adult life been an advocate to preserve and protect the environment for all the earthly creatures that are unable to speak for themselves.

As a young boy, Butch was born and raised in the shadows of the Warrior Mountains where he was taught by his grandpa the ways of the wild. He squirrel hunted on Brushy Mountain, trapped in Sugar Camp Hollow, searched for ginseng in Indian Tomb Hollow, and fished in West Flint Creek. He walked with his grandparents on old Indian trails including Black Warriors' Path, Sipsey Trail, and many others. He explored the deep canyons, rolling hills, steep bluff lines, and vast hollows containing beautiful waterfalls where he would stand in the spray to cool off on a hot day. He was nourished by the subsistence of West Flint Creek and surrounding hardwood bottoms, and molded from traveling the trails and paths his people once trod. He grew up with a fierce love for the Warrior Mountains in which his ancestors lived, died, and are buried.

In 1966 because of the love of his mountainous homeland, Butch became an advocate to stop the clear cutting of old growth woodlands that he roamed and hunted as a youngster. He worked to help establish the Sipsey Wilderness Area which was dedicated in 1975 and wrote weekly articles about the forest for the Moulton Advertiser. In 1992, Butch teamed up with Lamar Marshall and helped begin the Bankhead Monitor to fight the clear cutting and destructive practices by the United States Forest Service taking place in the sacred Indian Tomb Hollow. The Monitor became Wild Alabama and later Wild South. Butch served as Chairman of the Board of Directors until Wild South merged with the Southern Appalachian Biodiversity Project in 2006.

Rickey Butch Walker retired after some 35 years with the Lawrence County Board of Education during which he earned post graduate degrees in science, education, and supervision. He taught high school science for 11 years and served as Director of Lawrence County Schools' Indian Education Program and Oakville Indian Mounds Education Center until his retirement in 2009. In addition to his Master's Thesis, he has written several books including *High Town Path, Warrior Mountains Folklore, Indians of the Warrior Mountains, Indian Trails of the Warrior Mountains, Warrior Mountains Indian Heritage, Warrior Mountains Indian Heritage Student Edition, Doublehead: Last Chickamauga Chief, Chickasaw Chief George Colbert: His Family and His Country,* and *Appalachian Indians of Warrior Mountains*. Other titles pending publication are *Black Folk Tales of Appalachia: Slavery to Survival, Soldier's Wife: Cotton Fields to Berlin and Tripoli, Appalachian Indian Trials of the Chickamauga: Lower Cherokee Settlements, When Cotton Was King: White Gold of the Muscle Shoals,* and *Hiking Sipsey: A Family's Fight for Eastern Wildlife*.

You can find Butch's book at Amazon.com or www.Historicaltruth101.com.

You can also subscribe to his weekly blog at www.RickeyButchWalker.com or

http://rickeybutchwalker.blogspot.com to receive Butch's weekly updates on the historical research he is currently writing.

Bluewater Publications is a multi-faceted publishing company capable of meeting all of your reading and publishing needs. Our two-fold aim is to:

1) Provide the market with educationally enlightening and inspiring research and reading materials.

2) Make the opportunity of being published available to any author and or researcher who desire to be published.

We are passionate about preserving history; whether through the re-publishing of an out-of-print classic, or by publishing the research of historians and genealogists. Bluewater Publications is the *Peoples' Choice Publisher*.

For company information or information about how you can be published through Bluewater Publications, please visit:

www.BluewaterPublications.com

Also check Amazon.com to purchase any of the books that we publish.

Confidently Preserving Our Past,
Bluewater Publications.com

www.ingramcontent.com/pod-product-compliance
Lightning Source LLC
Chambersburg PA
CBHW050459110426
42742CB00018B/3308